The Trials of

C000262809

Terry Kirby has been [...] policing for ten of his eighteen [...] during which he has worked for local, regional and national newspapers. While working for the *Birmingham Post*, he received two awards for his crime reporting. After joining the *Independent* at its birth in 1986, he became the newspaper's first crime correspondent; he is also an occasional broadcaster and contributor to magazines. Born and educated in Birmingham, he now lives in north London with his wife, Marion, and three cats.

The Trials of
THE BARONESS

TERRY KIRBY

Mandarin

A Mandarin Paperback
THE TRIALS OF THE BARONESS

First published in Great Britain 1991
by Mandarin Paperbacks
Michelin House, 81 Fulham Road, London SW3 6RB

Mandarin is an imprint of the Octopus Publishing Group,
a division of Reed International Books Limited

Copyright © 1991 by Terry Kirby

The author has asserted his moral rights

Photographic acknowledgements:
No. 1, Press Association; nos. 2, 4, 5, 6, 7, 8,
12, 13, 15, 16, 18, Wilberforce family collection;
nos. 3, 17, 19, Central Television; no. 9, *The Times*;
no. 10, Desmond O'Neill; no. 11, Courtauld Institute;
no. 14, Veronica Bowaters; no. 20, News Team.

A CIP catalogue record for this title
is available from the British Library

ISBN 0 7493 0575 4

Typeset by Falcon Typographic Art Ltd,
Edinburgh & London
Printed and bound in Great Britain
by Cox & Wyman Ltd, Reading, Berkshire

Contents

Acknowledgements

In a story like this, it is inevitable that a number of people should have been prepared to give me their time, information and assistance on the understanding that I guaranteed their anonymity. They have their reasons for doing so. I have of course respected that wish and, where possible, have disguised their contributions. To them I give my wholehearted thanks.

Turning to those I can publicly identify, I must first express my sincere thanks to Christopher Mowbray, without whose invaluable contribution Chapters 9 and 10 would have been much more difficult to achieve.

I would also like to express my gratitude to Detective Chief Superintendent Barrie Mayne, head of West Mercia Police CID, for allowing me to talk to officers who investigated this most difficult of cases. In particular I should like to thank Detective Superintendent Ian Bullock, Detective Inspector Mike Cowley, Detective Inspector Derek Matthews, Detective Constable Andy McVicar and Sergeant Ray Heighway, who gave willingly of their time and responded to my requests for information with extraordinary patience. In particular, the help given by Detective Constable Robin Longmore was invaluable. I am also greatly indebted to my friend Allen Peach, the force press officer, for his considerable assistance.

It is of some regret to me that the officer in overall charge, David Cole, now retired as Detective Chief Superintendent and head of the force CID, felt unable to help with this account of what must have been his most interesting case. I did not feel able to meet terms which I considered would have devalued the enterprise.

By contrast, Sophia and Marcus Wilberforce talked to me at length openly and without precondition, for which I am enormously thankful. After expressing their feelings and opinions, they did not seek to influence my work, however painful it may have been to them personally. I am also grateful to them for the loan of a number of family photographs, for which they retain the copyright.

I also received some assistance, again without precondition, from Susan de Stempel, with whom I corresponded and whom I visited in prison. For her own reasons, there came a point where she decided to sever communications, which I obviously regret. Nevertheless, I should like to thank her for the assistance she offered.

Individuals whose help I must acknowledge for their assistance in compiling this account include David Crabtree of Central Television, Jesus Pardo de Santayana, Christopher Hurst, Albert Oslar, Simon Verdun, Dave Hill, Veronica Bowater, Geoffrey Bowater, Jo Corfield, Lynne Williams, Marie Osborne, Su Evans, Ben Scott, George and Jennifer Spencer and Dr Peter Acland.

I should also like to express my appreciation to Westminster Reference Library, the British Newspaper Library, the Catholic Central Library, Miss E. Willmott of the local studies department of Bradford Central Library, Harrogate Library, Shrewsbury Library, the Victoria and Albert Museum, Daniel Illingworth and Sons, and Colin Clark of the Bradford Undercliffe Cemetery Company. Thanks must also go to Sally Russell for secretarial work, Julia Kirby for research assistance and Guy Crawley of Number Eleven, Dinham, Ludlow, for hospitality. I am also grateful to Miss Margaret Duerden of Central Television and Christopher McKane of the *Independent* for their help with the photographs.

This book would not have been possible without the enthusiasm and encouragement of Lavinia Trevor, my agent, and the endless patience and unswerving support of Marion, my wife.

WILBERFORCE FAMILY TREE

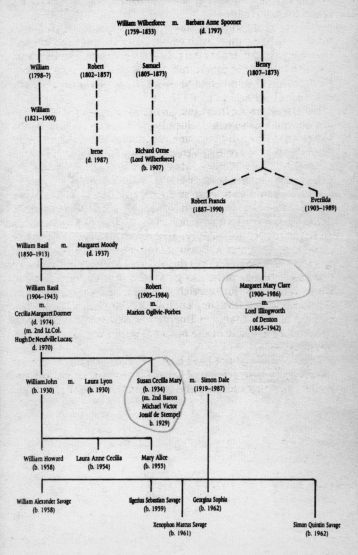

William Wilberforce   m.   Barbara Anne Spooner
(1759–1833)   (d. 1797)

William
(1798–?)

Robert
(1802–1857)

Samuel
(1805–1873)

Henry
(1807–1873)

William
(1821–1900)

Irene
(d. 1987)

Richard Orme
(Lord Wilberforce)
(b. 1907)

Robert Francis
(1887–1990)

Everilda
(1903–1989)

William Basil   m.   Margaret Moody
(1850–1913)   (d. 1937)

William Basil
(1904–1943)
m.
Cecilia Margaret Dormer
(d. 1974)
(m. 2nd Lt.Col.
Hugh De Neufville Lucas;
d. 1970)

Robert
(1905–1984)
m.
Marion Ogilvie-Forbes

Margaret Mary Clare
(1900–1986)
m.
Lord Illingworth
of Denton
(1865–1942)

William John   m.   Laura Lyon
(b. 1930)   (b. 1930)

Susan Cecilia Mary   m.   Simon Dale
(b. 1934)   (1919–1987)
(m. 2nd Baron
Michael Victor
Jossif de Stempel
b. 1929)

William Howard
(b. 1958)

Laura Anne Cecilia
(b. 1954)

Mary Alice
(b. 1955)

William Alexander Savage
(b. 1958)

Ilgerius Sebastian Savage
(b. 1959)

Georgina Sophia
(b. 1962)

Xenophon Marcus Savage
(b. 1961)

Simon Quintin Savage
(b. 1962)

Here's health to the man with a ragged shirt;
And no wife to mend it.
Here's to the one with plenty of money;
And a good wife to spend it . . .

Old Herefordshire drinking toast

1
A Sunday in September

Sunday afternoon in Shropshire: a dead time. Little disturbs this particular afternoon, in this part of the border country, in mid-September 1987. The wasps are lazy on a sunny autumn day. In this season it is sometimes cold at night, in the hills, where the colours show that the year is turning. Those spring lambs that escaped slaughter are growing coats for the winter; in the small orchards, the apples will soon be ready for picking. In the half-timbered and thatched cottages, in the solid stone farmhouses, in the few modern homes of the long-distance commuters, lunch is being digested and perhaps the television is turned to some old film. Children play on bicycles in the road and, because there is always work to be done, tractors rumble in the fields.

No motorways bisect this part of the world, this little corner of the Home Counties on the Welsh borders. Like so much else, they have passed them by. In the villages, the shops that opened in the morning for milk and Sunday newspapers have closed again; men walking their dogs stop to look in the windows, reading the handwritten notices announcing the next meeting of the parish council or of the Women's Institute, perhaps a jumble sale. The lanes are quiet and there are few sounds: now and then a car passes, containing a party on a drive and a stroll or returning home from luncheon with friends. A sudden roar and then all is calm again, leaving the magpies to reclaim their scavenging grounds. Sometimes there is the cry of a child fallen from a bicycle on to gravel or the distant, but curiously reassuring shriek of rooks in the trees. Country cats sit on sunny walls and watch the world, or prowl the gardens, where there are still autumn roses.

Among the scattered houses of Kempton, a hamlet at the head of a small wild valley that goes nowhere except into the low hills, all is quiet. There are no ancient houses or cream teas here to attract noisy visitors, for which the inhabitants are thankful. Suddenly, an engine ignites and a little Citroën car trundles down a rough private track. There is no reason to distinguish this car from any other taking the occupants home from a convivial meal, no reason to detect an urgency in its noises. At the bottom of the track, next to an ivy-covered lodge, there is a gate. The car stops and out gets its only occupant: a small, slim woman in her late thirties. She moves quickly to open the gate, returns to her car and drives through, before stopping again and jumping out to close the gate before driving away. The car passes down the tarmac lane that runs by the side of the meandering River Kemp, a tributary of the Clun, which created this pleasant little valley. The road is wide enough for only one car at a time to pass between the high hedges. It is about 4.15 p.m. on Sunday, 13 September 1987 and Giselle Wall is worried.

It was unlike Simon Dale not to telephone. Here was a man careful and meticulous about his habits to the point of utter predictability, not only as a result of the circumstances life forced upon him, but also because that was the kind of person he was. Besides, in a quiet, rural community, variation and spontaneity in life, even if desired, are difficult to achieve.

No, said Giselle to herself as she drove down the narrow lane, it was not like Simon at all. The previous Wednesday, when he had telephoned her home, she had been out. He had promised Tom, her husband, a nature-reserve warden, that he would call again to fix a time on Sunday for her to come to discuss the work she had been doing on his book. But there had been no call all weekend and now she was worried. Although he had been her employer, she was now working for free, sympathetic to this sixty-eight-year-old, tall, balding, almost blind man, who lived alone in the crumbling mansion. Its ownership was in dispute with his ex-wife, but Giselle tried not to get involved.

She had worked from May 1986 to July that year. 'Interests in history, archaeology and medicine', the advertisement in the job centre at Ludlow had specified, £1.98 an hour for fifteen hours a week, most of them at home. The house was tidy but huge, cold and spooky. As a Frenchwoman she was unimpressed by the English upper classes; she was also completely unable to understand his arcane writings on the Arthurian legends and the science of vision. But she had developed an affection for his courteous and gentlemanly manners, his dogged determination not to let poverty or blindness overwhelm him. And she pitied him, which was worse.

Against advice, she allowed his dependence upon her: she ran errands, did shopping, darned dilapidated shirts. And when she finally stopped work, in July, it was because such reliance was not good for either of them. But she wanted to let him down gradually and there was still a lot of work to be done, so she carried on for a while: checking references in Shrewsbury Library for footnotes in his Arthurian book. Her problem was that Simon's memory of the books he had used was poor and she could not locate them all. That was why she had arranged to go this Sunday, to discuss the next steps.

At lunchtime, she began telephoning, to ask if he wanted her to go that afternoon. No reply. She tried the operator, asking for the line to be checked. There was no problem, said the operator. Giselle was not unduly concerned, because he often visited friends for lunch, walking over the fields and being driven back. She kept trying, without success. She began to get worried. Although Simon's vision was reduced to a pinprick, he had no trouble getting about the house he had lived in for nearly three decades, using a combination of instinct and familiarity. But, Giselle told herself, he could still have fallen down the central staircase or have had a heart attack or some kind of seizure. She would never forgive herself if Simon were lying there now, injured or unconscious, unable to reach the telephone. Few others were likely to call. But he was probably out somewhere – no need to panic. She decided to go and see if he was all right.

The familiar journey took less than ten minutes. At the junction with the main road at the Hundred House Inn, closed for the afternoon, she drove across and continued for two or three miles through more open country until the left-hand turn at Hopton Heath railway halt. Here Simon would often wait for the train which took him to Shrewsbury and the library or grocers, asking the guard on the return journey to make sure the train halted.

Then came the straight stretch through the hamlet itself. On the left, fenced farmland; on the right, a garage. Then, amid trees, there was Heath Lodge, an attractive black-and-white thatched cottage, right on the roadside, opposite the T-junction with the lane to Leintwardine. She crossed the county border from Shropshire into Hereford–Worcester, but this is an area where the shape of the country counts for more than mere lines on a map. Several hundred yards further on the left, she came to two adjacent gateways. The first gate opened on to a drive curving away to buildings barely visible through trees. Giselle Wall drove down the second. She had no need to stop and open the gate – it was always open. The track plunged down into close, tall trees and shrubbery, a small copse that is home for rabbits, squirrels and abundant birdlife. After an opening in a stone wall, the trees thinned out, and there, ahead of her, across the small lawn with the rhododendron bushes, she could see Heath House.

Locals often say they prefer to see the Heath from the opposite direction to that in which Giselle Wall approached this Sunday afternoon, because it looks so much more attractive that way. It is as if the house has a divided character: a dark side and a light side, a blind aspect which often seems in shadow and a sunlit, open one, filling the emotions of those that know the house with a similar polarity, a mixture of love and hate.

Seen from the south-west, the front catches the afternoon sun before it dips behind the hills on the Welsh border, its rays reflecting on the ancient golden brickwork and glinting on twenty-one carefully proportioned windows. The house sits handsomely and squarely between the trees, separated by a sculptured hedge from a huge, undulating field, once part of its own grounds. In design it is simple: a flat front and two wings forming a U-shape; there are no gothic flourishes, flying buttresses or ornate towers. There is a pleasing simplicity to its lines: suggesting that the man who built it more than 300 years ago wanted a home, as well as a house. So again it divides: compact enough to be homely, big enough to be stately and exciting. One can still look at it and say: this is a proper house. But, close up, there are the cracks of the centuries. Giselle Wall was approaching from the dark side, through the trees.

She parked in the small space to the right-hand side of the rear of the house and got out. The warm afternoon was quiet – dead quiet. Birds may have sung in trees, cars may have driven down the main road, a breeze may have run through the trees, but she was unaware of any such sounds. She walked across the lawn and saw that the heavy wooden shutters on the ground-floor windows were closed; not like Simon, an almost blind man who loved the light he could barely see and would always open them during the day. She saw lights burning where there should not have been lights, not on this bright autumn afternoon, at the home of a man who watched every penny he spent.

In the corner of the house there is an ordinary red door, between a tall hedge and an outside chimney, approached by an irregular path which leads from an ornamental bird bath, dry and empty. She slipped through the gap between the hedge and the corner of the house on to the topmost of the three stone steps. She tried the door; it opened inwards. If she had not been worried before, she was now. Crossing the threshold, she saw a deckchair in her path on the floor of the narrow hallway, otherwise cluttered with gumboots, umbrellas and similar paraphernalia. A heavy bunch of keys lay on the floor. She paused because she had already sensed something in the air: a closeness, a heaviness, almost a warm richness: fetid.

Nervously, she did the polite thing anyone might do: she knocked firmly on the inner door in front of her. She knew it opened on to the large kitchen where he spent most of his days. Something within her clung on to normality: 'Hello!' she cried. 'Hello, Simon! Simon, hello?' Perhaps she would hear that familiar booming, sonorous, cultivated voice saying, 'Come in, my dear, come in. Let us get to work. All is well, all is well.' But she did not. She pushed open the door and released a hot, sickly, trapped heat that struck her in the face and then washed over her body in wave after wave, penetrating and pervasive. She had to squeeze her head around the door because it could not be pushed open any further and then, one second later, she looked down and saw why.

This is a part of the world where the black roots of history are still visible, poking through the placid green ground. These border counties between England and Wales used to be so bloody, so terrible, so full of mangled and hacked corpses, civil strife and angry warlords that it is almost impossible to believe, says Veronica 'Vicky' Bowater, one of Simon's friends, that it is all so tranquil nowadays, when there is hardly time to fit in all her social life. Now all that remains of Hopton Castle is a great stone stump surrounded by grazing cattle. In 1644, it was held for three weeks by the Roundheads against a siege of Royalists. When they finally surrendered, about twenty-five men and one maid were tied back to back, had their hands or arms hacked away and were drowned in a muddy pool. The castle was ransacked; one of its staircases is now in Heath House.

A few miles to the south of Heath House is Mortimer's Cross, where a monument is erected 'to perpetuate the memory of an obstinate, bloody and decisive battle' fought near the spot in February 1461, between the Yorkist Edward Mortimer, the Lord of Ludlow and Earl of March, later to become Edward IV, and Henry the Sixth. Four thousand men were left dead on the field and Owen Tudor, great-grandfather of Henry VIII, was beheaded at Hereford. Over the centuries, the hilltop castle of Ludlow, which still preserves its exquisite medieval buildings, was the seat of the lords of the Marches, eight miles east of Heath House. Elizabeth I gave Sir Henry Sidney, Lord President of the Council of the Marshes, permission to use torture on anyone whenever he believed it to be necessary. His instruments included an iron mask which fitted over the head and crushed it, slowly, by a turn of the screw. Some of these devices are still displayed in the small museum in the town.

For centuries, ever since Offa, King of Wales, rebelled against the English and erected a fortified dyke to keep their armies at bay, the English have fought both the Welsh and among themselves. And their blood was spilt on some of the most beautiful countryside anywhere in the kingdom. This is where the dark hills and mountains of the west mingle with the villages, dales and pastures of the English counties, and where, on spring mornings, or even on such warm autumn afternoons as this one, there can be a sudden waft of clear mountain air, sending a cool zephyr through the lush lowland valleys.

Fresh air was the one thing Giselle Wall most wanted now, as she lurched out of the kitchen at Heath House. She took in great gulps, standing in the doorway, turning her back on what she had seen as she opened the door and looked down. On the floor in front of her, his great balding, bloodstained head nearest her feet and stopping the door from opening further, was the 6 foot 3 inch tall body of Simon Dale, lying on his back, his arms bent backwards and his hands on his chest, as if clawing at his jumper. There was a large, bloody mark on his forehead.

She said afterwards that she had not seen any more blood, which is difficult to understand because there was so much around the kitchen. Something had happened: perhaps Simon had fallen down, hitting his head on the table – or something even worse, which for the moment her mind would not allow her to bring to the surface. She climbed into her car, started the engine and drove raggedly up the path, through the wall and the trees and out into the light again. At the road she turned right towards what she remembered as the nearest house: Heath Lodge. Giselle parked on the road and ran around the house to the back door and knocked, still shaking.

The door was opened by Marjorie Hollis, who lived there with her husband Mike, an antiques dealer. They had been entertaining another couple for lunch, Malcolm and Jennifer Barrett. Giselle Wall blurted out how she had gone to see Mr Dale – whom the Hollises knew by sight – but had found him lying in the kitchen, his head bloody, almost certainly dead. Mike Hollis dialled 999, and asked for an ambulance to come urgently, reasoning that Giselle was in no condition to know precisely what had happened to Dale, who might still be alive.

Hollis walked back down the road together with Barrett, following Giselle Wall, who drove her car. They reached the gate as the ambulance drew up and followed down the path, where it parked on the right-hand side. Standing on the lawn they waited apprehensively as the ambulancemen, John Abbotts and Jeffrey Timmis, walked across the back of Heath House and they entered by the kitchen door.

Abbotts followed Timmis into the kitchen, squeezing around the door. They both immediately saw the blood Giselle Wall had not noticed but, like her, were almost overwhelmed by the sickening heat and the smell of putrefaction. Abbotts went straight to the body to see if there was any discernible pulse in the neck: he realised at once there was nothing he could do for Dale. He was familiar with the posture: it followed automatically when the neck was broken. It was also clear that Dale had not died as the result of a simple fall. There was a lot of blood on the floor underneath the body and around Dale's head, on the table among the vegetables and on the other side, between the table and the sink.

The ambulanceman saw that the ring on the small electric cooker at the other end of the kitchen was on and seemed to be the source of the heat. He stepped around the table and crossed to the cooker, where there was a small saucepan with its lid on. He picked up the lid and, as he did so, the wooden knob came off in his hand. The heat had melted it away from its metal core, although the knob itself was cool. He tried to turn off the cooker, but for some reason the switch did not work.

The stale, heavy heat and the smell of death made it difficult to breathe and they went outside, gasping for air. Because of the wounds on Dale's head, it was an immediate possibility that this man might have been in a struggle with an intruder. Abbotts walked around the house looking, unsuccessfully, for signs of a break-in. He was the first person and by no means the last to consider it unusual that, if an intruder was responsible, there were no signs of a forced entry. He also looked for any other bodies: there was so much blood in the kitchen that they had wondered whether another injured person might be lying somewhere else in the house. Abbotts peered in through the windows, but could see nothing; they decided not to enter the house in case they disturbed clues the police would need.

As Timmis radioed his control room to contact the police, Abbotts advised Hollis that the best thing was to go back to Heath Lodge so that Giselle could recover; Simon Dale was dead, others would take over now. As they walked away, Abbotts stood there, his skin still clammy from the heat of the kitchen, and realised that outside it was a golden autumn afternoon. On the radio, Timmis was using the jargon of the emergency services: he was reporting a 'suspicious death'. No one had yet mentioned murder; its presence hung in the air between all of them.

Murder is not an act that pays much respect to normal working hours. Most of the people who would arrive at Heath House during the course of the evening were used to it: they did not do jobs where it was possible to hold as sacred any one part of the day or week. A great many murders, as any detective will explain, are relatively simple to solve, once you know what to look for, and in the majority of cases the culprit is caught within a few days or even hours. This is usually because the murderer is an acquaintance, friend or relative of the victim and there is a clear motive. Usually this is of an entirely personal and domestic nature, most often a squabble over love, property or money, sometimes fuelled by drink, that gets terribly out of hand and the killer flees, scattering clues, or is found sobbing by the body. It is a curious fact that many murder victims will have known their killers better than a lot of other people in their lives.

More difficult are the serial killers – the Yorkshire Ripper, Peter Sutcliffe, is the most obvious example – who strike without warning and never know their victims for long. But it is their increasing predictability of method that eventually leads to their capture, sometimes after many years and often because of their own mistakes. Worst of all for the detective is the random killing, the one-off lacking in either obvious method or motive, the one with the touch of the unusual or bizarre, which does not fit easily into any category.

This particular one-off fell within the area of the West Mercia police force, a medium-sized constabulary covering a large geographical area which comprises the predominantly rural border counties of Hereford–Worcester and Shropshire. The force had dealt with one other particularly vexatious case in recent years. In 1984, an elderly widow, Hilda Murrell, had been stabbed, beaten and left to die of hypothermia by someone who had apparently broken into her home near Shrewsbury. After an investigation frustrated by a paucity of clues, police concluded that she had been the victim of a random attacker whose initial motivation had been burglary. But the house contained nothing of much value, there was no evidence anything had been stolen and the reason for her being taken and dumped in a field was unknown.

It would have been just another unsolved murder, but for the fact that both MPs and newspapers made great play of her links with the anti-nuclear movement and the curious coincidence that her nephew, a naval commander, knew something about the controversial sinking of the Argentine ship, the *General Belgrano*, by the British during the Falklands War. There were strong suggestions that, for one of these reasons, she had been accidentally or even deliberately killed by some agents of the state, or those acting on their behalf, and that there had been a cover-up.

The open file and unanswered questions were an unwelcome blot on the record of Detective Chief Superintendent David Cole, the head of CID for the West Mercia police; it was his only unsolved murder.

As is so often the case, the first police officer to arrive was a local man, Sergeant Ray Heighway, one of the four officers based at Craven Arms, just a few miles up the road, where he had been radioed by Ludlow police station. With Abbotts, he went into the kitchen and walked around the body to turn off the cooker. They opened the cooker door and looked inside at something black and crusted. Dr Margaret Davies, the duty police surgeon, arrived to examine the corpse: Dale had clearly been dead for some hours, although how long it was not possible to say. She certified him dead. Sergeant Heighway, meanwhile, used the Heath House telephone to call Ludlow police station. They should notify the duty CID officer, Detective Sergeant Dave Clarke. 'And get the scenes-of-crime officers out,' he said. 'This looks serious.'

Many people were hearing the words Heath House and the name of Simon Dale for the first time that day. As soon as the ambulanceman had talked to his control room, a chain of events had been put in motion. Across the counties, telephones rang out, police radios crackled into life, pagers bleeped. Cole was called at home by the Worcester control room.

A murder investigation is a well-rehearsed ritual. As afternoon turned into evening, it was enacted at Heath House. Detectives are not the only people who investigate murders: the coroner's officer, who would care for the body, the video crew, to record the scene for posterity, the scenes-of-crime officers, the forensic scientists, the fingerprint experts, the pathologist, all arrived in succession to play their parts.

Among the first was Detective Constable Geoffrey Daniels. In the lobby, Daniels saw things Giselle Wall had simply failed to understand. To him, there were clear signs that some kind of struggle had taken place. He looked at the deckchair knocked on to the floor: one of its slats was broken. Plastic coat hangers had been pulled off hooks; there was blood on the walls. On the work surface, next to the sink, there were five sherry glasses: one had sherry in it and was of a different pattern to the others. Another had a crack in it and was unused, while the other three contained the dregs of some sherry. These told him a story at least: Simon Dale had received visitors, presumably not long before he had been murdered. He went to the body and – using tweezers because everything would later be fingerprinted – drew out Simon Dale's brown leather wallet from his pocket. it still contained his business cards, receipts, library tickets and £25 in notes. He put it aside for later examination. He looked properly at the body and saw that blood was still seeping from the back of the head. More blood was on the blue-and-white tiled floor: it was dried blood, black and flaking.

Meanwhile, Sergeant Heighway had met up with another arrival, Inspector Derek Matthews, the duty inspector at Leominster police station, who had been called at home. He lived a couple of miles away and went straight to Heath House. Although both men knew the area and its population well – Heighway had lived and worked there for seventeen years – they found it astonishing that Simon Dale had made so little impression on the surrounding countryside that neither man had ever met him.

They were all talking, in the easy, slow conversational fashion of Shropshire, to George and Jennifer Spencer, the nearest neighbours to Heath House, whose cottage is reached by the first of the two gateways on to the main road. Although their home is less than 100 yards from the house, and was once part of the estate, only the rooftops are visible through the wall of trees. Sergeant Heighway, who knew the couple well, had telephoned them from the house and asked them to come over. It was soon established that the Spencers had seen and heard nothing. It was normal for them not to see Dale for weeks at a time. The couple had known him since not long after he had first moved there, with his young wife and two children, in 1959. Differences in social background – Spencer worked at a nearby farm – had prevented the families becoming close, but they were on friendly terms, as neighbours, and their children had played with each other.

Mrs Spencer explained to the officers that although Susan,

the ex-wife, had left many years before, taking the children with her, she had been back a lot over the past year or so, working on the house with two of the children, Sophia and Marcus – pretty much every day, said Mrs Spencer, almost living in the little cottage on the other side, by the arch. But she did not think that Susan and Dale got on too well, because they both claimed the house was theirs and were involved in some long-running legal dispute. Of course, Mrs Spencer told the officers, she is not known as Mrs Dale any more, she is the Baroness de something, after her second husband. Susan and the children had not been seen for a couple of days though, which was surprising considering they had been almost every other day and that day had been so pleasant. Yes, said the woman, they would be the next of kin. A little while later, when he was free, Sergeant Heighway walked around to the Spencers' cottage with another arrival, Detective Sergeant David Clarke, for a second chat. Yes, said Mrs Spencer, Susan had made a point of giving her an address in case something happened: Forresters Hall, Docklow, near Leominster.

Evening became night. As the first arrivals waited for Cole and Dr Peter Acland, the Home Office pathologist, there was plenty to do. By now Heath House was no longer dark: it was lit brilliantly by spotlights, etching hard shadows on the ancient walls; dipping in and out of the light were a mixture of uniformed officers and casually dressed men going about their business or standing, smoking, making small talk. Strong tape sealed off the area immediately around the house; bright headlights shone through the trees.

Just after 9 p.m., Cole arrived. He was more used to this kind of scene than some of his colleagues in similar rural forces, for whom murders were relatively rare events. In addition to the Murrell murder, a clutch of other gruesome killings had somehow contrived to occur on his patch. No one could explain this; it was just the way things happened. Some might say that Cole did not discourage an appearance which might have been created for one of the more intelligent detective fictions. The bow tie, the balding crown, large glasses and an owlish appearance serve him well, particularly on television. Although he can be slightly ruddy of cheek and speaks with a soft West Country burr, he is no simple country copper. By 1987, Cole was an experienced criminal investigator.

But even the experienced investigator did not yet know how this one would go: whether he was facing the beginning of a series or the end result of a simple domestic argument. Heath House certainly had some of the same ingredients as the Murrell case: an elderly, slightly eccentric person and an isolated country house. But it was too early for certainties. There might be clear evidence of motive: an argument with a friend, who at this moment was remorsefully walking into his local police station; or perhaps a casual burglar sensing a quick in and out of a mansion stuffed, for all he knew, with valuable antiques.

Cole was quickly briefed by his detectives on the conversations with the Spencers and the obvious signs from the position and condition of the body. He and Clarke were detailed to go to Docklow. Their journey was necessary for several reasons: clearly this woman and her children were the closest relatives of the victim and still on some sort of speaking terms with him. Despite the divorce, they would have a right to know what had happened. And they had been in the area shortly before the murder – although precisely how long before was still in doubt. It was certainly possible they might have seen something.

Dr Acland arrived. He had been called at home in Birmingham. Like almost everyone else, he did not know where Heath House was; a police car led him from the village of Clun. A tall, pale man, Dr Acland has the morbidly cheerful disposition of those who confront death daily. He greeted Cole with easy familiarity and they went inside; they had stood over many bodies together, including that of Hilda Murrell; the pathologist was looking at possibly his 350th suspicious death.

Cole and Dr Acland examined the lobby and kitchen area carefully, treading on the duckboards now laid down to protect the potentially valuable evidence of the floor. They saw bloodstains about six feet up the lobby wall: this suggested that Dale, a tall man, had been struck by something while standing upright. Struck by what? Since there were a variety of domestic objects scattered around, it was possible that they could somehow have crashed down on him; the visible head wounds were not that severe: he could have staggered into the kitchen and collapsed where he had been found. It could still be an accident. As soon as it arose, they rejected this scenario: it did not explain the spray of blood which ran in an arc from the corner of the kitchen table near the door to the work surface surrounding the sink. It did not explain the bruising to Dale's throat.

There was little doubt this was murder, but the search for motive was more difficult; there was nothing immediately obvious to suggest one. It would always be that way. For the moment, although they saw no signs of a break-in, burglary would remain an option until the house had been fully examined – a process which could take days. There had been some kind of struggle in the kitchen lobby, but was this someone familiar being let into the house by Dale, or an intruder disturbed on entering? Who had drunk from the sherry glasses? Had anyone been about to share his meal? And which meal was it? Last night, or Saturday lunch? Or had he been lying there since Friday?

Dr Acland looked more closely at the body: decomposition had begun to set in; it was discoloured and gave off a nauseous odour. Dr Acland realised that rigor mortis had been and gone, suggesting that Dale had been dead for up to thirty-six hours. But the heat of the kitchen had accelerated deterioration of the body; it would never be possible for Dr Acland to determine with the accuracy that is normally available just when Dale had died. They allowed the body to be removed and taken to Hereford mortuary for the post-mortem examination. Just before midnight, Simon Dale left Heath House for the last time: finally sightless.

Matthews and Clarke had spent some time finding Forresters Hall. Docklow is little more than a scattered strip of houses along the main road in Leominster, about twenty miles to the south of Hopton Heath. They were looking for a large building but were directed by the local pub to two adjoining cottages, set back off the road. Just after 12.30 a.m. they parked in the road, opened the gate and walked down to the cottage on the left. In darkness, they passed several cars and knocked firmly on the door. No reply. They knocked and then hammered on the door. They heard stirrings inside. No one came to the door. They kept hammering and shouted who they were. It was clear that whoever was inside did not want to come to the door or even open a window to enquire who was knocking in the middle of the night. Matthews went for a stroll, peering in through the windows of three smart cars and one large white van. In the rear of one of the cars, an estate, he saw something glinting. He peered closer and saw what he thought was a long bright metal rod: a poker.

Eventually the lights came on. A young man opened the door, wearing a brown jumper over his pyjamas. He invited them straight into the house. He asked if they were policemen. They replied that they were and asked why it had taken such a time to answer the door. He said it had taken so long because there had been a lot of drunks around and he had telephoned the local station in Leominster, only to be told that it was the police themselves doing the knocking. Matthews thought his attitude was curiously belligerent.

As the conversation was continuing a woman appeared, fully dressed in a smart, flecked two-piece suit. The Baroness Susan Cecilia Mary de Stempel, formerly Mrs Simon Dale, and once Susan Wilberforce, invited them into the lounge. They were faced with a fifty-three-year-old, straight-backed woman of medium build and above-average height. Her hair was black and unremarkable, cut short. Parts of her face were deeply etched with wrinkles that were not unattractive in the way that they cut through the pale skin. She had two other distinguishing features. One was her mouth, which is strong and small, and often appears tightened and pursed, as if in permanent disapproval of the world around her. The second and strongest feature was her eyes: they are so much of a dark blue, they can appear almost black; they are well spaced, but deeply set. They do not always look at you directly, preferring to look down or sideways, but when their gaze turns upon you, as it now turned upon the two police officers, and the lips tighten just so much, it is difficult not to feel at some disadvantage.

The two officers sat and introduced themselves, Matthews and the woman facing each other across the fireplace. She did not ask why they were there, so Matthews said there was 'a problem' at Heath House. The police officers, working in a comfortable, rural area, were used to the tones of the upper-middle classes and the landed gentry, but her voice, although quiet and unemotional, had a particularly acute timbre. She asked, 'Has he burnt it down?' Without asking the officers why they had arrived in the middle of the night, she explained, in precise tones, that her ex-husband had known she wanted to sell Heath House, which she still owned and which she had recently been working on in order to improve its value. That was why she thought he might have burnt it down.

She sat next to her son, a jobbing gardener, Xenophon Marcus Savage Wilberforce, normally known as Marcus, nicknamed 'Nimmi' by the family because of his early affection for Elgar's Nimrod Variations. The two officers saw a slim, pale, diffident man, who looked considerably younger than his twenty-six years. His hair was straw-coloured and untidy and his small eyes, when they looked at the officers, were light blue. The detectives thought he looked nervous, because his knees were knocking together. When he spoke, he was more stammering and hesitant, but used the same tight-lipped, flat and unemotional tones as his mother.

Matthews said no, that was not the reason why they were there; Heath House had not burnt down. He asked if anyone else was in the house. The woman said there was. Matthews asked if she would fetch them. She went up the stairs and roused her other two children. After a short while, in which the others had sat in uncomfortable silence, Simon Quintin Savage Wilberforce appeared, then twenty-three, nicknamed 'Pigga', a younger but taller and more solid version of his elder brother. He wore a jumper and jeans. He was accompanied by their sister, Georgina Sophia, usually known by her second name, then twenty-five, a woman of medium build, with light-brown hair, blue eyes and what was once known as an 'English Rose' complexion, wearing a nightdress and dressing gown. There was something about her which gave a firmer impression than her brothers had, although she, like Marcus, looked far younger than her years.

They sat there and waited for Matthews to say something. Faced with their blank expressions and the distinctly awkward atmosphere, he took the plunge. He was very sorry, he said, but he was there to tell them that Simon Dale had been found dead at Heath House that afternoon. Deliberately, he added no further details, waiting to be asked for more, waiting for them to behave like an ordinary family. They did not. They continued to look at him, and stirred and shifted a bit, but otherwise there was no reaction. No one burst into tears or cried out. Sophia asked flatly if the death was 'inside or outside'. He said it was inside, that the police were making enquiries and informing them as next of kin. They continued to look at the two officers in a way which Matthews found quite unnerving. Punctuated by long pauses, the conversation continued for some time. Matthews does not remember describing the death as 'suspicious', although the four people he faced say he did, but he did not volunteer any details. The woman asked him several times if the house had been broken into. Matthews said police had found no evidence.

Matthews then asked about their movements over the weekend. The woman said the last time she had seen her husband had been the previous Friday, when there had been visitors to Heath House and she had taken the number of a caravanette parked in the grounds. She had been to the house twice on the Saturday and had not seen her husband; they had all stayed at Forresters Hall on Sunday. She told him a little more about the situation at Heath House. Matthews asked some routine questions about names and ages and who else needed to be notified. He said the police would be back later that day to carry out more detailed interviews. Matthews wondered what they thought he was there for.

The police officers left, the older woman seeing them on their way. In the driveway, Matthews asked if he could look into the Peugeot estate, which the woman said was hers. When she opened it, he bent inside and pulled out the poker from the rear footwell. As he held it up, the object gleamed in the moonlight, it was so highly polished. The woman asked Matthews if he was taking the poker away. When he said yes, she did not ask why.

The two police officers returned to Leominster police station. Matthews, clutching his trophy and ruminating on his encounter, wondered how this woman and three younger people, none with any visible means of financial support – and he knew that because she had said she needed to sell Heath House – managed to buy and run four new vehicles and live in a cottage crammed with expensive furniture, some of which was clearly too big for the place. He remembered a huge statue that might have been more at home in a garden and a large, dominant chandelier. As the car sped through the dark country night, he pondered on the strangeness of these people.

The night's work was far from over; for some, once it was broken, there could be no easy peace in the county that night. While the two policemen were at Docklow, a few miles to the south, on a cold slab at Hereford mortuary, the body of this woman's former husband lay naked. Bending over it was Dr Acland. He was surrounded by a number of others, including Cole and Dr Norman Weston, a scientist from the Home Office forensic science laboratory in Birmingham, who had also been called at home. The movements of Dr Acland's knife were painstakingly recorded by the video crew.

Dr Acland cut the body open and looked for internal bleeding. He prepared samples for analysis for alcohol and drugs. Turning to the head, he counted five separate wounds across the top of the forehead and the top of the back of the head, which seemed to have been caused by perhaps only two or three blows, none of which had been strong enough to crack the skull. But the most substantial bruising had been around the larynx. The damage to the throat, rather than any of those to the head, he realised, had been the cause of death. These blows, or more probably just one single blow, from a thin implement, he suggested, had shattered the larynx, causing the explosive arc of blood around the kitchen. He would estimate that the blow which had killed Simon Dale had been struck with the force which would be needed to drive a nail into a block of wood.

2
Old Families, New Money

The disconcerting woman with the black eyes and chilling accents carried upon her shoulders the accumulated but decaying weight of the centuries. She is the great-great-granddaughter of William Wilberforce, a name which will always be associated with the abolition of the slave trade. But Wilberforce also founded one of the great English landed-gentry families, and the woman encountered by police is a principal member of the current generation.

The name of Wilberforce ripples through the English establishment in a kind of minor key, connecting with, but rarely dominating, its major themes. Among their three pages in *Burke's Landed Gentry*, the Wilberforces are linked to all the great institutions – the public schools, Oxbridge, the law, the army, the civil service, both the Catholic and Anglican Churches and, by marriage, to many similar families.

The name of Wilberforce emerged out of the Dark Ages and into medieval Britain as the name of a village between York and Pocklington in what was once the North Riding and is now the county of North Yorkshire. The village was in a forest, renowned for its herds of wild boar, which earned it the name of Wild-Boar-Foss, later contracted to Wilberfoss. The lordship of Wilberfoss was passed by marriage from the de Kyme family of Lincolnshire, and in 1153 a Benedictine convent, later called St Mary's Convent, was established in the village and Henry II granted the convent a charter, naming William, son of Illgerus de Wilbefoss, and Osbert, son of Robert de Wilbefoss, as benefactors.

In 1643, about the time Heath House was being completed, William Wilberfoss, a grocer, is recorded as Mayor of the town of Beverley in Yorkshire. His grandson, another William, also became Mayor, in 1674. By this time the tradition had been established that the first son of the family was christened William, although in recent generations they have been known alternately by their second names. Thus the present head of the family, Susan's brother, was christened William John, but is known to everyone as John Wilberforce. His son, born in 1958, is the present William Wilberforce.

The grandson of William Wilberfoss became the first William Wilberforce and subsequently Mayor of Kingston-upon-Hull in 1722, where he had married the daughter of a leading merchant of the town, then part of Yorkshire. Their grandson was William Wilberforce, the abolitionist, who was born in August 1759 into what had become a prosperous, although essentially provincial, merchant family.

After studying at St John's College, Cambridge, William Wilberforce quickly made his mark on the national political stage, being elected MP for Hull in 1780 when he was only twenty-one. He would represent various constituencies in the county for forty-five years. At first, the young politician availed himself of the pleasures of London, particularly gambling at Boodle's, and enjoyed the company of Pitt the Younger and of Sheridan. However, according to a fellow Yorkshireman, G. C. Heseltine, he was 'inwardly religious' and, on a European tour in 1784–5, underwent a conversion.

In a somewhat caustic appraisal in his book, *Great Yorkshiremen*, Heseltine lambasted Wilberforce for coming close to being 'the greatest prig in English history'. Heseltine sums up Wilberforce in terms which might easily be applicable to his descendant, Susan: 'He possessed and cultivated a native tenacity and persistence, a hardness of mind and purpose which is the conspicuous quality of his kind.' Whether Heseltine's other conclusion applies to her is a matter for debate. He said: 'He fought all his life against powerful opposition and won a final and complete victory.'

He became one of the guardians of the nation's morals, helping to set the tone for the Victorian era. He was among those who founded the Church Missionary Society, the British and Foreign Bible Society and the Proclamation Society for the Suppression of Vice, and spent, according to one contemporary account, 'most of his fortune in philanthropic objects'. But he was no particular friend of the poor and, although a pacifist, supported the parliamentary bill which banned meetings of those protesting about the wars with the French as the cause of their poverty. 'His outlook was too narrowly bounded for him to see the whole truth,' said Heseltine, who observed that this 'pious little shrimp' would forever be associated with the 'soul-deadening gloom' of the Victorian Sunday.

But it was the ending of the then prosperous slave trade that became the true mission in life of William Wilberforce. He was the leading abolitionist in the Houses of Parliament, first introducing a bill in 1789. Three years later and largely due to his own tireless advocacy, the House of Commons carried a motion supporting its gradual abolition. But, due to opposition in the House of Lords, a series of bills supporting total abolition failed, until one eventually became law in 1807. The cause of abolition fired the man and he developed a reputation as an orator as well as a thinker and a writer of tracts. Boswell observed him speaking in Yorkshire: 'I saw a mere ship mount upon the table and as I listened the ship grew and grew until the ship became a whale.' Even Heseltine was prepared to acknowledge some qualities: 'He was an example of that strangely rare phenomenon in representative government, a man who in his principles and personal qualities represents his own people.' It was on his deathbed in 1833 that he heard of the final measure, the passing of a bill to compensate slave traders, which would ensure that all reason to carry on the business was lost. He was buried in Westminster Abbey.

William Wilberforce brought the Wilberforce family into the forefront of public life, ensuring that the name would always be associated with qualities of honesty and service; but it also sowed the seeds of the discontent and divisions that were to rack the family almost 200 years later. In May 1797, he married Barbara Spooner, who came from a prosperous family in Warwickshire. She gave him two things any Victorian gentleman would have wanted: four healthy sons who all went on to have long and illustrious careers and, something the Wilberforces had not previously obtained, property.

Markington Hall is a large mansion house built during the seventeenth century by the Spooner family and surrounded by several thousand acres of rolling Yorkshire farmland between Harrogate and Ripon. It became the family home of the Wilberforces, entitling the head of the family to the lordship of the Manor of Markington. The settlement lies between upland dales and lowland farmland, at a point where the

Pennines shelve down towards the Yorkshire Wolds and the eastern coastal plain. As at Heath House, one can sense in the breeze the calmness of meadow and pasture with a whiff of cool mountain air, the rush of fast streams and a hint of dark peaks just out of sight.

But, unlike the glowing brick of Heath House, Markington Hall is grey stone, reflecting the sombre countryside. Lying in the centre of the village, it is a solid, neat but once rambling building, small enough to be a family house and large enough to be impressive. Its garden, stretching along the roadside to the left of the house, is attractive and the product of much hard work by Laura, the American-born wife of the current Lord of the Manor, John Wilberforce. It is a mixture of flowerbeds and graceful lawns, surrounded by tall trees. A stream flows down the middle of the garden, and in front of the house there is a small bridge and a weir. Clusters of daffodils grow on the lawns in spring and geese can be seen wandering.

At Markington, between 1798 and 1807, Barbara Wilberforce bore her husband four sons, who doubtless all played in this very garden: William, Robert, Samuel and Henry. Many of their grandchildren and great-grandchildren became part of the drama which brought the Wilberforce name into the courts and the public spotlight in ways which would have horrified the 'pious little shrimp'. The divide between (on the one hand) William and Samuel, who sided with the established Anglican Church, of which their father was such an enthusiastic supporter, and (on the other) Robert and Henry, both converted to the Roman Catholic Church, echoed down through the generations.

Robert was born in 1802, went to Oxford, was ordained in 1826 and married the daughter of an archdeacon of the East Riding, a post he himself went on to hold. His wife died after two years of marriage, a few days after the birth of their second son, Edward, who went on to become a barrister and leading judge. In 1854, Robert entered the Roman Catholic Church and became a close associate of the great English Catholic, Cardinal Newman, who founded the Oratory School in Birmingham. A number of Wilberforces have been among its pupils, including, in the 1970s, Marcus and Simon Wilberforce.

Samuel, born in 1805, was successively Bishop of Oxford

and of Winchester. His wife Emily, daughter of the Rev. John Sargent, MP for Queensborough, bore him four sons. The eldest, Samuel, became a judge in India and was the father of Richard Wilberforce, now as Lord Wilberforce of Kingston-upon-Hull a respected ex-judge who for eighteen years sat as a Law Lord, a contemporary of Lords Denning and Scarman.

Henry, born in 1807, was the youngest. He married his sister-in-law, Mary Sargent, youngest daughter of the Rev. Sargent, briefly became vicar of East Farleigh in Kent before joining the Roman Catholic Church in 1850 and then becoming editor of the *Catholic Standard*. His grandson, Robert Francis Wilberforce, became a barrister and a diplomat serving in the Vatican City and New York. Both Robert Wilberforce and his cousin, Lord Wilberforce, became embroiled in the events which rocked their family in the late 1980s.

But it was the branch headed by William, the eldest son, which was most devastated by subsequent circumstances. He failed to make as much of a mark as his brothers, although he was doubtless a worthy MP for Hull. It was another three generations before the main line of the family was to distinguish itself.

By the 1900s, the Wilberforces had been totally bypassed by the industrial revolution sweeping through the nation during the Victorian era. While elsewhere in Yorkshire other families were making money from wool, coal and iron, the Wilberforces continued serving the Church, the law and the armed forces without ever giving rise to captains of industry or self-made men or women. That is not to say the family lived in poverty: they maintained a large house and grounds, as well as running an estate and a quarry, which provided a regular income. Nevertheless, the house was believed by some to be in need of considerable restoration and there was no substantial financial base for the family as they entered the new century.

The Lord of the Manor was William Basil, who lived the life of a country squire. By now, this branch were staunchly Roman Catholic, and Markington had its own chapel. William Basil's wife Margaret was a devout Catholic from an old Irish family, who, fuelled by her convictions, was said to have given to charity a significant portion of the remaining family wealth. Their first child was a girl, born on 23 November 1900, and she was named after her mother as Margaret Mary Clare Wilberforce, later to become Margaret, Baroness Illingworth of Denton.

The Illingworths, the family into which she would marry, were among the great wool dynasties of Bradford – 'Worstedopolis' as it was known – the greatest textile-manufacturing centre in the country. With undisguised but understandable pride, they were summed up perfectly by the *Yorkshire Observer* in 1920: 'The Illingworths are among the leaders of the markers of modern Bradford and the men who gave England its pre-eminence in the wool trade. They have been a family of hard-working, honest, keen businessmen who, at the same time, were foremost in the public service of their city and have contributed five Members of Parliament. They are fine, sturdy types of Yorkshiremen – men of strong character and a high sense of public duty.'

The dynasty had been founded by Daniel Illingworth, who on 23 May 1860 had watched with pride as his son Henry and his daughter Margaret married the sister and brother Mary and Angus Holden, children of Isaac Holden, founder of the largest wool-combing concern in the world, later created a baronet. The joint wedding formed a relationship between the two wool families that was cemented six years later when Alfred Illingworth, Daniel's elder son, succumbed to a third sibling, marrying Margaret, younger sister to Mary and Angus. Albert Illingworth was the middle of the three sons of Henry and Mary, born on 25 May 1865, just two months before the engines began to turn at Whetley Mills, the site chosen for the family wool-spinning business in Bradford. His father was a partner in the firm and a wealthy man, and the Illingworth sons enjoyed the best possible education.

Percy, the youngest and brightest, at first overshadowed his elder brothers. After Rugby, Cambridge and the Bar, he became MP for Shipley in 1906 at thirty-seven and successively Chief Secretary for Ireland, Parliamentary Secretary for the Treasury and Chief Whip. He was at his peak when he died in 1915, *The Times* calling him 'one of the most popular figures in the House of Commons'.

While the influence of the family steadily grew both as leading industrialists and as provincial politicians, Albert was educated at private schools in London and Switzerland and joined the family firm. At the age of thirty, in accordance with tradition, he married a Holden girl, Annie Elizabeth Holden Crothers, a member of a branch of the family which had extensive wool-combing works in France. Although they were married for more than thirty years they were childless because of his infertility, due, it was widely believed, to an attack of mumps in his youth. But she remained the loyal wife in Bradford and London. Albert became the senior partner in Daniel Illingworth and a director of two Holden companies. By 1910, like his father before him, he became president of Bradford Chamber of Commerce and a leading figure in the town's industrial life.

At fifty, he emerged from his brother's shadow to stand for Parliament as a Coalition Liberal. He was returned unopposed in November for the Heywood constituency in Lancashire after the death in the Dardanelles of the sitting MP and was immediately appointed to a number of key government committees on industry and post-war reconstruction. Successful in politics as in business, a year later he was made Postmaster-General in the War Cabinet by the new Prime Minister Lloyd George.

The Times damned him with faint praise: only after pointing out that he was 'a brother of Mr Asquith's favourite Chief Whip' did the Thunderer acknowledge 'a notable appointment'. In fact, the composition of the Cabinet he joined was acclaimed as a bold political stroke, since it introduced into the government a group of ministers who had experience of commerce and industry, including a number who were not members of either House of Parliament. He was made a Privy Counsellor and remained Postmaster-General throughout the war years, making a loyal, if unspectacular, contribution. His speeches around the country were always on domestic issues such as the postal services and the need for post-war reconstruction.

In December 1918, the first proper elections after the war saw Albert Illingworth elected member for the Heywood and Radcliffe division and he remained Postmaster-General in the new government until 1921. But the immediate post-war period was clearly a time of great stress for all, and government ministers worked long hours. At Otley Petty Sessions, on 4 July 1919, the Postmaster-General, of all people, was fined £3 for possessing an out-of-date dog licence for the animals he kept at his Yorkshire home, at Denton in Wharfdale. He cited 'pressure of public business in London' in mitigation. Later that month he was confined to a nursing home, forcing both him and his wife to miss the victory procession in London. The next year, the trouble was worse: nerve strain leading to high blood pressure, reported *The Times*, meant that Mr Illingworth had joined 'the growing ranks of ministerial invalids'. He went to Monte Carlo to recuperate. But the writing was on the wall and in May 1921 he retired, accepting the customary peerage from a grateful nation and becoming the first (and only) Baron Illingworth of Denton. Although an active Liberal peer, effectively his political career had peaked.

He returned to the business world, but that of the boardrooms of London, rather than the mills of Bradford. By now he had sold the company, then the last-remaining large Bradford wool firm still in private hands, for £780,000, of which he would have received a sizeable share, since he was still chairman and co-owner, with his brother Harry and two cousins.

As is still the case, big companies liked to have on their boards politicians with government experience, mainly because of the wealth of knowledge and contacts among the corridors of power they bring with them, and Lord Illingworth enjoyed a new lease of life in a number of lucrative appointments, including directorships of the Ford Motor Company in Britain and of the National Provincial Bank and its foreign arm, the Lloyds and National Provincial Foreign Bank. It was perhaps no surprise in 1930 when he joined the Conservative Party.

All was not entirely well on the domestic front. Lord Illingworth's inability to have a family may have been responsible for the first Lady Illingworth turning to drink. There were long periods of separation with either Lord Illingworth in Monte Carlo and his wife in London or vice-versa. Lady Illingworth was sometimes, according to *The Times*, 'recuperating after a short illness', although her drinking became public knowledge. Inevitably, there were rumours of his womanising. They divorced in 1926.

He is said to have met Margaret Wilberforce during a shooting party on the grouse moors. Whatever eyebrows may have been raised or family displeasure expressed at a woman marrying a man twice her age were probably outweighed by the evident suitability of the match of a couple clearly very much in love, who both enjoyed parties, socialising and the good life. It would have been distasteful to have mentioned the fact that he was very wealthy but it was family rumour that an earlier engagement – to Charles Dormer, later Sir Charles, the fifteenth Baron Dormer and head of the same Dormer family that her brother William had married into – had been opposed on the grounds that he did not have enough money. However, also according to family lore, there was nonetheless resistance from the Wilberforces because the Illingworth money was considered by some to be not quite the right kind of money – they were, after all, self-made men, from an industrial background. This was just too much for some of the Wilberforces, with their long history of selfless service to Church and state.

There was certainly one other major problem for the family in giving its approval. The Catholic Church does not recognise divorce and at the insistence of the family, supported by her younger brother Robert (who had considered entering the Church at one point), Margaret and Lord Illingworth waited four years until the first Lady Illingworth died in a nursing home in 1930. But although the period was deeply frustrating for both, it did allow Lord Illingworth, then living in Belgravia, to complete the purchase of a house in Grosvenor Square, in Mayfair, and spend a considerable amount of his money on renovations for his young bride.

They were eventually married on a rainy day in November 1931 by the Abbot of Ampleforth at St Joseph's Church in the village of Bishop's Thorton, the neighbouring village to Markington. Whatever differences may have existed were put aside for the wedding, a thoroughly Yorkshire affair. The bride was given away by her younger brother William, then Lord of the Manor and later Susan's father, before a full cast of Wilberforces, Illingworths and Holdens, as well as tenants from the Ramsgill estate of the Illingworths and from the Markington Hall estate. The *Yorkshire Observer* reported that because of the rain 'a more wretched day for a wedding could scarcely have been possible'. The church was filled with villagers, while others stood outside, eager to see this great politician from London marry the lady from the Hall. The reception was held at Markington but the couple did not remain in Yorkshire for long – Grosvenor Square beckoned. The house at number 44 would become the focal point of the new Lady Illingworth's life; its opulent surroundings would first be a home, then a source of envy and ultimately of wealth for her niece, Susan, more than half a century later.

'The very name of Mayfair', says the first of two volumes on the Grosvenor estate in the *Survey of London*, 'has become a byword for quality, not least because of the strong and characteristic architecture and the total absence of mean or derelict streets.' Sir Thomas Grosvenor, from an ancient Cheshire family, acquired the 1000 acres of meadow and pasture in 1677 on his wedding to Mary Davis, daughter of a scrivener (in modern terms a broker or notary) of the City, who inherited them on her father's death.

The eight acres of the Square were developed between 1725 and 1731. Of the fourteen four-storey, many-roomed houses on the south side, most were leased by Sir Robert Grosvenor, fourth Baronet and Whig MP for Chester, to MPs and assorted dukes or earls. Number 50 was occupied by the Hon. Anne Vane, mistress of Frederick, Prince of Wales, and number 43 by the Duchess of Kendal, mistress of his father, King George I, whose statue dominated the ornamental garden in the centre of the Square. The first occupant of the forty rooms of number 44 was Oliver St George, son of an Irish baronet, and Whig MP for Dungannon in Ireland. He bought the house for £3400 in 1730, only to die the following year. His widow, like Lady Illingworth, lived on alone for many years, and following her death in 1747 the house had a number of owners until it was sold to Lord Harrowby in 1804.

The Square and the house were then at the zenith of the social life of London's political world, and Lord Harrowby was a fitting occupant. A member of an important family, MP for Tiverton in Devon, he probably bought the house to celebrate his appointment as Foreign Secretary under Willam Pitt.

Between 1812 and 1827, Lord Harrowby was Lord President of the Council in Lord Liverpool's Cabinet, which regularly dined together at the private homes of its members. On the evening of 21 June 1815, they were dining at number 44 when the Duke of Wellington's aide-de-camp, Major the Hon. Henry Percy, arrived in a chaise and four amid much commotion to bring news of the great victory over Napoleon at Waterloo, three days earlier. The Meissen dinner service on which they were eating is still kept at the Harrowby family home in Staffordshire.

This habit of dining together gave rise to another footnote in history for number 44. The early 1820s were a time of economic distress and radical unrest and one of those rare creatures, an English revolutionary, Arthur Thistlewood, heard of this regular event. He planned the assassination of the entire Cabinet at number 44 on 23 February 1820, and hoped to carry their severed heads through the streets of London. Lord Harrowby heard of the plot and, although the Duke of Wellington planned to carry on with the dinner and have the assassins caught by guards posted outside the house, the rest of the Cabinet ordered the arrest of the conspirators. They were captured as they left rooms in Cato Street, which gave the affair its name, and were later hanged. The dinner was cancelled.

In 1913, the house was bought by Sir Ernest Cable, later Baron Cable, a merchant, whose earned, rather than inherited, money underlined the social changes taking place. Although by the 1920s the total number of peers, baronets and knights living on the estate remained the same, their own background was slowly altering. Some of the older residents were moving to mansion flats in Park Lane or Belgravia, selling their homes to businesses or to the new money, made from industry and commerce. Foreign missions were attracted by the fine, spacious houses. In 1910, the *Survey of London* notes, there was just the Italian Embassy on the Grosvenor estate. 'By 1921, there were seven embassies and legations, four in Grosvenor Square alone.'

There were still a large number of houses in private hands. 'The ritual of the social season continued and in the unfashionable months, cruises to the Mediterranean or the West Indies . . . but cocktail parties, "by far the cheapest way of entertaining" and "cheap cabarets and intime night clubs" were replacing the lavish private receptions of Edwardian times.' New money was taking over from old. By the 1940s, the titles of around half the peers resident on the estate had been created since 1900. One of them was Lord Illingworth of Denton, who bought number 44 from Baron Cable in 1927.

*

Number 44 had been renovated extensively and decorated sumptuously on behalf of Lord Illingworth for his young bride. The morning room was in Spanish green and gold and contained a portait of the new owner in his Privy Council robes. In the panelled drawing room, with its Adam ceiling, the antique furniture was upholstered with silk; a marble-topped table was placed in the centre. Every room was full of fine furniture and thick carpets, antiques and objets d'art of all types, clocks, mirrors and ornaments, thick drapes and curtains. At the end of the paved garden, decorated with neo-classical statues, benches and tubs of flowers, there was a temple. On its pediment was the Illingworth coat of arms.

The couple enjoyed their wealth in a house built for such pleasures. Lady Illingworth was young and attractive, as tall as her still vigorous husband, and took to her new home and life with gusto, shedding generations of Wilberforce austerity. And it was only natural that he, with a full and active career behind him, no longer troubled by ill-health, would wish to relish his money and his autumn years in style, in his newly decorated and historic home and with his young wife, showing her off to London society. While the rest of the world suffered from the years of the Depression and Nazism began to dominate Europe, they enjoyed a blissful existence as hosts to diplomatic and political London; they became regular faces at all the grand occasions, the balls, the race courses, the grouse moors.

Number 44 saw at least two dinner parties a week. The food was sometimes served on silver plates decorated with the Illingworth crest; the glassware and china were exquisite. The guest lists were duly recorded in *The Times*, a combined roll-call of the House of Lords and the London Diplomatic List, drawing upon Lord Illingworth's by now extensive political, diplomatic and business contacts. She became what her belated obituary was to call an 'indefatigable hostess', assisted by a dozen or more servants. There was racing at Ascot and winters in the South of France. In 1934, Lady Illingworth had her picture painted twice by the society artist Philip de László – renowed for his portraits of the nobility – and hung them in the drawing room. In 1936, they attended the Coronation of King George VI and had their pictures painted in the robes they wore on the occasion. Velvet draperies hung in Westminster Abbey for the Coronation were obtained and turned into upholstery for the armchairs in the morning room. The new Lady Illingworth took great interest in the history of the house and declared that she would give a ball every year on 21 June to mark the anniversary of the news of Waterloo reaching London. But Yorkshire and the Wilberforces were not forgotten; despite the determined Anglicanism of her husband, she remained a devout Roman Catholic; in 1933, she opened the Wilberforce Centenary Exhibition in Hull and took a keen interest in the anti-slavery cause. She remained, always, deeply fond of Markington Hall, where she had grown up.

There were few concessions to the growing threat of war, and life continued in the same luxurious manner until the late summer of 1939. But when war came, with the threat of the bombing of London, their beloved Grosvenor Square was reluctantly abandoned for the comparative safety of Markington, at that time unusually empty. Both her brothers, Robert and William, were away at war.

Lord Illingworth had already devoted time, money and energy to Markington, doubtless gratefully received by the Wilberforces. In addition to work inside the house, he had paid for the renovation of the adjoining barn and outbuildings. One part was converted to house the family chapel because, he said, he was 'fed up with the workers from the estate marching through the house to attend Mass every week'. After taking up residence at Markington, Lord and Lady Illingworth did their bit for the war effort. She joined the Voluntary Aid Detachment and became a commandant. Part of Markington was given over as a billet for senior officers of the Canadian Army, one of whom just happened to be a friend of the Illingworths, General Harry Crerar. It is said that he and his colleagues planned the Allied invasion of Sicily from the kitchen.

By this time, Lord Illingworth was in his early seventies. He had made a new will, leaving everything to his second wife but showing his continued opposition to her faith by introducing the condition that she did not enter a convent or join any religious order. It may have been more of a private joke than anything else; although a devout Catholic, Lady Illingworth clearly enjoyed her social life far too much to contemplate anything so drastic.

He died on 23 January 1942, at Markington after a short

illness. On his death, Lady Illingworth inherited, as planned, the entire estate: £5000 in cash, jewellery, wines, at least one Rolls-Royce, 44 Grosvenor Square and £288,000 on trust. It was enough to keep her in comfort for the rest of her life.

The funeral at Bradford Cathedral was very much a Yorkshire affair. Lady Illingworth was comforted by her two brothers and surrounded by many other members of the Wilberforce, Illingworth and Holden families. The city itself was also present: the Lord Mayor, the Town Clerk, the President of the Chamber of Commerce, representatives of the National Provincial Bank, of the Worshipful Company of Weavers and, of course, although no longer the family firm, of Daniel Illingworth and Sons, all came to pay tribute.

After the ceremony, the cortège swept back past the Cathedral and up the Otley Road, climbing above the back-to-back brick and grey stone terraces of the families of the mill workers, now fighting the war, along Undercliffe Lane and then left into the Undercliffe Cemetery, where in the central promenade are the graves and monuments of the Holdens and Illingworths. On that January day, for those Wilberforces who had never been there, it would have been an extraordinary sight.

Not just the Holden and Illingworth families, but during Bradford's heyday of Victorian capitalism, many more of the town's leading industrialists and prominent figures vied with each other, in death as in life, to create the most portentous or exotic monuments as their tombstones among the twenty-five acres of the Undercliffe Cemetery. At their more concentrated and ornate in the centre, they resemble closely packed skyscrapers, bizarrely represented in the finest of the Victorian gothic funerary art as columns, needles, obelisks, steeples, draped urns and a multitude of Celtic and Roman crosses, standing harshly silhouetted against the skyline of Worstedopolis.

By far the most solid and substantial is the Holden family tomb, a square monument with double columns on each corner, topped by barrel vaulting and a cupola, and the Illingworth mausoleum, a grey granite, mock-Egyptian temple, sealed with bronze doors, guarded by two sphinxes and decorated with the insignia of the Sun God. It is said that when Sir Isaac Holden was ordered by his doctors to take a rest from overwork he went

to Egypt and described the monuments of that country in letters
to his children, thus providing inspiration for the tombs of the
pharaohs of the wool trade. Forget the temporal powers of mill
owning and civic duties, all the monuments seem to say, here
is real and lasting power over the generations.

That January day, as his forebears looked on, Lord Illingworth
was laid to rest under the more simple monument to his grandfather, Daniel, a tall marble column topped by a draped urn
which had been erected by Lord Illingworth's father. As the
coffin was placed in the vault among those of his father and
grandfather and the great stone slab was slid back into place,
Lady Illingworth will have repeated to herself the vow she
made at Grosvenor Square, knowing that their age difference
would inevitably shorten the full life they shared. As a Catholic,
she knew they would be reunited eventually, but she wanted
something else. 'When I die, I want to be buried here with
Albert,' she vowed. It was not to be. And the woman who
would deny Lady Illingworth her vow was her niece, Susan,
then just seven years old.

3
Two Suitors

Susan Cecilia Mary Wilberforce was born on 6 May 1934, at a house belonging to her godparents, a family called Hibberd, in Queen's Gate, which lies between Hyde Park and South Kensington in west London. 'My first memory', she says, 'is of my nanny lowering the rail at the side to peer into my cot.' The nanny, shared with other children, and an endless round of distant relatives, rather than her parents, are the dominant figures of Susan Wilberforce's early life.

She was the child of Lady Illingworth's younger brother William, born in 1904, and his wife Cecilia, who came from another landed Catholic family, the Dormers. While the Wilberforces were mayors of Beverley, the Dormers were already among the nobility, having been soldiers, diplomats and landowners since Sir Robert Dormer was created the first baronet by King James I in 1615. The present Baron, at the time of writing, Joseph Spencer Philip Dormer, the sixteenth, inherited the title from his brother on his death in 1975. He is an unmarried elderly landowner in Warwickshire on whose death the title will pass to Geoffrey Henry Dormer, a descendant of the eleventh Baron, and Susan's uncle. 'They are all frightfully eccentric. Most of the men are gay and the women are gardeners,' says Susan.

Cecilia Dormer was the daughter of Captain Edward Dormer, of Dorset, and Vanessa Borwick, whose father was Lord Borwick, from yet another wealthy landed family. Thus the marriage of William Basil Wilberforce and Cecilia Dormer had cemented links between three of the great landed families of England. William, aged thirty when his daughter was born, and in India as a captain in the 1st Battalion of the King's Own Yorkshire Light Infantry, one of a number of Wilberforces to serve the regiment, already had a son and heir, William John, born in 1930.

Until Susan was in her late teens, she and her brother led a rather rootless existence, shifted between relatives, homes and schools, a process caused partly by the dislocations and deaths of war, partly by their variety of relatives and also by English upper-class schooling methods, which contrive to keep the children as far away from the family home as possible. It was something Susan's own children would also have to suffer.

When her father's army career took him and her mother to India, she was sent to live with Dormer relatives. Susan remembers Gwendoline Dormer explaining that she was not Susan's mother, that her mother was the woman sending postcards from distant lands.

When their parents returned to the United Kingdom, her father was even less of a visible presence. 'I can just remember him reading a newspaper on the day the war broke out. And once he came and took us for the weekend to a hotel in Uckfield in Sussex.' It was the last time she would see him. Lieutenant-Colonel William Wilberforce was killed in action in Tunisia, by a sniper's bullet, while on loan commanding the East Surrey Regiment, a curious body for a Yorkshireman to be leading. He was awarded the Distinguished Service Order. He died, Susan discovered later, on her ninth birthday, and she realised she had never really had a father, just a memory of a man who was 'very good-looking, very tall'. The effect of the loss of a barely known father on someone so young can only have been traumatic. Even if Susan did not then recognise it as such, the lack of a father was to influence the ultimately disastrous choice of the two most important men in her life.

It might have mattered less if she had had some other central core to her existence. But she had neither doting mother nor stable family home. Her mother, Susan would later confide to her own children, 'never really liked girls', and so Susan seems to have been simply treated as a burden to be shifted on to as many relatives as possible. 'Cecilia liked men. Girls were just something to be tolerated,' said another member of the family.

By the time of the death of her father, she was a boarder at St Mary's Convent in Ascot, like all convents a place of strict rules and regulations, reinforcement of orthodoxy and, just in case she needed any more, emotional repression. Weekends were spent with her great-uncle Sir Cecil Dormer and his wife Lady Mary, who lived nearby; holidays were sometimes with her mother and other relatives, sometimes at Markington. 'A sweet thing, running about Markington around then. She had lovely curls,' said one cousin of Susan shortly after the death of her father. At school, she acquired the nickname 'Chubby'.

In 1949, when Susan was fifteen, she was sent to Paris to continue her schooling, although by this time it was clear that she was not the academic type. Not that it was so important in that era. She was staying with friends of her mother, the Comte and Comtesse Ogier de Lesseps, and attending a convent school in the Rue de Lubeck, near the Arc de Triomphe. Susan treated it as an adventure. 'Every morning I would get up and go off about seven-thirty. And I would return about four-thirty in the evening and they would think I had been at the school. In fact I had been wandering the streets all day, exploring Paris. I cannot remember what happened as a result. I expect I got a lecture about it.' After about a year, it was back to St Mary's for another year to study domestic science, 'because I felt I needed to learn something about real life'. She ended her education without a single qualification.

In 1950, her mother Cecilia had married again, this time Lieutenant-Colonel Hugh de Neufville Lucas, from a Scottish family, who was an officer in the Indian cavalry and an international polo judge, which meant they spent a lot of time abroad, leading what someone later described as a 'rather glamorous life'. Cecilia also suffered from the disfavour of the Wilberforces for marrying a divorcé, although this may not have worried her unduly.

Cecilia, a woman of strong personality, never particularly liked the other Wilberforces, considering them a little straitlaced, nor the Illingworths, possibly because they were 'new money'. She certainly never had much of a relationship with her sister-in-law, the one who actually was on the beneficial end of the Illingworth money – possibly as a result of jealousy. After the war she had taken delight in planting creepers to cover the plaque Lord Illingworth had put up to mark the work he had carried out on Markington. The effect of all this was to distance Susan's mother from Markington and the Wilberforces and from her own daughter, in whom, it was made clear, she was not that interested. Although Susan would always get on well with her mother and also with her stepfather, whom she liked, their marriage meant she had even less of a stable homelife than before. Crucially, she also carried with her, drummed in from an early age, her mother's dislike for the Illingworth name.

But it was her aunt, Lady Illingworth, on whom she was now thrown. At Markington, where Susan was now living, the chubby, lonely teenager formed a close friendship with Lady Illingworth, or Aunt Puss as she was called by the family because of her love of cats. Following a period of mourning for Albert, Aunt Puss had moved into the White House, a cottage just a few hundred yards from the gates at Markington, where she would remain for nearly ten years. 'We used to walk around the estate together,' Susan remembers. 'She knew the names of all the estate workers and they all knew and liked her.' Since both had lost the men closest to them within the space of a few months and Susan now lacked a mother, it was not surprising that a sympathetic relationship developed.

Although Susan was on good terms with her brother John, there were certainly no suggestions that he had a rebellious nature. At Markington and at Ampleforth, the great Roman Catholic school run by monks, John had spent all his time in his room studying Latin and Greek and was to graduate from Oxford with a first in classics. He was, according to everyone who knew him, quite, quite brilliant. The one thing he did share with his sister was complete control of his feelings.

It is an unfortunate fact that children who come from broken or dislocated homes or who simply lack, for one reason or another, the closeness and warmth of a stable family life find it difficult to express their own emotions or conquer an inbuilt natural reserve and shyness as they grow up. And so it appears to be the case with Susan and her brother, neither of whom had received any kind of encouragement towards openness through their schooling or their family background. In their late teenage years, first John and later Susan would display those facets of their characters that would later be described, in variations on the same theme, as cold, aloof, calculating and emotionless in the case of Susan, and bookish, reserved, aesthetic and emotionally controlled in the case of John. In effect, they were two sides of the same unemotional coin.

In the wake of her mother's remarriage, Susan was left at rather a loose end. She was too young to be the lady of Markington, and anyway it would be assumed that John, as Lord of the Manor, would eventually be entitled to occupation of the house. Besides, she would be more or less on her own at Markington, since Aunt Puss had declared her period of mourning over and was determined to return to London and Grosvenor Square.

Both Lady Illingworth and her other brother, Robert, born in 1905, a successful solicitor after Oxford and war service, became concerned about Susan's future. With Cecilia living a new life, mostly in Scotland, and John away at university, these two comfortably wealthy relatives felt responsible for the welfare of the daughter of their late brother. It was an assistance they would give, both willingly and unknowingly, for the rest of their lives.

There was talk of Robert, known as Uncle Wee because of his great size, assuming some legal responsibility for Susan, which never came to anything, but he certainly accepted that he would help her out financially. They agreed that Susan should go and live in Billericay with him and his wife Marion. (Marion was, according to everyone who encountered her, very non-Wilberforce, a dashing, glamorous Scotswoman who had earned herself a reputation as a courageous pilot in the Royal Air Force Auxiliary during the Second World War, ferrying aircraft around the world.) And Aunt Puss would help Susan by realising a long-held ambition of her own: she had never had a daughter to 'bring out' as a debutante on the London social circuit, now reawakening after the post-war austerity. Susan, whose own mother was unavailable, would provide the perfect opportunity for Aunt Puss to have a surrogate mother–daughter relationship.

Early in 1953, as Susan was preparing for her debutante season, she and John divided the spoils. Their father had died without making a will, their mother had remarried, so they simply divided up the estate as they saw fit. 'John was going to the Foreign Office and getting married and I was going to live in London, so we just cut it apart,' said Susan. 'I had most of the farmland [about 2000 acres, including a quarry] and John had the house. It seemed a better idea than having half of each. Then we went around the house spinning a coin to divide up the contents. It seemed the most sensible thing to do.'

*

'Summer has reached London at last,' trilled Jennifer's 'Social Journal' in the July 1953 issue of the *Tatler*, the first full year of the new Elizabethan age. It was certainly a summer to make the most of, for, as the new Queen was crowned at Westminster Abbey, the upper echelons of London society shook off the post-war gloom and indulged in an orgy of self-congratulation and celebration, determined to show that nothing had been changed by years of war and social and economic upheaval. Despite all the changes wrought by the Labour Party in the late 1940s, now that the Conservatives were in power again it was more acceptable to stress background and superior breeding. Most of those involved would simply have seen it as a reaffirmation of what they considered to be most correct about the world.

The *Tatler*, of course, was more concerned with enjoyment than needless speculation about the changes in society. There were more things to worry about than the grim past or the uncertain future. After the blissful agonies of the Coronation and all its pomp and splendour, its positive ranking of society by invitation, London was informed that it could relax and really begin to enjoy life: 'Parties and dances, Ascot, Wimbledon and Henley all lie ahead, with their own special brand of pleasure and delight,' gloated the *Tatler*, which advised: 'For complete relaxation – between coming from luncheon and tea and going out to dinner – lie flat on your back with your feet raised. . . .' Many of the other pages of the *Tatler* were filled, as they are now, with glowing, detailed, slightly breathless accounts of this social maelstrom, bolstered by as many titles, names and frocks – 'looking sweet in white lace' or 'beautiful in a dress of peach satin and tulle' – as can be crammed into one paragraph, accompanied by many, many pictures.

But pride of place belonged to the debutantes, beneficiaries of that peculiarly English custom of presenting the young women of the gentry into London society in or about their eighteenth year, when they are considered the right age to 'come out' from childhood into the adult world, celebrated by the throwing of a lavish dance or ball and climaxing in their presentation to the Monarch, in this case the new young Queen. A debutante's season comprises obligatory attendance at the dances of all her friends, or of the daughters of the friends of her mother. It is inevitably an excuse for a good deal of gratuitous socialising and competition between mothers as to who can mount the most flamboyant occasion attended by the best selection of prospective husbands for their offspring. The pictures in the *Tatler* that month were of young women in gowns chosen by their mothers and young men in dinner jackets which made them look older than their years, gathered, as the captions reported, 'sharing a joke' or 'sitting one out', or even 'discussing their plans for the evening'.

Back in Grosvenor Square, reopened for business once more, Lady Illingworth could not have been happier. Not only was the London society she had loved before the war in full swing, but she would stage Susan's coming-out ball at the house. This in itself was something of coup. Few people in those days could boast a London property suitable for such an event. Albert had been unable to provide his wife with a daughter, but his money would allow Margaret to indulge Susan instead.

Susan, now nineteen, hated it. 'She'd had her eyes on me for ages, she'd always wanted to do it.' Forced to live at Grosvenor Square — 'dusty because she couldn't afford the full staff any longer' — Susan would get up very early and rush downstairs when the post arrived to sort through all the invitations and hide all the ones that she did not want to attend.

In that July's *Tatler*, amid all the inebriated jollity, there is one of those rare photographs which capture something the photographer probably never intended to find: a frozen moment that means more decades later than it ever was meant to say at the time. Standing awkwardly against the rich backdrop of one of the rooms of the Grosvenor Square house is a chubby-faced young woman, her small mouth nervously pursed, her dark eyes wide, with just a hint of fear about them, her shoulders drawn slightly back. Susan, in a rather plain ball gown, clutches, perhaps more tightly than she needs to, the chain of a small purse, almost as if it is her only protection.

Next to her is the altogether more imposing figure of Lady Illingworth, resplendent in richly decorated gown and tiara, shoulders squared, ready for anything. Nevertheless, there is a slight hint of hesitation about her manner, as though something has just passed between them, or as though she knows all is not well with her charge.

The occasion merited a whole page in the *Tatler*, but frustratingly little text. 'The only remaining private house in Grosvenor Square was a very gay scene,' it reported. 'Over 300 guests were present at one of the more memorable dances in this summer. An occasion such as this in Grosvenor Square brings memories of past elegance.'

There is one other picture of significance, a small one, tucked away in the bottom right-hand corner. 'The Hon. Robert Maude, son and heir of Viscount Hawarden, with Miss Camilla Minioprio and Miss Diana Birbeck,' it says underneath, showing the trio sitting against what is clearly an outside wall in the rear garden, none of them looking directly into the camera. In the background, unnamed but clearly visible between the two women, is a smaller figure, her back to the wall, leaning slightly forward and looking, with that characteristic direct gaze, right into the camera, apparently all alone at her own party. A foretaste of isolation.

Most of those present did not remain her friends for long – they were just part of the shifting social circle of wealthy young bucks and does, invited whether they were known to you or not. When one guest, who knew Susan, was asked later about the evening, he said he had difficulty distinguishing the occasion from all the others: 'There were just so many dances then.' He remembered Susan though: 'A sweet girl, as I recall, pleasant and quiet, round-faced and sort of baby-looking.' A fellow debutante has a slightly more critical view: 'She was a rather gauche little flower, but with these dark eyes and a calculating look about her. She was a bit of a loner – she would never get into a corner and have a giggle with the rest of us girls.' Another young man on the circuit put it this way: 'She was very pretty, but also very intelligent. She had this streak of toughness about her which she didn't always show, except when she had to, if you see what I mean.'

For Susan, much of the season and the occasion itself were uncomfortable, leaving few pleasant memories. 'I came out and went back in again as quickly as possible,' she said. In the eyes of the others she also failed, during her season, to find a husband, at least not immediately. She had already received one proposal from a rather unusual young man mingling among the throng in 44 Grosvenor Square that night, who had just been sent down from Oxford. It would be thirty years before she took him up on it.

Michael Victor Jossif Walter de Stempel was twenty-two, a familiar but slightly exotic figure amid the members of fashionable London who gathered at that party. Although thirty-seven years later, at his trial for defrauding the woman whose generous hospitality he was enjoying to its fullest extent that June evening, his own counsel would describe him as 'a congenital liar', 'a monumental snob' and 'a man without courage', to those gathered at Grosvenor Square he was 'a rather entertaining sort of chap'.

Many of the young people, in their white ties and ball gowns, formed a loosely knit group based around shared public schooldays, distantly related families, Oxbridge colleges, debutante balls, parties at Claridge's and the Ritz. For them, Michael was an enjoyable character, slightly eccentric for one so young, good to have around, who would invite you to parties but warn you not to come if you did not have white tie (although everyone did).

Only his three wives and four children appear to have made any impression upon him. He never seemed to get close to his many male acquaintances and friends. Or, at least, they will not admit to it now, stressing that yes, they knew Michael, of course, 'everyone did', but never that well. Three decades ago, however, when society people in London were having fun, Michael was good to know.

One friend, who despite falling victim to what might be described as 'advantage-taking' by Michael, still remembers him fondly. 'He made us all laugh. He had a strong personality in a mad sort of way. He was quite dotty.' When confronted with accusations about certain dubious behaviour, Michael was insouciant: 'He just sort of whistled away, you know, as though nothing was the matter, blaming it all on his unhappy childhood.' Another old acquaintance put it differently: 'He had the gift of the gab, he would talk his way out of anything. Do you know, I saw him a couple of years ago in the King's Road and he was exactly the same as he used to be? I just can't understand how anyone can change so little in thirty years.'

His father, Victor de Stempel, was a White Russian bearing

an ancient Latvian title, which enables Michael to call himself Baron de Stempel, although it is fair to say he uses the prefix only when it suits him, and it has no particular standing in this country. *Debrett's* does not recognise it, a fact likely to trouble him. Victor de Stempel was, in contrast to his son, 'quiet and dignified, a proper gentleman', say those who remember him. According to his son, he was a former guards officer in the army of the Tsar. He fled Russia after the 1917 revolution and spent some time in Holland, before arriving in London in the 1920s. In 1928, Victor married Dawn Beaumont, the stepdaughter of a member of the Dunkels family, leading diamond merchants, and was employed by the company. Michael, the only child, was born in 1929 and the couple were divorced in 1932. (Five years later this led to an extraordinary action for slander in the courts in which Victor de Stempel claimed that his former wife's step-father had made malicious statements about him – specifically, 'Victor is a Jew-hater' – to his cousin, Otto Dunkels, so that he would dismiss Victor from his employment. And dismissal in the diamond trade implied only one thing – theft. After a long, tedious but highly publicised case, Victor won £6000 damages, an enormous sum in those days. He subsequently spent his time between France and the Channel Islands.)

Michael was brought up largely by his mother and her step-mother, who was the beneficiary of a good deal of Dunkels money, at a house near Windsor. He went to Beaumont, a Catholic public school now closed, run very strictly by Jesuit priests, and then to Stonyhurst, in Lancashire, still a well-known Catholic school, attended by many Wilberforces. Along came National Service and he was commissioned into a Catholic unit, the Royal Ulster Rifles, becoming a second lieutenant. He decided he rather liked it, and developed an abiding interest in medals, which fitted well with his other growing passion: genealogy, heraldry and particularly his own lineage. 'He became obsessed with titles and all that sort of thing. It became very important to him.'

By now, Michael was following the path of his type and class. There was little else to do but go to Oxford. He gained entry to 'the House' – Christ Church – where he studied modern history and first met and befriended the classics scholar John Wilberforce, although it is difficult to understand what he would have had in common with the quiet and studious John. It is far more likely that Michael felt he simply had to get to know anyone who bore the illustrious Wilberforce name.

It was in John's rooms at Christ Church, in the autumn of 1952, that Michael had first met Susan. The relationship that was to have such a catastrophic effect on both their lives and on those of their families had an inauspicious beginning. 'I'd gone up to see John in his rooms at the House,' recalled Susan, 'and he apologised for having to go out and left me with this little friend. Michael bored me to tears droning on about the Dormers and the Borwicks. He was so fascinated by my background. My brother came back and he had that look in his eye, you know, as though he half expected me to react against Michael. Some time afterwards Michael asked me to marry him. I refused, of course. But he kept on asking and eventually I did, many years later.'

Although across Europe the great social and economic shifts in the post-war era had swept away the old orders and aristocracies as well as their countries, in some parts of society it was as though change and decay had never occurred. In Grosvenor Square, Lady Illingworth entertained, furiously, evoking a past, not of hard-earned Yorkshire money, or of the Wilberforce faded gentility, but of an even grander age, that for which Grosvenor Square had originally been built. And in London and in Oxford, Susan and Michael seemed determined to maintain this world, of inherited land, large houses and great names.

In Oxford, there were many wealthy young people from some of the great British and continental families. This naturally reinforced Michael's growing fascination with his own background and anything remotely connected with titles, pedigree or famous families; it also confirmed for him and Susan that their particular place in society was entirely correct. Their circle of friends included Desmond Guinness, from the famous brewing family; Michael Dormer, later to become a genealogist himself, from Susan's mother's family; Rupert Loewenstein, later a banker and social figure; the Earl of Mexborough, an Irish peer; and other members of French and Spanish families. 'There was a close-knit group of people from very old families and they were always discussing their pedigree. Anyone not from a famous family just wasn't allowed in. They gave parties to whom people whose names were "old" were usually the only ones invited. The question of intellectual achievements didn't bother them. It was only the family name that was important. It was all very amusing if you were part of it – they all had a wonderful time with their own parties and social life,' said a friend of the time.

For a while, Michael divided his time between London, where he lived with his mother in Flood Street in Chelsea, and his rooms at Christ Church, said to have been among the best in Oxford. But he did little or no work and was sent down in June 1953 at the end of his first year after failing to pass his preliminary examinations.

Whether he ever worked after Oxford is a questionable matter. He certainly spent several months in Paris studying history and philosophy at the Sorbonne and playing the Parisien. On his return, some of his friends insist that, for a while, he was the deputy director of medals for the War Office, having first obtained a short-service commission with the rank of captain back in the Ulster Rifles. This is said to have come to a swift end when some question of serving in the Korean War was raised. It must simply be stated here that the Ministry of Defence has no record of this posting or of any de Stempel serving as an officer in the Ulster Rifles, but they could be wrong.

Other friends from the era believe the Ministry's version to be correct. Michael has never done a proper day's work in his life, they say, although with his cronies he would always be dreaming up schemes for making vast amounts of money. There was no evidence of anything illegal, just schemes. One acquaintance describes a typical plan: 'A group of the young men became friendly with a snobbish millionaire who wanted titled people to come to a party. So Michael and his friends hit upon the idea of charging the millionaire so much per title. He offered them a fortune for the Duke of Edinburgh.' It was clear that, even then, money and the making of money was becoming an obsession with Michael.

But he would never do anything to earn it himself. He claimed to be fluent in Spanish, Italian and French and he could certainly read Russian, although there is little sign that he put any of this to much use. Later he was to use his personal friendship with a diplomat to claim that he worked for the Costa

Rican government; at one point he worked for a Texas-based financial company; he would describe himself as an economist or 'in import and export'. His first wife said later that he never worked during the period of their marriage.

Certainly the furious social round of the early 1950s would have left little time for a proper job. Whether in London or Oxford, he lived the lifestyle of a young socialite, mostly among the same loose circle of debutantes and wealthy but idle young men. He was, of course, spending heavily. His mother would bail him out whenever necessary, paying his bills at the tailors and bootmakers. The Dunkels money made them well off and gave Michael little sense of value. An Oxford acquaintance recalled how once Michael had told his mother he needed a new pair of boots and she sent him £10, a ridiculous sum in those days. He would receive cheques for £1000 to cover his expenses, more than generous for a young student. This vagueness about money was something of a family characteristic. 'Michael would never steal, he was never dishonest. He just wouldn't pay his bills. Ever. If he actually signed a cheque, it would bounce,' said the friend.

And the bills came only from the best kind of places: his clothes were made in Savile Row and Jermyn Street and he had a number of suits in the fashion of the time for Edwardian dress – tight, three- or four-buttoned jackets, narrow trousers – shirts from Turnbull and Asser and ties and stiff high collars from a particular shop, Washington Tremlett, near Savile Row. Shoes were handmade in St James's and he sported a silver-topped cane.

He would take tea with the other young bucks at Fortnum and Mason's, dine at the Ritz, where they would address him as 'Monsieur le Baron', which pleased him enormously, and dance at nightclubs, particularly a place called Millroys, near Hyde Park Corner, and the Green Room, run by a Baron von Roth, who turned out to have assumed rather than inherited his title. (When he was found out he sold his rather glorified memoirs of the period to a Sunday newspaper before going to live in the United States.) There were many parties: everything seemed to be an excuse for a party. Everyone tried to recapture the heady days long before the blight of war: the debutante balls, birthday parties, parties simply for the sake of it which would carry on until dawn. Although there were inevitably suggestions of wild promiscuity and a little cocaine indulgence (reportedly in the basement of one particular hotel in St James's), most seemed to acknowledge that much of the purpose of the round, indeed it was the specific purpose of the debutante balls, was for the younger ones to find partners, which is what Michael and Susan did, although initially not with each other.

Michael enjoyed his social life to the full, adopting the behaviour of the Edwardian gentleman in fin-de-siècle London, secure in his position among the upper strata of society – not the kind ever to visit a jazz club in Soho. Someone who once arrived with him at the Savoy recalls: 'The taxi pulled up outside and Michael just sat there, obviously waiting for the taxi driver to open the door for him, which the driver clearly had no intention of doing. Eventually Michael banged his cane several times on the partition and ordered the man to do it. But he gave him a rather large tip. Women just loved that kind of attitude.'

The story also illustrates his disregard for anyone he considered to be his social inferior. This grew worse with his interest in pedigree. At Oxford he had attempted to research the origins of the title of baron, which he claimed was the oldest of all titles. Despite his strenuous efforts on an essay, working day and night to the point of exhaustion, it was laughed at by genuine academics. He spent much time studying the *Almanach de Gotha*, the continental version of *Burke's Peerage*, examining the pedigrees of himself and his friends. He stopped having Spanish lessons when he discovered that his tutor came from an important Spanish family; he decided that it was wrong for a man from such a noble background to teach another and they would become friends instead. When he introduced or talked about someone with any kind of title, or even distantly related to a title, he would always make a point of mentioning it, as in 'My friend, ——, whose great-uncle is the Duke of ——, whether this was relevant or not.

When he went to Madrid, he was rather taken by the right-wing government of General Franco. He made several return trips over the next few years, claiming to have studied in Salamanca, although this seems unlikely. 'Michael rather liked the sort of authoritarian government in Spain at that time, with the working classes kept under. This to him was the natural order of things,' said a friend. The same, untitled friend, tells another characteristic story: 'He was just incredibly conscious of class and nobility, very patronising to the people who waited on him and served in shops. We once arrived at the Ritz and I was wearing a smart new duffel coat, which I was very proud about. When I gave it to the cloakroom attendant, Michael tipped him generously and apologised for the habit of the Marquis for wearing odd clothes.'

He was keen to promote his own lineage wherever possible. 'I have never seen him so crestfallen', said the friend, 'as when he was told that he did not qualify to become a Knight of Malta.' At his twenty-first birthday party at the Hyde Park Hotel, the evening had culminated with a band playing the Imperial Russian Anthem. No one knew the words, but everyone understood the point.

Women liked all this. In those days, his flowery language, extravagant behaviour and ludicrous snobbishness, although they attracted excited but totally inaccurate speculation that he was homosexual, were far more normal and stood out a good less than they would today and made him attractive to some women. He had a number of affairs and was usually to be seen in the company of the daughters of ambassadors and other diplomats, some of them highly attractive, but was reputed to have been less interested in beauty and figure than in names. He would be seen only with a certain type of girl; those from lesser families had no interest for him. But Michael knew his place: he once turned down an invitation to have an affair with a daughter of the Romanovs, the Russian Imperial family, on the ground that he was a mere nobleman and she was 'several degrees above me'.

Intermittently sharing his obsession with pedigree was Susan. By now, after spending two years dividing her time between Grosvenor Square and her Uncle Robert's home in Essex, she had finally settled into a flat of her own, in Philbeach Gardens, Earls Court. She had begun to develop a taste for good furniture and filled it with pieces brought down from Markington. She had a small sports car, her spare room was often occupied by friends overnighting in London and she enjoyed the part of the young girl about town. She was learning to play the piano, taking private music lessons, and for a time, she said, worked in a lowly capacity for the interior designer David Hicks. She was otherwise untroubled by work. A former lover said: 'She often had absolutely nothing better to do all day than consult old books about her family. She knew all about families and their names and titles.'

She was a slight loner among the social crowd in which she and Michael mixed, an unemotional girl with a steely intelligence, who preferred the company of men, in the broadest sense of the word, to that of women of her own age and type, possibly because in those days, and in particular in the world in which they moved, women shrank back from being strong characters. A friend said: 'Susan was very precocious, not like all the other girls. She was much more at home with men and had no women friends at all. It was very difficult to take her unawares in any way; she would always have something to say in reply.' Although some described her as a 'a bit tomboyish' and critics might have said she was plain, as she grew older she lost some of the weight of her youth and developed into a smart and presentable young woman.

Susan was still on cordial terms with her brother, who had now married a woman from a prominent New England family, Laura Sykes. The two women would never get on. Laura was, according to those who met her, variously described as 'tough, masculine, mannish' and it was claimed that she had married John following the breakdown of another relationship. Perhaps one reason why Susan and her sister-in-law never hit it off is that Susan resented Laura's apparent enthusiasm for playing to the full the part of a member of the English gentry – Susan, by her strict criteria, could never have accepted her as such.

The ex-lover says that Susan wanted to be seen with the 'smart crowd' at all the fashionable occasions. She considered herself among its leading figures. He said: 'She was very jealous when one woman with a foreign title arrived and began to dominate the scene. She was very upset. But she was very, very sensitive to flattery, that was how men would get around her.'

One who was constantly subjecting her to flattery was Michael, still pursuing her with some vigour. After her initial rejection, their paths continued to cross on the rather narrow social circuit of St James's, the Ritz and Mayfair. He was invited, along with all the other men about town, to her coming-out ball and by the mid-1950s she was seeing him regularly, although often as part of a larger crowd of friends, a loose grouping of people, some of whom were sleeping with each other.

Their mutual fascination with pedigree created a strong bond between them, gossiping and making fun of those names they considered lesser than theirs or those people who used titles or forms of address they were not entitled to. Some friends say this attitude underlaid everything they did. 'It was where their thinking started from,' said one. Thirty years later, Michael's second wife, Francesca Tesi, would complain that when Michael resumed his affair with Susan they would spend all day in bed discussing their ancestors.

Their bond may have been cemented by an equally mutual recognition that they both, because of their own particular natures, stood slightly alone, even in the densest of crowds and amid the jolliest of parties. When they were together, friends said, these two young people were just that little bit different: some fire had been ignited between them that was to last for nearly four decades and even now may not be wholly extinguished. From the beginning it was one of those relationships which can survive the inroads of other parties, including wives and husbands. There was clearly an accord, a mutual fascination which transcended all else. If they were not sleeping together by Susan's coming-out party, then it was not very long after that they did. Whether he was her first lover is unknown. He was not the only one before her marriage. One friend of both put it this way: 'Sex was always there between them, hanging in the air. But they would go off and have affairs with others and then get back together again. There was nothing difficult about it, it was one of those sort of relationships.' That made it all the easier for her to go and marry Simon Dale.

When Susan first rejected Michael's hand in those rooms in Christ Church, she did not know that the man whom she would first marry and have five children by, and for whose murder by bludgeoning she would eventually stand trial, was then working in a first-floor office above bank chambers on the other side of the city. For Oxford, to those that know it, is a city divided, some have said, 'between town and gown'. And if Susan, John, Michael and their circle were representative of the 'gown' then Simon Dale, ex-Royal Engineers and an architect working for his father's firm, was quite definitely 'town'. But he was also, like Michael, something of a snob, desperate to enter the world of the upper classes, and he had a growing interest in large country houses, with which, of course, Susan was certainly more familiar. He was also slowly going blind.

Thomas Simon Savage Dale was born in Oxford in 1919, one of four children of Angela and Thomas Lawrence Dale. The family were prosperous but distinctly rooted among the emerging provincial middle classes. Lawrence Dale (as he was known) was a successful architect and enthusiastic Freemason, well known among the small businessmen and city officials. A pipe-smoking, stocky man who wore tweeds and a bow tie, he would take lunch with friends each day at the Cadena Café, just down the road from his offices in the centre of the city. He was architect for the Oxford diocese of the Church of England and was sufficiently prominent in city life to become embroiled in a controversy over a plan to push a relief road for the city through Christ Church Meadows.

All the children were educated at public schools. Simon went to St Bees in Cumbria and then to Cambridge to study architecture at Christ's College. But already he was suffering from the severe myopia which would ruin his life and marriage and probably prevented him seeing his killer before the fatal blow was struck. Later in his life, he would suffer from progressively severe retinal haemorrhages, which caused a gradual and irreversible deterioration in his vision.

By the time Simon Dale's call-up for National Service came in 1939, his eyesight was so bad it threatened to bar him from duty. He cheated by memorising the eye-test card beforehand and entered the Royal Engineers. He had a thoroughly undistinguished war, spent mostly away in India from the action, but rising to the rank of captain. His eyesight caught up with him and he was invalided out in 1944. He returned to England by way of the Seychelles and spoke little of the war afterwards.

In the immediate post-war years, Simon completed his degree at Cambridge and then his postgraduate studies at the North London Polytechnic before joining the family business. In the offices above the bank chambers, the other employees would call Mr Dale Senior, now a widower, 'Sir' and Simon Dale 'Mr Simon', as he, in the eyes of one visitor, 'wandered in and out, not doing very much at all'. By now the business was past its height.

It is easy to see how Simon Dale would find this comfortable but mundane atmosphere somewhat restricting. Despite his receding hairline and fading eyesight, for which he wore thick glasses, in the words of his old friend, the publisher Christopher Hurst, he still 'cut something of a dash'. He was six foot three inches tall, fair, good looking in an unconventional fashion, had an engaging smile and what was described as 'a Guards-officer voice' that belied his more prosaic background. Not only was he a fine conversationalist, he had the experience of life and a wide range of interests extending far beyond architecture which made him agreeable company to all.

Simon put these abilities to good use when playing the part of the bachelor about town with enough money and looks to enjoy himself. He would frequent Oxford parties and was regularly seen in the company of younger, attractive women, driving about in his open-topped Lagonda, regardless of his poor eyesight. Although, as someone observed, all the Dales were 'extremely plain people', Simon Dale clearly exerted, in his own way, considerable sexual magnetism. He had a number of successful relationships before marrying Susan and remained attractive, both personally and intellectually, to a wide circle of women of all ages, right up until the day he died.

Working with his father with the expectation of eventually taking over the business, although it clearly provided a respectable position within Oxford itself, was not enough for Simon. He began to develop the kind of firm opinions on a variety of subjects that would divide his friends. In the mid-1950s he turned his attention to road routes, having his views on the proposed Oxford bypass quoted in the *Oxford Times* and his proposals for the inner London ring road warmly commended by John Betjeman in the *Spectator*.

Simon also wanted to move away from the image of a local architect, with a limited field of operation, into something slightly grander. He decided that his future lay in renovating the country houses of the gentry, giving him access by proxy to the class to which he clearly aspired. 'Simon wanted to move from provincial to county,' says Hurst. Others suggest he was a bit of a social climber – a snob, even.

A job with Claude Phillimore, an experienced and reputable architect with a practice in Kensington, gave him the opportunity he sought. Although he would remain a partner in his father's business for several years (until Dale senior's death in 1958), Simon left Oxford behind him and moved into a flat near Gray's Inn Road owned by his sister Alison, later to become secretary to the Institute of Landscape Architects.

Working for Phillimore must have seemed a world away from the offices in Oxford. He was travelling around the country meeting various members of the great, and not so great, families, spending time with them discussing their needs and plans. But he knew he was fighting a losing battle against his sight, which was steadily getting worse. Consciously or unconciously, he needed an escape route. 'He found it by marrying into a class he had been courting professionally for some years,' observed Christopher Hurst.

Susan met Simon some time in the spring of 1957, when she was twenty-three and still living in Earls Court. She was temporarily estranged from Michael, refusing his renewed offers of marriage on the grounds that he was too unreliable and fickle. One day at her flat, he threatened to commit suicide by jumping out of the window; she called his bluff and told him not to be such a bore.

The meeting took place at a gathering at the home of a family called Powell, who had engaged Dale to work on their country home, Sharrow Hall, near Ripon. He asked her to dinner, she accepted, and they were married six months later. The wedding took place at an Anglican church, St James's, the parish church of Clerkenwell, on Clerkenwell Green, and near where Simon was then living. Susan was never a particularly strong Catholic, so the Anglican nature of the service probably meant little to her. The wedding was remarkable for who failed to attend, rather than for the handful that did. Susan's mother did not. She was in France, with her new husband. Susan's brother John was in Berlin. The best man was Robert Clifford, an old friend of Simon's. Susan said afterwards that it was a very quiet affair.

Some said it was held in secret; that she had made a curious marriage.

As with so many relationships, Susan Wilberforce and Simon Dale provided each other with everything that they wanted in life but had yet to find. In 1957 Dale was charming and worldly, and desperate to move among those classes to which Susan so effortlessly belonged. Susan, while not necessarily attempting to leave her origins behind, found she had stumbled upon a means of both manifesting her rebellious side and giving her something solid in life to hold on to.

Simon represented a rejection of some of the values her immediate family – principally Uncle Robert, her brother John and to some degree her Aunt Puss – held dear. He failed on a number of grounds: he was not a Catholic, he was from the middle classes, he was considerably older than her and he had neither land, money nor even title to provide means of support for a young woman used to most of the best things in life. This may well have explained the meagre turn-out at their wedding.

Under normal circumstances, Susan might have shared this view of Simon. But, by his age and maturity, he must have provided her with something that she lacked in her so far rather peripatetic and shallow life: a stable centre, a father figure to replace the one she had never really known. She was also deliberately rejecting the traditional suitors who had hitherto surrounded her: the Michaels and the young army officers. Simon, with his solidity of character, would have had little in common with many of the young party-going creatures whose company she had enjoyed. He was something different and exciting, not quite a bohemian maybe, but as an architect he certainly carried a different aura from that of most of her friends. He appealed to the side of her which was attracted by fine furniture and interior design. Of course, it may simply have been the capricious act of a twenty-two-year-old girl designed to show her independence from Michael.

From the point of view of Simon, she bestowed upon him the weight of the accumulated history of the Wilberforces and all they stood for; it was doubtless a burden he was happy to shoulder. Some say he felt sympathy for her: seeing her as a rather forsaken character, a little rich girl without her parents and in the care of her aunt and uncle. Her income, furthermore, would help fund the work on the house he was thinking of buying. Whether he considered it as a cushion for a career that would become progressively more difficult to pursue is unknown, but it would be foolish to rule it out for lack of evidence. It also seems that Dale may have hidden the extent of his blindness from his new wife. Susan later said that she did not know about it until after they were married and conceded that it could 'possibly' have prevented their marriage.

It is also obvious that she appealed to him because she was an attractive young woman, fifteen years his junior, able to rescue him just in time from becoming a middle-aged bachelor architect. Friends spoke of a sexual magnetism between them, an animal side to the relationship, which may have rendered all other considerations null and void.

They bought a light and airy two-bedroomed first-floor flat in a mansion block in the Old Brompton Road, then and now a fashionable and expensive part of London. Simon was a man of taste; Susan was developing her own and the furnishings were probably better than might have been seen in the homes of comparable newly-weds. Susan bought some of her own antiques and furniture from Markington; they installed attractive carpets and curtains. No one knew she had already left him once, briefly, in the November after their wedding: 'It was for just a day. I went back of course, I was already pregnant with Alexander. The thing that annoyed me most was that he was too busy to notice my absence all day.'

The birth of their first son, William Alexander Savage, in July 1958, eleven months after their marriage, may have eradicated whatever slight cracks had begun to appear. A friend who visited them at the flat said: 'Simon was a much more relaxed and softer person than before his marriage. Susan had a definite physical, animal vigour about her; she was young and attractive, wearing a light summery dress, and there was Alexander crawling across the floor. It was a very pleasant scene.' But despite their appearance of being settled, they had both decided to leave 1950s London behind them and begin a new life. Dale was enthusiastically showing his visitor photographs of a large mansion house somewhere on the Welsh borders and in the middle of nowhere, which they were intent on buying. He said it was called Heath House.

4
Family Life

'I was appalled when I first saw it,' said Susan. 'The thistles were seven feet high. We had to buy a scythe to find our way in. Eventually, I fell in love with it. I find old houses so romantic, all my family do.' But, if it had not been for the political ambitions of another member of the Illingworth family, Heath House might never have been put up for sale to the newly married couple so cheaply. And a lot of trouble might have been avoided.

Heath House was built about 1620 for John Heath, a squire on the borders a few miles west of the fortified town and castle of Ludlow, seat of the lords of the Marches. Ludlow was then an important strategic base and market town, surrounded by lush farmland dotted with small villages and hamlets and, to the west, the Welsh hills. Apart from the county town of Shrewsbury, to the north, the essentially rural, sparsely populated character of the area remains the same today.

The house lies isolated, amid the fields, on the road heading south from the cluster of cottages at Hopton Heath, a hamlet taking its first name from Hopton Castle, a mile to the west. To the north-east and south-west are the tidy villages of Clungunford and Leintwardine, lying in the valley of the River Clun. The house faces south-west, inclining itself towards Wales at exactly the point where the undulating English countryside begins to steepen into Welsh hills.

Towards the middle of the seventeenth century, after the Civil War, it was extended, a second wing added, and a massive, extravagant wooden staircase was taken from nearby Hopton Castle, ransacked following the siege of 1644, and installed as a centrepiece of the house. Wood is a dominant feature of the inside of the house, with ornately panelled rooms and one long wood-panelled passageway. Although altered and extended over the centuries, the basic U-shape of the house and many of the original Jacobean features, both inside and outside, remained untouched until the twentieth century. For

200 years, Heath House, what remained of the castle and the surrounding Hopton estate were owned by the Beale family.

In 1880, the estate was purchased by Sir Henry Ripley, a political and industrial contemporary of the Illingworths in Bradford. Sir Henry, who had made his fortune in wool-dyeing and had been chairman of Bradford Chamber of Commerce, was elected MP for Bradford in 1868. In a celebrated controversy, he was unseated after an enquiry heard that his supporters had extensively bribed voters with beer, food and drink-laden transport to the polling booths. He was re-elected MP for Bradford in 1874 and defeated in 1880 by Alfred Illingworth, uncle of Albert (later Lord) Illingworth, formerly Liberal MP for Knaresborough.

This prompted the award of a baronetcy to Sir Henry and his retirement to Shropshire, where he bought the Bedstone estate and village and where he had built Bedstone Court, a huge, mock-Elizabethan mansion, although he lived there for only a few months before his death in 1882. But by this time he had also purchased the adjoining Hopton estate and Heath House. The family had no use for Heath House and it was rented out.

In 1903, the second baronet died and was succeeded by his son, who also decided to rent out Bedstone (it is now a school) and live elsewhere. His mother, Eugenie, the Dowager Lady Ripley, moved into Heath House and, under her, it enjoyed a rich period. Lady Ripley lived with a companion, cook, housemaid and butler–chaffeur and enjoyed her social life. There were children's parties and occasional balls for the adults. A local woman who went as a child remembers 'lovely big sunny rooms; it was always a very sunny house'.

After her death in 1941, the house was briefly leased as a girls' school and in 1946 given by the then Lord Ripley to his son Hugh, a decorated soldier newly home from the war, as a wedding present. But his wife wanted neither the house nor the 100 acres with it, mainly because of the cost and the size. The couple never lived there, preferring Surrey, where he commuted to the City.

Throughout the late 1940s and the 1950s the house was alternately empty or divided into flats and rented out. The costs of maintaining it soared, and although Sir Hugh Ripley enjoyed a successful business career (he became a director of Johnny Walker, the whisky distillers) the estate was declining. There was never enough money to restore the house to its original glory. By 1959, Heath House was being sold piece by piece – panelling, fireplaces and floorboards were being taken out and sold. It is said that some bits now repose in a public house in Leominster and in a hotel in Shrewsbury. After being stripped, it would be demolished. When Mr and Mrs Dale came along, the Ripleys breathed a sigh of relief.

An earlier plan to restore Aramstone House, a large but elegant eighteenth-century mansion near Hereford, had fallen through. Then Simon heard one day from the Society for the Protection of Ancient Buildings that Heath House, this wonderful borders mansion, was on sale cheaply, but he would have to move quickly because demolition loomed. He went by train the next day. After some hesitation Susan agreed. They exchanged contracts three days before it was due to be demolished. After a period living at Brimfield, near Tenbury Wells, Susan and Simon, together with their children, Alexander, eighteen months old, and Ilgerus (an old Wilberforce name) Sebastian Savage, born just two weeks previously, moved into Heath House, at Christmas 1959. She had paid £2000 for a semi-derelict shell, surrounded by five overgrown and untended acres. They had found their ruin.

Susan and Simon's motives for this move were quite simple and must have made good sense at the time, however unrealistic they appeared with hindsight. The newly married couple planned to realise their shared ambitions to have a substantial country home of their own by restoring Heath House using the money from her inheritance and his architectural and practical skills. It was not a real wrench to leave London since both came from the provinces and neither felt particularly at home there. Simon positively wanted to live in a large house in the country; Susan was already quite used to such homes. Even more importantly, her mother and stepfather were now living at Bishop's Castle, a village just a few miles to the north of Heath, and it may well be that Susan hoped for the parental help and support any young woman might anticipate when embarking on such an enterprise. They would not live entirely on Susan's inheritance and income because, although Simon would give up full-time employment with Phillimore, he would carry on working from home.

'My heart sank when I saw what they were planning,' said Simon's friend Christopher Hurst. 'An attractive house, but I was extremely doubtful whether anyone should take on a project like that, costing so much money, time and effort to make habitable, let alone live there. I wondered if they knew what they were doing.' Sophia strongly and firmly believes her mother simply followed Simon's ambitions: 'She was only in her early twenties after all and had been living in big houses all her life – they were natural to her. I don't think she really knew the scale of what she was taking on.'

There is some force in this argument: if Susan had really assessed her husband's career prospects, which promised only a diminishing income at a time of rising expenditure on the house while she was trying to raise a family, it is possible she would have held back. But she did not, perhaps because she had clearly found a means of asserting her independence; of showing her family she too could have her Markington. Perhaps also she was convinced by the certitude and enthusiasm of an older, more experienced person. But, if Susan had gone on in the hope of some help from her mother, she must have been disappointed when Cecilia and her husband decided, not long after Susan and Simon arrived, to move to the other end of the country, to Devon. It can only have seemed like another sign of her mother's indifference.

It is not difficult to imagine what it was like at first, in winter, with two young children, in this huge, half-dismembered house, surrounded by trees and isolated from such neighbours as there were, in an unknown and inward-looking part of the country, their car, a Rover 90, just about the only link with the outside world. But they survived, treating it as a big adventure. For the first five years, they lived in one of the flats on the top floor. On the ground floor, between the exposed joists, they grew lettuces, joking about leaving it like that so that dinner-party guests could reach down for salad.

The twin demands made upon them by the house and their children occupied the Dales to the exclusion of just about everything else. There were few local people to make friends with anyway; the nearest neighbours were farmworkers and no one in the hamlet of Hopton Heath would have had much in common with either of them. The lack of a social bridge, such as a shop or pub, cannot have helped. Apart from a formal acquaintance with various Ripleys, Susan did not appear much interested in making friends; the gauche young London debutante was becoming the lady of the manor. 'She was a bit snooty to begin with, high and mighty, rude about everybody,' said one woman who knew them well. 'She talked about local people in a rather mocking way, rather making fun of them.' That set the tone from the start. Word spread about the new lady of Heath House. She did invite some people, of 'her type', for drinks, where she played 'the perfect, charming hostess' according to one visitor. This may have been slightly unfair on Susan. Some friends explain her rectitude and lack of emotion as simply the shyness of a private person. Although among friends of her own age in London it may have been less noticeable, now in the unfamiliar country among strangers she might have erected barriers which appeared unattractive and maintained her privacy in order to cover up a painful shyness. And it may not have been just Susan; friends of Simon from both pre- and post-Susan days described him as a snob, careful about his friends.

One way or the other, they never became a real part of the community, though it was of course a diffuse one. No one ever really got to know them beyond the kind of casual recognition neighbours reserved for each other. And so, from the polarised attitudes and their understandable preoccupations, from Susan's desire for privacy, however it was motivated, there was created a cocoon around the family, into which Susan's three youngest children were born. It was a cocoon she later strove to keep them in and from which they have only recently completely left, to emerge blinking into the daylight.

They had plenty to occupy themselves. The first anniversary of the arrival at Heath House was celebrated by Susan's third pregnancy and Xenophon Marcus Savage was born on 2 July 1961. Georgina Sophia came along on 14 August of the following year and it was another two years before Simon Quintin Savage arrived, in April 1964.

The work on the house was extensive, with builders labouring in it for years. It was cleaned and decorated from top to bottom. They replaced some of the fireplaces with better ones, often marble. They gradually refitted floorboards; Simon rebuilt part of the central staircase. A series of crumbling eighteenth-century outbuildings which formed a kitchen wing on the left-hand side of the house were knocked down and an archway formed out of the old kitchen window to take the path from the rear around the front of the house. The arch linked the house to a small, two-bedroomed cottage, which for many years they rented out. They built a new kitchen and fitted it out with a huge Aga, modern units and a long, solid refectory table. They installed an underfloor central-heating system in part of the house. (It rarely worked properly and the house was always cold.) They worked long and hard on the grounds, hewing, weeding and trimming, tidying the paths, creating a rose garden and clearing the splen-didly large but overgrown walled garden, with its ancient apple trees. Susan, true to her Dormer blood, would always be an enthusiastic gardener, with a genuine love of attractive land-scapes, which she eventually passed on to her son.

The family moved gradually into other parts of the house as they were completed. It was furnished well: some items came from Markington but a lot of very good furniture came cheaply from the antique sales thriving on the then regular demolition of country houses. There were paintings and family portraits on the walls, one set of eighteenth-century female Wilberforces and another of Wilberforce husbands and wives. There were tasteful wallpapers, drapes and fabrics. There was a harp in the music room, an elegant table and chairs in the dining room. By the time they finished, there were twenty-seven rooms in the house, including the huge and sumptuous panelled drawing room and adjoining music room. There were a dozen bedrooms, four bathrooms, two halls, study, workrooms and the kitchen.

The Dales were simply maintaining the style of Susan's fore-bears: the Wilberforces and the Dormers, even the Illingworths and Ripleys. The children would attend the best schools; the house had, for a short time, a governess to look after Sebastian and Alexander and a woman to help Susan with domestic duties.

All around them, in the late 1950s and 1960s, the great patrician families, the landed gentry, even the newly rich, were fading rapidly, victims of mid-twentieth-century social and economic changes. They could no longer claim to be the dominant forces of society or public life; there were no more Conservative grandees, but a socialist government, led by Harold Wilson. In this Britain of the National Health Service, the unions and the Beatles, country houses were being knocked down, estates like the Ripley lands divided, grand houses like those in Grosvenor Square sold as prestige offices: how else would they have obtained and equipped Heath House? Susan, with the inherited values of her class, and Dale, in his embrace of them, were swimming against the tide.

It would have been a realistic enterprise – and still is for many – if there had been enough money. But there simply was not. If they had chosen to live in London or in a smaller country house needing less work, they could well have lived in some comfort, like many of her kind, supported by a husband with a decent job. Dale did not even have that. And they were in huge Heath House.

Susan would later say that it was only her abilities that kept the family together for ten years. Most work on 'the Heath', as they called it, was funded by Susan, selling all her inheritance from Markington, in total about £35,000. They lived and fed an increasing number of children on the small income from her family trust money, about £1000 a year.

For some years, Simon had carried on with architectural work – he designed for Phillimore in London and worked on houses at Coldstream, on the English–Scottish borders, at Clovelly in Devon and elsewhere in Shropshire – but it diminished in proportion to his eyesight. The house and children absorbed what money he earned; Susan's inheritance gradually disappeared. Even £4000 placed in trust for Sophia by her godfather, Francis Rose, was borrowed to pay for repairs to the house. The fact that it was never paid back was a source of considerable acrimony between Susan and Simon for years to come.

Her determination that the children would have a good education had been under threat until rescue by the intervention of her uncle, Robert Wilberforce, now a senior partner in a firm of solicitors in London and a director of Guinness, the brewing firm. As they had kept an eye on Susan when she was younger, Robert and Aunt Puss, although not approving of her marriage or her chosen life, felt an obligation to look after the children, their great-nephews and great-niece. Lady Illingworth sent a van-load of furniture when she finally left her home in Grosvenor Square; Robert contributed towards the schooling of their children.

During the latter half of the 1960s the older children were mostly away at school and distanced from the everyday relationship of their parents. The boys all spent a year or two at the nearest village school, at Wigmore, south of Leintwardine. At seven or eight, they were despatched to the fashionable preparatory school of Ludgrove, near Wokingham. Sophia went to Wigmore, then to a village school at Craven Arms.

There were arguments between their parents, but they rarely intruded in what they recall as a largely idyllic, if somewhat reclusive childhood. One of the sons said: 'There were happy family occasions and in many respects we had an ideal childhood: we lived amid wonderful countryside, in a beautiful house with all those rooms. We had a large garden and there were ducks, geese, a donkey and a cat.' Marcus was said to be particularly fond of the animals, but his memory is more downbeat: 'I can remember very little of my childhood, it was so mundane and ordered and with so little to break the routine.'

The children each had a room on the top corridor of the house; their windows facing the elegant deer park which the house had once called its own, the Welsh hills in the distance. For children, the house with its huge rooms, its nooks and crannies would have been a delight. The atmosphere was relaxed and Susan was, after all, trained in domestic skills; there were family mealtimes around the big table in the kitchen, the one their father was later to stain with his blood. There were always cooked breakfasts and, in the evening, stews and hotpots, tripe and 'adventurous things like that', according to Sophia. They may also have involved the cheapest cuts of meat.

Their childhood friends were mostly various cousins, but, once they were all away at fee-paying schools, friends inevitably came from other parts of the country, and there were no invitations to stay from Susan. It was the first manifestation of what would later become an obsession with her own privacy.

The origins of this desire for privacy, which she shares with her brother, can be found in their background. The Wilberforces are simply a particularly private, introverted family from the kind of upper-class stock that leads other nations to comment on the 'British reserve' and the lack of warmth towards each other and their children. In Susan's case, reinforced by her surroundings, it became a defence mechanism, initially to cover her growing financial insecurity, later her criminality.

One of the children said: 'My mother just did not encourage visitors. She was always immensely house-proud, everything had to be done properly or not at all. So, often, it was simply not done. We would not bother. My parents regretted that we didn't socialise as much as other children, but it was never encouraged. It was also partly because there were so many of us, we found enjoyment in each other's company. We were not so much self-contained as self-sustaining.'

There were no family holidays; perhaps day-trips into Wales or the coast, but little else. There was one single foreign trip, some time in the late 1960s, when Aunt Marion took them for a wonderful week in Normandy. Susan's desire for privacy and the lack of money meant there was little socialising; she was never one for parties anyway.

Guests were mostly Susan's relatives. Although Susan was a long way from the prosperous lives of Uncle Wee and Aunt Puss in London, there was regular contact by letter and telephone: both visited Heath House once or twice during the early 1960s. Aunt Marion, to whom Susan would always remain close, was a more frequent visitor. A remarkable woman who would fly and ride to hounds well into her eighties, she would zoom up from Essex to Heath House in a 1930s Hornet Moth, swooping low over the roof and flapping its aerofoils in greeting before landing at nearby Shobden aerodrome.

Susan's brother John, rapidly becoming a successful diplomat, made what one observer called 'a state visit'. John and Laura had three children of their own, the eldest being William, born in 1958. Relations between John and Simon were somewhat formal, perhaps reflecting the coolness between Susan and her sister-in-law. When they later corresponded, they addressed each other as 'Dear Dale' and 'Dear Wilberforce'. Another visitor was an old friend of Susan's from London social circles called Anne Simeon, whose relationship with Susan would later take on a somewhat different hue. They shared a mutual friendship with Michael de Stempel, who also came to stay.

Susan married Simon when Michael was in South America for a long period. When he returned, he did not spend much longer as a single man. It may have been pure coincidence that a few months later, in November 1957, Michael announced his engagement to the debutante daughter of an army colonel. It ended after six months. The following year he married Christina Macdonald, a dark, half-Spanish farmer's daughter from Kent. By now, Michael was an interesting enough figure to attract the newspaper gossip columns. In January 1959, alongside a picture of Michael (looking roguish) and his bride (looking pleased) the *Daily Express* reported that the happy couple were rather confused about something.

She told the reporter: 'Michael has never had a job and I don't suppose he ever will. I don't think he wants a job.' He said: 'I have been in the import–export business for about two years. It keeps me quite busy. This is really rather embarrassing. My fiancée is half-Spanish and a bit vague about these things.' She then added: 'We are both very idle.' In typical fashion, the Baron said they would live 'either in London or Costa Rica'. The report also inaccurately described him as an Oxford graduate.

The couple lived in Notting Hill, surviving on his allowance from his father, then in France. They had three children in a few years: Tatiana, Andrew and Sophie, which made their finances even more difficult. Michael, who did not have a job, would spend a good deal of time in bed, socialising in the evening. Christina later described their existence as 'hand to mouth'. By 1966, they had split up. The following year Michael married Francesca Tesi, a fiery Italian woman who would later work as a translator. In May 1968, Michael again made the newspapers, although in more serious circumstances, when he was fined £60 for shoplifting goods worth 18s 4d from a supermarket. Michael, who said he earned £6000 as an economic adviser to two embassies, had pleaded not guilty, claiming he had absent-mindedly pocketed the goods his five-year-old son had knocked off shelves while riding a shop trolley. In 1970, Michael and Francesca had a son, Alexander, who was, to their distress, educationally subnormal. Some would later say he was the only person about whom Michael ever really cared.

He had never quite lost touch with Susan, visiting Heath House at least once with each wife. Michael liked the Wilberforces; he enjoyed the hospitality at Markington, where he had visited John, and at Grosvenor Square, where, he claimed, he had developed a friendship with Aunt Puss. He enjoyed Heath House. Relations between him and Simon were surprisingly good because they both found so much to look down on in each other that they enjoyed having the opportunity to do more of it. Michael liked Heath House so much that on one visit he began having his post directed there.

The physical position of Heath House, the period of renovation and the lack of money increased the family's sense of isolation from the rest of the world, which was busily enjoying the 1960s, and reinforced the cocoon. This was compounded by Simon's increasing self-absorption, born out of his frustration at his inability to support his family as an architect. He turned his attentions to a variety of subjects, some of which obsessed him and about which he developed his own theories. And, as these too failed, the frustrations exploded into anger.

Susan later claimed they had no social life because of Simon; his children say they simply saw less and less of him. 'He would just shut himself away and work on his obsessions. If you were in company and he began talking about things, it put people off; you would see their eyes glaze over.' Susan said that Simon's strongly held views on so many matters led him to argue with everybody, often simply for the sake of it. 'He was going to convert to Catholicism [possibly for their wedding] but had a huge row with Ronnie Knox [the theologian] and gave up the idea. He didn't know anything about it as usual.' He always had schemes and ambitions. 'I would have to say to him, "No, Simon, we cannot do that, we have the children to feed."'

Sebastian believes that his father had an unusually active and enquiring mind. 'He was a fearless thinker, driven by a desire for a sense of achievement in his life,' he later told friends. Later, Simon would take up archaeology, Arthurian legends, Celtic myths and dowsing, writing two unpublished books. He had ideas for system-built housing developments and to turn

Heath House into a conference centre. He drew up plans for sash-window locking devices and snow scrapers and made a number of successful and unsuccessful patent applications. But, as his own eyesight failed, he began to study the causes of his own shortsightedness.

Locked in his study, reading with the aid of his contact lenses, spectacles and magnifying glasses, he absorbed everything he could lay his hands on – including the seminal work on the subject, Duke-Elder's *Systems of Ophthalmology*. He took issue with established medical opinion and paid for the construction of a model of the eye to help support his theories. He wrote to everyone in the field, seeking approval and agreement to conduct lengthy and expensive research to prove him correct, but his tortuous, wordy style undermined any worth in his ideas. The experts invariably replied that, while his ideas were thought-provoking or worthy of further consideration, they were not able or prepared to go any further in subjecting them to serious examination.

Simon made much of the encouragement and ignored the underlying tone of rejection, which served to convince him even more of the merit of his idea. Sebastian later said he 'brooked no opposition'. 'I have reached certain conclusions which apparently have merit. It is now up to the experts to work on them,' he pompously informed one newspaper reporter who went to see him. Eventally, in 1970 (and almost certainly to Susan's chagrin), he paid for the publication of a lengthy pamphlet entitled *Sight Without Glasses*. Its ideas may have been worthy, but it was an impenetrable read. Susan took to calling him Birdbrain.

Susan would later claim that it was in the mid-1960s, as his own brooding and sense of failure increased, that Simon became physically and sexually aggressive towards her. He would shut himself away, she claimed, for up to three weeks at a time in his study, emerging only for food and/or sex. Susan later claimed: 'He was very sexually active and very aggressive, but it certainly was not loving. He simply needed sex to satisfy himself.' This may be somewhat disingenuous: friends had already observed the strong physical attraction between them, and Simon would later claim that Susan had only married him as a stud, to provide the many children she wanted.

The purely physical assaults began, Susan claimed, not long after the birth of Simon junior in 1964. Much of the evidence for the physical assaults comes from Susan herself, mainly after her later arrest by police, but with some support from the children. They were mostly too young or at school, and could not have known what had really transpired between their parents. As a behavioural trait, it was certainly completely at odds with what was known of his personality before and after his marriage, when his friends would describe him as the gentlest of men. No one remembers any manifestations of violence outside his marriage.

It may have been that in the confined atmosphere of Heath House, confronted with the failure of his architectural career, his inability to support his house and family and the growing rejection of his theories, his intellectual frustration manifested itself in strong argument, which would sometimes turn to physical anger. Years later, Jo Corfield, who was his last secretary/reader, also provides corroboration for this suggestion: 'Simon was unable to express himself in writing in the way that he wanted. On a couple of occasions when I told him that his writing needed to be more plain and simple he would go very tight and angry. He was a very big and strong man and he certainly had a temper, so it is not difficult to imagine he might have been unable to control it at times, although I cannot believe it was to the extent Susan claimed.'

Susan said: 'I was absolutely terrified of him. He was a big man and he seemed to get bigger. He was terrifying when he had one of his attacks. He seemed to swell all over.' She said she suffered permanent back pain where he used to hit her and that he threatened to kill her and throw her body down an old lead mine between Bishop's Castle and Shrewsbury. She gave her solicitor a map reference for the spot because it would have been difficult to find. Another story was that he dug her grave in the garden, although this may really have been in pursuit of his by then growing archaeological interests.

The children remember an increasing number of arguments and some violence. Marcus said: 'My father did not beat me, but I saw him beat my mother; he kicked her in the back violently.

I remember being frightened of him. He was so frustrated at his fading sight it would just simply explode into a rage.' Another son said: 'My parents were both incredibly strong-willed characters and both had a very clear idea of what they wanted. It was inevitable they would clash. Although I did not actually see it because I was in the next room, I very clearly remember the row when my father hit my mother on Easter Day 1968, a fact which was used against him in the divorce proceedings. But that is the only occasion I recall.'

The relationship deteriorated beyond repair as Susan struggled to cope with his moods and violence, the lack of money, the demands of home and family. She eventually decided that, at some point, she was going to have to leave him. When asked why she had not done so earlier, Susan responds simply: 'I believed in keeping the family together.' In reality, her options were few: she had only a small source of income and nowhere to go. Susan eventually moved into another bedroom. Simon, she said, would come in and demand sex.

An opportunity presented itself when her mother, now widowed again, said she wanted to move back into the area. Susan had kept in touch with her mother and stepfather after they had moved to Sidmouth in Devon, and the children had all been on holidays with their grandparents. Now Mrs Lucas, in her seventies, had decided to spend her last years near to her daughter and grandchildren. She knew Susan's marriage was disintegrating and told her she would buy somewhere that Susan could have as a bolt-hole if needed, to be hers on her mother's death. Mrs Lucas chose Mellington House, a large, imposing Georgian house in Weobley, an attractive village twenty miles south of Leintwardine. Simon was even induced into doing some design work on alterations to the house, unaware of his wife's plans. As she was about to move to Weobley, Mrs Lucas, a heavy drinker all her life, suffered a stroke and was forced to enter a nursing home outside Hereford, where Susan made regular trips to see her. She told Susan that Mellington House, large and unoccupied, would be hers.

In 1972, Susan, now thirty-eight, sought divorce on the grounds of Simon's unreasonable behaviour. Although still living together, they were barely on speaking terms and the size of the house allowed them to live separate lives. She cooked for herself and ate alone or with the children when they were at home. He would emerge from his study or workroom when the coast was clear and prepare his own spartan meals.

She carried on living there after the divorce was granted. 'Where else was I supposed to go? I was waiting for him to leave.' It was, after all, Susan's house, bought with her money. Clearly, he had no intention of leaving, and relations became unbearable. In September 1973, when all the children (including Sophia, now attending a convent in Brecon) were at school after the long summer holiday, she grasped her opportunity. 'I took my handbag and went to Weobley.' She also took the car. The children were not told until later. 'When we went home from school, we just went back to Weobley, rather than Heath House. It was as simple as that. But it was also a great relief,' said Marcus. They enjoyed Weobley; it was a good-sized house, warm and full of nice furniture.

But they did not forget their father. Although, through his reclusiveness and the breakdown of his relations with their mother, he had become a sad and marginal figure in their lives, the four oldest, in different ways, remained deeply fond of Simon. Alexander, fifteen, and Sebastian, then thirteen, both at Shrewsbury School, were able to remain close to him, visiting Heath House regularly. In Sebastian's case, it was at the expense of his relationship with his mother. All three younger children would spend time, by arrangement, at Heath House during school holidays. 'We were sad there were no more invitations,' said Sophia. But Simon junior, the youngest, would remain more attached to his mother, in her cocoon. All of them changed their names from Dale to Wilberforce.

The effect on Dale was simply to intensify his previous behaviour. He was not a man normally to share his feelings, even if there had been anybody about to share them with. He appears simply to have become a more brooding, isolated and embittered figure than before. The energies expended on his theories were now turned towards defeating Susan's attempts to evict him from what he now believed was his house.

Although legally the house was Susan's, the divorce agreement said that it was to be sold, the proceeds apportioned between them. But he did everything to avoid this actually happening. In mid-1974, the house was surveyed and put up for sale. Unfortunately, the property market, which had boomed in 1973, giving a value to the house of more than £100,000, slumped in 1974. Heath House was put up for sale in June at only £75,000. These were uncertain economic times, a Conservative government had been thrown out amid the industrial-relations crisis of the three-day week in February 1974 and replaced by a minority Labour government.

Any potential purchaser would have been deterred not simply because of the possibility of a Labour government increasing taxes but also because there was what amounted to a sitting tenant. Simon, at his most dogmatic, firmly told visitors – surveyors, estate agents, lawyers, potential purchasers – that he was staying put, because the settlement was still all up in the air, whatever nonsense his wife got up to and however much she claimed it to be hers.

Then came another bitter blow, an event still surrounded, fifteen years later, by a certain amount of family mystique. In August 1974, Mrs Lucas died. Susan, who had visited her mother every day for months, cried at the death. It was, her children remember, the only time they ever saw her cry, until one particular moment much later.

Her grief was aggravated by what occurred next. Although Susan had been expecting to inherit the house she and her children had lived in for a year, the will specified that the house, its contents and all other possessions must be sold and converted into a trust. John would receive the bulk of the capital and income, with the income only from two-fifths of the estate going to Susan, along with the furniture from the bedroom and drawing room. She would get an income of about £1000 a year. She also inherited her mother's car, an Austin 1300, in addition to the Peugeot she had nurtured since leaving Heath House.

When asked about her mother's will, Susan tends to shrug her shoulders. 'She bought it [Weobley] for me in the first place, realising I'd have to leave Simon at some stage. But she forgot to alter her will so that at the time of her death it was sold according to the terms of her [original] will.' Effectively, John benefited rather than Susan, perhaps as a result of Mrs Lucas's old-fashioned belief (according to Marcus) that women would always be provided for by men. What happened between Susan and her brother over the sale of the house is unclear, but it evolved into his offering her room to stay at Markington. She had no option but to accept.

The net effect of all this should not be underestimated when weighing up what came later. Here was a women with five young children, needing money for their education and food for when they were all home, already excluded from the house she had expended so much time and energy upon, being, in effect, turned out of another home by her own family. Her mother had been absent, one way or another, for most of her life; it must have seemed like the final rejection.

The children wonder whether their uncle John could have done more to share his benefits with Susan. 'Perhaps he simply did not realise the position we were in,' said one of the children. 'You have to understand John's character to appreciate how it could happen. He might simply have been unaware.' He did, after all, make an offer of accommodation in the vacant wing of Markington, where his wife Laura was in residence.

It was hardly a good idea, given Susan's desire for privacy, the fact that she and Laura were not on friendly terms, in addition to the damage to her considerable pride. But she had no other option or money. It was a disaster. 'Markington was freezing cold. There was no heating and no carpets,' says Sophia. Relations also cooled. 'There was also no privacy, which annoyed my mother. She became angry when she realised that she could not lock the door which connected the two wings of the house.' They stayed just a few weeks. One day, according to Sophia, her mother 'simply took off without telling them where she was going'. Susan's relations with John and his family would never recover from this episode. John would later say that Susan was unhappy to be parted from her 'social circle', although it is debatable precisely which circle he was referring to.

Now when the children returned from school – by now Marcus and Simon were attending the Oratory School, the Catholic public school at Reading – they went to the little market town of Ross-on-Wye where, for a year, Susan rented a two-room flat from some friends. It was very cramped, particularly when the children were there. 'Mother was terribly secretive about Ross. She did not want anybody to know we lived there,' said Sophia. 'When I went up to visit Markington with Alexander, I was told not to say anything about where we were living.' Susan explained that this was all to do with the legal battle with Simon, but embarrassment over her reduced circumstances may have had more to do with it.

Although the children would always remain very close to each other, their paths had begun to diverge. From about this time, Alexander and Sebastian would begin to distance themselves from the financial and physical arguments of their parents, acutely aware that they could be used as instruments by both sides. And there is no doubt that the split was even more painful for them, since they knew their father better, than it was for the younger children. Although they both accept that it was an almost inevitable consequence of the clash of personalities, like the children of many divorced parents their feelings and emotions are torn. And that was bad enough without what transpired afterwards.

As the eldest, Alexander had initially borne the brunt of looking after the other children following the divorce, acting as surrogate father on trips to Markington. But since the late 1970s he has mostly carried on his life in other countries. After two years at Oxford, he spent a year in Malaysia before returning to graduate in modern languages. He then went to Japan, where he was employed in the Ministry of Foreign Affairs. Later he worked briefly for Sotheby's in New York before returning to Japan to begin a new career as a banker. Throughout, he kept in touch with his mother by letter and telephone and when returning from abroad would visit his parents in their respective houses. And regularly he would send his mother, brothers and sister money to keep them out of debt.

In April 1977, for Sebastian, seventeen years old and studying for university, it was extremely difficult. Forced to sleep under the kitchen table, he was unable to concentrate on his work. When he refused to take sides in the dispute with his father, in a rage Susan drove him to Heath House and left him there.

Of all five, Sebastian, who physically resembles his father all more than the others and whose defective eyesight he has inherited, was possibly the most distressed by the split, choosing to go to his father at Heath House or sometimes to Markington when not at school or at Hull University, where he studied theology. Over the ten years after leaving Ross, he would see his mother twice, briefly. He kept in close touch with his younger brothers and sister, maintaining contact through Alexander at Oxford. When the children all met, it was on the strict understanding that they never discussed the financial affairs of their warring parents. Sebastian remains the most defensive of his father's memory, while being totally realistic about his failings. He was the last to change his name to Wilberforce.

In the middle of the hamlet of Hopton Heath is the railway station: a flower-bedecked platform on the rural branch line running south from Shrewsbury into the Welsh hills. In the bleak years after Susan left, it became Simon's principal link with the outside world. Still a physically vigorous man, he would stride up the road to take the train to Shrewsbury to visit the library and the shops. It is still possible to stand on the little bridge over the line and imagine this tall, tweed-jacketed man, two bushy white billows of hair either side of a gleaming pate, standing alone on the platform in the morning breeze, waiting to hear, not see, the up train, which would arrive glistening from the Welsh rains. He would return later in the day, carrying his ground coffee, his loaf of bread, his library books and photocopied articles, after asking the guard to make sure the train stopped for him.

Simon described his own semi-blindness as 'like looking down a shrinking straw' and it was as though he had aimed that straw like a telescope at certain fixed points to which he returned again and again. Living in Heath House for so long enabled him to memorise its doors and staircases, its nooks and crannies, its dark passages. His familiarity with the house was such that visitors often did not believe his blindness. 'It is also', he said, 'one of the reasons why I do not want to move to somewhere unfamiliar.'

He developed his own methods of dealing with the problems blindness brought. When cutting the lawn at the front and back of Heath House he devised a special method of placing either white plates or a sheet as a marker so that he could see which way he was heading. He was supremely unembarrassed by his affliction and would speak with good humour when it got the better of him. Sebastian later recalled: 'He would cheerfully and with some hilarity recount his latest mishap, such as the time when he solemnly walked off the bridge near Hopton Heath into a stream ... fully clothed and carrying a walking stick and a briefcase full of shopping.' Once, deliberately pulling on mismatching gumboots, he confided that since everyone thought him mad he might as well give them something to talk about.

He had been given a white stick, but had it knocked away during a trip to Shrewsbury by a gang of hooligans: he never bothered again, preferring a tall, roughly cut wooden staff for the country, a conventional walking stick for the city. He refused to learn braille. The rural calm of the area allowed him to walk almost everywhere. He would stride into Leintwardine to the butchers, up to Hopton Heath to buy vegetables. When he made friends locally, he thought nothing of walking miles across the fields to lunch.

Simon lived in dignified simplicity, eking out his savings, mostly the residue from the sale of a house in Winchester which he had been left by his parents. He usually cooked every other evening and developed cheap, well-practised dishes – toad-in-the-hole, mince rolls, lamb stew – that would last him two nights. He made jam and marmalade. He bought uncut white loaves, which lasted precisely two and a half days: two slices toasted for breakfast, two with Cheddar cheese and two tomatoes for lunch. The indulgences were fruits in season, always freshly ground coffee and sherry, and later, when he had someone to share it with, wines from Tanners in Shrewsbury. His clothes, originally of good quality, became worn and patched over the years. He slept grandly, in a single four-poster bed in a first-floor bedroom.

He was not a recluse, simply starved of opportunities to enjoy company, when Sebastian or Alexander were not about. Shorn of a family and with no real friends from his earlier life, the lack of social contact with the surrounding community during the early years now took its toll. The fact that there are no local people who had more than cursory contact with Dale during this period signifies a great deal.

Two visitors were his old friend from Oxford days, Christopher

Hurst and his wife. 'I hadn't seen him for almost twenty years [this was 1978] but he didn't look any different and spoke as vigorously as ever. Simon told us that Susan left him when his sight packed up. He said she was trying to get him out but he was afraid that, if she did, he would be on the streets. He said there was no question of selling up and out. There was a pile of correspondence with his lawyers on the table.' Hurst added: 'Upstairs, he showed me the nurseries, still full up with children's stuff, toys and cots everywhere, just like they had been abandoned, like the *Marie Celeste*. He seemed to be rather lonely and I wondered how the hell he managed.'

5
From Damask to Docklow

Just as Susan had placed herself in a time capsule by going to Heath House, so had Lady Illingworth. But hers was in the middle of London. By the late 1950s, number 44 was the last private house in Grosvenor Square, a sole reminder of the old in a setting more and more dedicated to the new.

Almost as if in defiance of her isolation, Lady Illingworth continued with the enthusiastic socialising that had become her hallmark. Indeed, it was as though she lived only through her guests and her hospitality, as she may have lived the part of a proxy mother through Susan's debutante season. While everyone has something to say about Susan's personality, Lady Illingworth is usually recalled only in terms like 'charming, a great beauty' or 'very much the *grande dame*'. Few would get to know her well. One typical recollection sums up the prevailing impression: 'She had become a very grand lady. I just remember everything being very well appointed and properly done, all in very good taste. The dining room had red damask walls. We ate off the most wonderful silver and in the middle of the table there was this marvellous pair of silver galleons.'

There were dinner parties, cocktail soirées and balls, including the by now traditional June celebration to mark the news of the victory at Waterloo reaching London, which, guests recalled, often climaxed in a re-enactment of the great scene itself. She was assisted by a small staff, including cook, chauffeur and butler, but only about half the number she had employed before the war. There were old friends from the Diplomatic Corps, politics and industry, and, to a lesser degree, some members of the various families whose lineages met through her: the Dormers, the Wilberforces, the Illingworths. In 1957, her proximity to the United States Embassy led to her having as house guests the bulk of the US delegation to disarmament talks then being held in London.

Financially, Lady Illingworth was more than comfortable, though not, as some later made out, fabulously wealthy. The money invested on her behalf by her late husband would eventually realise about £45,000 to £50,000 a year, depending on interest rates; there was nothing to pay on the house and she had a separate income from a reasonable amount of shares and other securities held in her own name. In addition to an incalculable amount of antique furniture, books, paintings, jewellery and ornaments, there was also the value of the house itself, which, despite short-term changes in the property market, would always be substantial. She still ordered a car to take her around whenever she needed one and spent a holiday every year with old friends in Monte Carlo.

While it may have seemed that time was passing Grosvenor Square by, in fact it was running out. Influenced perhaps by the post-war construction boom in Britain, the Grosvenor estate revived a dormant plan to redevelop parts of the Square. Although the house had been scheduled as a building of historic and artistic interest in 1957, the London County Council had failed to make a preservation order on it. In 1959, the estate sought permission to demolish the house and neighbouring properties to make way for a 'neo-Georgian block of flats, a new building for the Indonesian Embassy and a hotel'.

The proposals mortified Lady Illingworth, who mobilised a number of establishment figures in support of her campaign for its preservation. She also took a step which was to increase the public interest in the house. In the 1900s, during renovation work by an earlier owner, a wall painting was discovered in the first-floor drawing room. Although this had excited considerable interest, it was covered up some years later, at first temporarily, and later completely by Lord Illingworth in the late 1920s. In 1960, Lady Illingworth asked builders to remove the panelling and so reveal the painting, a series of scenes of figures in seventeenth-century costume, rumoured to be the work of Hogarth or William Kent, although eventually deemed to be by a follower of Louis Laguerre, a minor French architectural painter. Among those called to see the painting was Sir John Summerson, curator of Sir John Soane's Museum in Holborn, who described the house as a 'fragment from another world'.

The battle over the house led to a planning enquiry. 'I love this beautiful old house and should like to be able to go on living here,' Lady Illingworth said to the *Daily Telegraph* reporter on the day. Sir John told the enquiry that the house enshrined the 'the whole feel of eighteenth-century London'. But it was not to be. In June 1961, the Ministry said that the original Georgian character had been altered and the house was not of such importance that it should stand in the way of redevelopment.

Ironically, the publicity attracted great interest in the house when Lady Illingworth, playing the hostess again, opened it to the public on 21 and 23 June that year. It was particularly appropriate to open it on the 21st, she said, because the original news of the Waterloo victory had been brought on a Wednesday and that year the day again fell on a Wednesday. Takings went to the Seaman's Hospital Society at Greenwich.

By the time the lease finally expired in July 1967, the site had been bought by her old friend Maxwell Joseph, the property developer, for a new hotel, to be called the Britannia. 'I wanted to spend my last days here,' she told friends and, devoted hostess to the end, threw one last party for 200 people, attended by, among others, the Russian Ambassador, the Marquis of Bristol, the Earl of Verulam (a former neighbour) and the Conservative politician Reginald Maudling and his wife.

The following weeks were spent packing the results of thirty-six years of a rich life at Grosvenor Square. The forty rooms were emptied and all the fine furniture, silverware, china, glassware, clocks, prints, watercolours, ceramics and books were packed up. Down came the wall hangings, the curtains and drapes, also all packed away. It would all go into storage until she needed it again – van-load after van-load of the heavy goods, mainly the furniture, left Grosvenor Square for the storage depot of Giltspur Bullens, the removals company, where it would await further instructions for eighteen years. Still more was carted around to the Kensington branch of the National Westminster Bank – Albert's bank after all – which would look after the valuables: the silverware and jewellery. A van-load went to her nephew John at Markington, where she might one day live. And another went to her niece, Susan, who was now renovating and furnishing her own house, on the Welsh border. She would need it.

Aubrey Appleton, then a young foreman for Giltspur Bullens, later to become its managing director, made a number of trips to

Grosvenor Square during that summer of 1967 to help with the packing and transporting. On one occasion, Lady Illingworth took him down to the extensive cellars underneath the house, where the fine wines and unwanted furniture were kept. One of the cellars was used as a strongroom for particularly valuable items.

Lady Illingworth told him that she dreaded going down there and did so infrequently; the lights were fused and it was difficult to see clearly. But his eye was caught by something he was never to forget. In one corner there were a number of gold bullion bars, shining in the gloom. Lady Illingworth agreed with him that they should go to the bank vault.

Lady Illingworth had not decided where to go after Grosvenor Square. She was a still a vigorous woman in her late sixties and, while her style of life was fading fast, she had many more years to look forward to, but nowhere to spend them. She had no close family of her own and would almost certainly have been reluctant to impose upon any of her relatives, such as Robert, out in Billericay, or cousin Richard, the recently created Lord Wilberforce, a Law Lord. She could almost certainly have bought herself a substantial mansion flat somewhere fitting in central London, but chose not to for reasons never fully explained. While Markington, once her family home, must have beckoned, half of the house was rented off to help pay for the upkeep. Also, John Wilberforce, her nephew, had just returned to London to take up a post at the Foreign Office as the assistant head of the United Nations department; his wife and family would want to live at Markington.

For a brief period, she decided, she would go and stay at the Connaught Hotel, close by Grosvenor Square, while she looked around for somewhere suitable. After a few months she moved in with a spinster cousin, Irene Wilberforce, also in her late sixties. Irene was a great-great-granddaughter of William Wilberforce through the abolitionist's second son, Robert. Her father was Sir Herbert Wilberforce, a barrister and stipendiary magistrate who had been both president and chairman of the All England Lawn Tennis Club at Wimbledon during the 1920s and 1930s. Irene had never married and had lived for many years in a huge but gloomy ground-floor mansion flat in York House, Kensington Church Street, just off Kensington High Street. Lady

Illingworth moved in for a short stay that was to last sixteen years, paying rent, never moving in her furniture.

These two elderly, rather genteel ladies were probably largely unaware of the fundamental changes in society taking place all around them. While Lady Illingworth had been somewhat immune from them in Grosvenor Square, her new home was another matter. Kensington High Street in the late 1960s was one of the centres of fashionable London, but a different fashionability from that once enjoyed by Lady Illingworth. It was a culture centred on the preservation of youth rather than its treatment as a chrysalis from which fully grown adults suddenly 'came out' and turned into clones of their parents. In her retreat to York House, Lady Illingworth symbolised the retrenchment not just of a generation, but also of a way of life.

By now, number 44 had been demolished. After two years she went, on 21 June, the day of the Waterloo Ball, to view the new hotel taking shape on the site. It was, she said afterwards, a very fine building, but she missed the old house terribly. The wall painting had been taken to the Victoria and Albert Museum, where it is still displayed on a staircase, the last surviving fragment of the last proper house in Grosvenor Square.

For a decade or more, Lady Illingworth consoled herself by maintaining as far as possible her former lifestyle, though she did so mainly away from York House, where she would never entertain. She still received many invitations to attend receptions and cocktail parties at embassies and art galleries – as many as four a night. She reciprocated by hosting elaborate lunches in a hired suite at Claridge's. She would visit Richard at the House of Lords and take tea at the Ritz. She enjoyed going to the races and a regular feature of her day was checking the early racing results in the London *Evening News*.

Although the Rolls-Royce she had kept in the mews behind Grosvenor Square was now garaged at Markington (and was eventually sold in the early 1970s) she would be picked up at York House and driven by Albert Oslar, her part-time chauffeur since the mid-1960s. There was a wide circle of friends and relatives. There were also various Wilberforces who visited York House from time to time.

Closest was John, who spent long periods living at York House during the 1970s when on attachment in London. In 1972, he was posted to the Washington Embassy as Counsellor and then Head of Chancery. In 1975, he returned to London and York House when he became head of the defence department of the Foreign Office, dealing with arms control and military assistance, before spending a year at the Royal College of Defence Studies, which trains senior civil servants as well as army and police officers for high-ranking posts. He had clearly been earmarked for the most important positions.

Aunt Puss's relatives might have been forgiven for thinking her range of friends and stream of invitations would always keep her occupied and that their attention was superfluous. But outside the family there were a great many acquaintances and only a few close friends, such as the Duchess of Leinster, widow of the penniless Duke of Leinster, who still lived in a top-floor flat in Grosvenor Square; Sir Maxwell Joseph, whose home she would visit for dinner; and a city stockbroker, Robert Strauss, who would invite her to lavish parties at his home in Sussex.

Oslar recalled: 'She had a wonderful life. Enjoyed herself enormously. She was a lovely person. I rarely heard her complain about anything. A lovely old lady, very serene and gentle, always a smile, always well dressed. People often ask me what she was like and, you know, all I can say is she was like the old Queen Mum. You know, always nice.'

She was certainly still considerably wealthy as well as being generous with her money. 'When we arrived at a racecourse she would often press a twenty-pound note into my hand and say, 'Go and have a bet yourself, Mr Oslar.' She often forgot she had paid me and would send another cheque. I would ring her up and say, 'M'Lady, you've paid me twice again.' She simply told me to just put it into the bank and not to worry. 'Course then I just didn't charge her for a few trips until it balanced out. There was nothing but the best all the way down the line. She never bought anything that was cheap.' She dined at Prunier's in St James's and the White Tower in Fitzrovia; her wines came from Berry Brothers and Rudd in St James's; her chocolates from Charbonnel et Walker in New Bond Street.

Years later, Lady Illingworth is still remembered fondly by the portering staff at York House for the glorious Christmas presents they would receive, as well as the glittering gold jewellery she wore when picked up by Oslar for a night on the town. The head porter recalls several visits with her to the bank to return jewellery she had taken out for some special event.

Oslar is illuminating on the subject of her affection for gold: 'She once got very pleased when some gold-mining company announced some deal or find or whatever. She said to me: "Got a tip about that in Monte Carlo, Mr Oslar, made of a bit of a killing on it . . ." The Lady Illingworth was very keen on Kruger-rands, always wanted to know when the price was going up or down. I was sitting in the kitchen at York House with Cathy (the housekeeper-cum-nurse) one day, waiting for her to get ready, and she comes in with a gold cigarette box in her hand. It must have been about eight inches long. She gave it to me to hold and feel the weight. She said she had bought it for someone but liked it so much she had decided to keep it for herself.'

Throughout the two decades Oslar drove Lady Illingworth, becoming an intermittent confidant, she never mentioned Albert or the grave in Bradford. But it was clear Albert was still very much on her mind. Oslar said: 'Just the once I said something critical about Ford cars, like them being of poor reputation, if you get my meaning. Well, the look I got from her was pretty awful and I realised I had said something wrong and shut up. Found out afterwards that her old man had been on the board or something.'

As the twilight of Lady Illingworth's years neared, her thoughts turned to her vow to Albert, made more than thirty years before, to be laid to rest in the Illingworth vault next to him, in the Undercliffe, overlooking Bradford. In 1975, she reorganised her affairs, opened fresh bank accounts in Kensington and Ripon, near Markington, and made a will, using the family solicitors, Theodore Goddard and Co., who had drawn up Albert's own will in the 1930s. The second paragraph of the 1975 will made it quite clear: 'I wish to be buried in the place reserved for me next to my husband at Undercliffe Cemetery near Bradford.'

The will also disposed of the bulk of her estate equally between her nephew John and a distant Illingworth relation, Lucy Kilfoil, who lives in South Africa. There were other small bequests, including ones to John's son William and to her nephew Jamie Illingworth, a London businessman. She also left £1000 to Alexander, Susan's eldest son, then a teenager, the only bequest to Susan or her family. No reason for the bequest was ever made known by Aunt Puss.

It is what Lady Illingworth left out, rather than what she put in, which is most significant. At this point, she had barely been in contact with Susan for five or more years, presumably because of her displeasure over the divorce. She almost certainly knew Susan was in dire financial straits; she had helped her out before, staging her coming out and sending the lorry-load of furniture. And Lady Illingworth was unquestionably a woman of some generosity. A conscious decision to reflect her strong opinion of the divorce, something Catholics did not contemplate easily, may be why Susan was excluded from the will. Had she herself not had to wait for Albert to be freed naturally, by God's intervention? But it also has to be acknowledged that Lady Illingworth may have believed that, since Susan was then at Weobley, her immediate future had been taken care of by her own mother. For either reason, there would be no money for Susan; Alexander would benefit, since he was the eldest and therefore likely to have need of money soonest.

This may have been only one of the reasons why it soon became suggested among the family, particularly by her brother Robert, that the will was carelessly drafted and the bequests apparently made at random.

The lady of the manor had been reduced to the lady of the bedsit, counting the pennies. Birdbrain's stubborn resistance at Heath House, which Susan now ran out of emotional and financial steam to fight (and would do very little about for several years), had also destroyed her relationship with Sebastian. At Markington, Laura was in charge, while John worked in London; she had rejected their hospitality in pursuit of her own independence. The divorce and family upheavals had also put her out of favour with her staunchly Roman Catholic relatives.

Aunt Puss had made her point firmly in the will. Uncle Wee was also said to have been unhappy about Susan's situation, although whether he withdrew financial support is unclear. His relations with his niece were odd: although he gave her considerable sums of money over a number of years and took a keen interest in her affairs, after she left Heath House he did not visit her or see her again until very late in his life. At this point relations were sufficiently cool for Aunt Marion to be forced into making what Susan described as 'secret' trips to see them, still sometimes flying up to Shobden and also helping out financially.

There is no proof that at about this time Susan learnt that John and his children, growing teenagers like hers, would be the beneficiary of Aunt Puss's will, although it became common knowledge among the rest of the family. Her children think it unlikely – because of the split between Markington and Susan – and say that the most obvious conduit for the information, Aunt Marion, made a point of never gossiping over family business. Nevertheless, the possibility remains that Susan did find out, at about this time, that Aunt Puss had made no provision for her or her four youngest children, while making a substantial one for John, who already had Markington and had benefited from their mother's will. It would have been like twisting the knife in the wound. It may well have shaped what happened later.

In late 1977, they were on the move again. This time back north to Docklow, a straggle of houses and a pub, five miles east of Leominster on the road to Worcester.

The previous year, through her Aunt Marion's visits to Shobden aerodome, Susan had become friendly with a curious character called Louis Wood, otherwise known as Woody, the chief flying instructor, a heavy-drinking, womanising former commercial pilot in his sixties who lived in a caravan on the airfield. It was a strange affair, possibly born out of Susan's isolation and her still, even in her mid-forties, overwhelming need for a strong masculine presence in her life to replace the one she had lost when so young.

He had helped them find a cottage known as 1 Forresters Hall Cottages, one of a pair, which everyone locally referred to as Forresters Hall. It was just big enough: a galley kitchen and two rooms downstairs and two large and one small bedroom upstairs. There was a decent-sized garden at the rear and a large drive at the front. The two cottages were shielded from the main road by a tall hedge.

1 Heath House.

After the divorce

2 Susan de Stempel gardening at Docklow.
3 Forresters Hall, Docklow.

4 Simon, Marcus and Sophia outside Heath House, around 1974. After leaving Heath House, Susan would take the children back to look at their former home.
5 Susan and Sophia at Markington, sometime in 1975.

Family life

6 *Opposite:* The children at Markington in about 1975.
From left: Sebastian, Alexander, Marcus, Simon and
Sophia.
7 Susan at Docklow with Oats, the cat
they bought for Aunt Puss.
8 Sophia cutting Simon's hair, in the garden
at Heath House, in 1979.

Lady Illingworth

9 With Lord Illingworth, leaving the Royal Academy, 1937, after a private viewing.

10 A woman in her prime. Outside her beloved number 44 Grosvenor Square, in 1961, shortly after learning that its demolition was unavoidable.

11 The portrait of Lady Illingworth by Philip de Lazlo, one of many paintings which hung in Grosvenor Square, which Susan obtained.

12 and **13** With Sophia and Michael, in the garden at Docklow in the spring and early summer of 1984, as the money was beginning to flow through Susan's accounts.

16 Sophia, outside Heath House,
after her release from prison, autumn 1990.

17 Sebastian and Alexander outside Hopton Church after their father's memorial service.
18 John Wilberforce in the 1970s. **19** Detective Inspector Mike Cowley.

20 Michael de Stempel,
leaving court during the fraud trial.

A strong tribal sense had now enveloped Susan and her three youngest, remaining children. They formed a close unit in their cocoon, bonded and strengthened by rejection and adversity, reinforced by Susan's private nature. There was very little for any comforts, but mother always provided. She had shepherded them from Heath House, through Weobley, Markington and Ross and, armed with her strength of personality and purpose, would continue to look after them, to shelter them from the travails of the world. In return they gave her their unblinking devotion. It was them against the rest.

Money was extremely tight. The school fees for Marcus, Simon at the Oratory and Sophia at St Ursula's Convent in Brecon came to at least £5000 a year, funded mainly by Uncle Wee and, in Marcus's case, also by his godmother, Charlotte, Lady Reay. But Susan still needed to pay the rent and buy food, particularly when the children were at home. The £2000 a year from family trusts was simply not enough. Bills often went unpaid, clothes were old and Susan took up knitting. The limited nature of their lives during the later 1970s is perhaps best typified by the fact that so few local people became friendly with them at Weobley or Docklow. The clichéd neighbourly assessment, 'They kept themselves to themselves,' actually had the ring of truth.

There does not appear to have been any thought in her mind of getting a job, even if anybody had wanted to employ a forty-three-year-old woman of impeccable breeding and no qualifications. She seems to have occupied her days with house-keeping, clothes repair and gardening. Michael, an intermittent visitor, claimed she wrote letters to him stressing how they were starving, had no heating, how it was five miles to the nearest shop and they had no petrol for the cars. He said he began sending her money, eventually totalling £28,000.

Sophia left the convent, possibly because of cash shortages, after gaining eight O-levels in 1978. The nuns there are diplomatic in commenting about their ex-pupil, beyond saying that she had a very good academic record. In July of the following year, Marcus left the Oratory, with six O-levels and two poor-grade A-levels, after what must have been an unhappy schooling. His teachers remember a pleasant but solitary and shy individual, who looked like a third former even in the sixth and was sometimes picked on by the other boys as a result. They knew of the family problems, which they are certain contributed to academic under-achievement. He was encouraged to pursue a career in landscape gardening, since he appeared to have a genuine interest in something which also suited his personality.

Both went to Hereford Technical College to retake their A-level examinations, each obtaining three passes. None of the three younger children would have enough qualifications to go on to university, although Sophia studied for, but failed, her Oxford entrance examinations. Marcus thought he wanted to be a landscape gardener, Sophia was unsure.

At Docklow, life was limited. Casual callers were rare and there was nowhere to go in the evenings apart from the pub down the road. Marcus, Sophia and Simon, now also back at Docklow after the Oratory, had few of the opportunities for social life enjoyed by urban teenagers. Anyway, that was not their style. 'Marcus is not really the kind of chap that you slap across the back and drag down the pub,' said one acquaintance of the family. (By contrast, according to those who know him, Simon junior appears to be almost the complete opposite.)

The combination of boarding school, country homes, small towns and villages meant that their experience of life was limited, their available circle of friends narrow. They were not followers of fashion or music. 'They were just a bit other-worldly, not at all modern young people,' said another acquaintance. Friends would later say how innocent Sophia and Marcus always were; that the innocence of their rural childhood had never really left them. One of the children later put it another way: 'I am afraid we simply don't know many people.' Evenings at Docklow would be spent with their mother, working till late in the garden (in the summer), watching television or reading middlebrow thrillers. Susan would often take her food upstairs.

They had often accompanied their mother to the flying club at Shobden, where, in addition to meeting Woody, she took some flying lessons, perhaps hoping to emulate her aunt's spirit of adventure. (Simon junior would also later take flying and parachuting lessons at Shobden.) But probably the more important attraction of the club was the bar around which a social life revolved. 'Susan was very vivacious and could turn the charm on, but of course she was much better looking then than she is now,' recalled one former club member. 'She seemed to spend most of the time in the bar and I don't think she did much flying.' Susan, occasionally accompanied by Sophia and Marcus, would be seen disappearing into Woody's caravan.

But Woody was hardly a reliable character. In December 1979, after a hard night's drinking at a local pub, forced by floodwater to abandon the Austin 1300 on temporary loan from Susan, he tried to walk home to his caravan through appalling weather. They found him the next morning on the runway, face down, dead from heart failure brought on by exposure. The inquest accepted this version of events, although why his trousers were down and he had gravel between his buttocks was never explained. Susan, who gave evidence at the inquest, always maintained that there was something funny about his death, because of some of the people with whom he was involved. Her children say that the pain of his death was reduced by the fact that the relationship had been nearing its end at the time.

This was one of the few highlights of an otherwise predictable, limited lifestyle which persisted relatively without incident for a number of years. 'But then we had always been isolated, all our lives,' said Marcus. 'We were like a desert-island family, Mother, my brother and sister and myself. All the trouble brought us so close together, we were in a sort of bubble of our own making. And we were happy. We would laugh and have fun and go to Wales and things like that. We were so happy we never noticed that much of the outside world or the lack of money.'

Susan had. Already, and almost certainly through gritted teeth, she had begun selling some of the good-quality furniture she had brought from Markington and Heath House to help keep them afloat, paying for the bills Uncle Wee did not cover. That was one way of providing for them, her children. She believed, as she said, in keeping the family together. Or what was left of it.

In 1982, Michael reappeared on the scene. Although he later claimed he had been giving Susan money for some time, his visits had been rare. He had been a regular fixture during the

Weobley period, when things had improved for a short while and there had first been talk of him and Susan getting married. Susan backed out when she discovered that he was actually still married to Francesca.

Now, divorced, Michael wanted to resume the relationship. She readily accepted him. He was not exactly bearing gifts, but he had some money and was expecting to inherit £150,000 from his father. While this was a sizeable sum, most people who knew him would not have expected it to last for long.

So a little money was injected, along with a little variation, into the lives of those at Docklow. Michael became a regular visitor, almost living there, returning to London at weekends to look after Alexander. But it would be too cynical to believe the motive was only money. Susan was quite probably feeling short of male company; her later letters would show a real love, or at least passion, for Michael. The relationship blossomed; he paid attention to Sophia, Marcus and Simon; they thought he was entertaining to have around. Susan and Michael began to talk of a future together; he encouraged her to do something about Heath House. Everyone said how happy things were between them all.

Not long after this, Marcus went to Thames Polytechnic, at Dartford, to study landscape gardening, living in halls with the other students. Sophia realised that she too needed to break from the claustrophobic atmosphere of Docklow, now that her mother had Michael for regular company. The natural move was to London, where Sebastian and Marcus now lived. She had nowhere to stay; she could not join Sebastian, staying with Uncle Richard, Lord Wilberforce, while working in London, because there was not enough space and she hardly knew him.

She had the idea of staying at the big flat of Aunt Irene's in Kensington, which she had last visited twelve years previously. It had been nearly ten years since Aunt Puss had been unhappy about the divorce; she was an old woman now; time was a healer. And, after all, Uncle John and many other members of the family had stayed there, Michael had been there, and had not Aunt Puss, herself something of a long-term lodger, looked after Susan, her mother, all those years ago, when she, a young girl from the shires, the same age as Sophia, had first set foot in the big city? Sophia wrote to Irene, asking if she could come and stay and look for a job. The answer was yes. Sophia, aged twenty, like her mother almost thirty years before, was going to live with Aunt Irene and Aunt Puss in London.

By the time Sophia arrived at York House in the autumn of 1982, the passage of time had reduced the pace of Lady Illingworth's life a great deal: she was older, and she went out less and less, although still taken by Oslar. Everyone agreed she had aged after falling down and breaking her hip in 1979. After a period of convalescence in Yorkshire, she became less active and less sociable. The invitations from embassies had dropped away; to them, she became a figure from the past. Many old friends were dead, her trips to Monte Carlo stopped and she retreated into York House: the principal visitors now from among her family. They included Lord Wilberforce, now also retired, and his wife Yvette, who went about once a week. Their house was nearby; Sebastian, studying law, would also call, to see both his great-aunt and his sister. Younger members of the Illingworth and the Wilberforce families would drop by infrequently. Lady Illingworth would spend Christmas with her now retired and ageing brother Robert and Marion in Essex, arriving loaded with presents.

Sophia found the atmosphere at York House a little stifling. Conditions had deteriorated. Lady Illingworth was eighty-two, Irene somewhere in her seventies, and Cathy Whelan, the housekeeper, was sixty-three. Everyone who went there agreed it was what might be expected when three elderly ladies had lived together for many years: it was dark, dingy, musty and in need of a decent redecoration. Part of the problem was that the flat was on the ground floor and almost always in shadow, rarely receiving any sunlight. The front overlooked the forecourt to the flats, the rear windows gave on to the inner yard and service entrances. Albert Oslar remembers the 'dilapidated feel' and the dominant feature: 'Hat boxes everywhere, dozens of hat boxes.' Another visitor spoke of a plethora of handbags and, in Lady Illingworth's room, old boxes of soap and suitcases containing Elizabeth Arden make-up. Most of the furniture, once of impeccable quality, was getting a little worn. A few yards away, fashionable west London hummed; inside, it could have been another age.

Having lived together for so long there were inevitably arguments between Aunt Puss and Irene, petty disputes over domestic matters that resulted in loud voices but little else. Monica Makra, Irene's niece, said they would 'scrap like children'. Aunt Puss had lived a grand, sophisticated existence and was still a woman of strong personality, who, in her heyday, had alienated some members of the family with her often deliberately provocative rudeness, designed to encourage people to stand up to her. Irene was almost the opposite, a spinster with limited experience of life and quiet manners. Cathy was a religious woman with old-fashioned, straightforward views, almost obsessively protective of her charges and conscious of their well-being – she would prepare a hamper if Oslar were taking Lady Illingworth on a long drive. She ran the household firmly and rebuked Sophia for running up telephone bills talking to friends. But the abrasiveness between Irene and Lady Illingworth does not appear to have been pronounced enough to support the subsequent suggestion that it was one reason why Aunt Puss wanted to go to Docklow. York House may have been unsuitable, but she was more likely to have been unhappy because she wanted to go to Markington, not because she wanted to leave.

At this time it was abundantly clear to everyone – apart, that is, from Sophia – that Lady Illingworth was becoming more and more absent-minded. Oslar would check with Cathy by telephone to see if she really was going where she said she wanted to go, whether she was ready and expected at the other end. 'There was one occasion when I took her to have tea with some relatives in Datchet, near Windsor. I dropped her off and said I would be back at a certain time. When I arrived, she didn't come out. After a while I knocked on the door and was told she had summoned a taxi to take her back to London and had already left. That was how forgetful she was.'

Another visitor who noticed instances of Lady Illingworth's absent-mindedness was Elizabeth Gregg-Smith, recruited by Robert in 1981 to look after his sister's financial affairs. They were in chaos, she said. Masses of old correspondence and bills had to be sorted out; she put them into four accordion files. She said Lady Illingworth had become vague and sometimes unaware of what was going on around her. Her hand had to be guided to sign cheques and she could read only with difficulty, using a magnifying glass.

With, initially, only a small circle of friends in London, Sophia had time to spare and began to chat with her aunt in the evenings after work. They grew very close and would spend time together in Sophia's bedroom, where Aunt Puss would be the beneficiary of Sophia's ability to talk and gossip at length. There is no reason to suppose that the relationship was not a genuine one from the point of view of Sophia, and undoubtedly for gregarious Aunt Puss her young relative's buoyant personality was a welcome relief from the somewhat dour attitudes of her other companions. They would have a drink, usually a gin, together at York House, go for walks and shopping and sometimes eat at an Italian restaurant around the corner in Kensington Church Street.

It is clear that at this point Lady Illingworth still considered Markington to be her country home, although whether she was ever given direct encouragement to go there is unclear. Some years previously she had suggested she could renovate an old mill in the grounds for her home; the idea was never pursued. She certainly spoke of Markington a great deal and with some fondness; she would write asking for transport to be arranged to take her there. After all, she had grown up there, returning there frequently in the late 1930s and early 1940s when her brother had been away in the army and Cecilia and Susan away with other Dormers. She and Albert had spent a lot of time there and Albert had poured money into the house; he had died there. Her other brother Robert, his health deteriorating, and Marion were now staying in one wing of the house. She may have felt that she had a right to be at the house as well.

But, strictly speaking, the ownership of Markington and the lordship of the Manor – the direct line – had passed from her late brother to her nephew. In 1983, John and his wife Laura were in Cyprus, where he was British High Commissioner, and two of their three children, William, then twenty-five (sometimes with his girlfriend), and Anne, twenty-nine, were occasionally living in one part of the house. Lady Illingworth did make two trips to stay at Markington in 1983, on which, Sophia says, she accompanied her; her aunt, she adds, was only 'tolerated'.

There was the gap in generations between Lady Illingworth

and her Markington relations; she would have a very different feeling about the house from theirs: she had known it all her life; but had not lived there for any length of time during the three decades they had known it as their home. William later conceded to police that there had been times when he had said it was not convenient for Aunt Puss to visit.

How much of this was understood by Lady Illingworth is impossible to say. She was becoming senile, but the disease is progressive and periods of lucidity mingle with those of confusion. This may explain the differing accounts of the severity of her condition. It is entirely possible that by the end of 1983 she had accumulated some vague sense, possibly misplaced or exaggerated, of rejection. She was not being offered the opportunity to spend her last years at Markington; she may have felt she were no longer wanted. She told the others at York House that she might go for a stay at Markington anyway, uninvited.

The Markington Wilberforces later made it clear that they had been concerned about conditions at York House and there had been some discussion about how long Cathy would be able to cope. They may simply have postponed any kind of decision. William later told police: 'I was sure she didn't really want to move deep down and such an upheaval at her age would not have been good for her health.' But other members of the family felt it was wrong that no one made more of an effort to look after her at York House. In November 1983, while passing through London on his way back to Cyprus, John went to see her. He realised with a shock that her condition had worsened and that she was now clearly senile. He was unable to do anything; he flew out the next day. But he came to the conclusion that for the time being his aunt would be best left in familiar circumstances, with those already able to care for her. He was never to see her again.

One day the following February, Father Ignatius McDonnell, a priest at the Carmelite Priory near York House which she had attended for more than ten years, was surprised to see Lady Illingworth enter the vestry in what to him was a confused and agitated condition. She asked him to get a chauffeur-driven car to take her to Markington. He called for a mini-cab. While waiting for the car to arrive she remained apparently confused, once asking him to take her to York-shire.

She arrived at Markington some hours later, after being charged £500. Oslar got the summons from Cathy a few days later. 'Anne and William wanted me to come and take her away because Mr John was away and there was no one to look after her.' When he arrived she was sitting, waiting packed and in her coat, in the kitchen. She asked who he was and Oslar had to explain that he had known her for twenty years. She was gently steered to the car for the drive back to London. 'I got the impression they were anxious for us to leave.' At York House, he handed her over to Cathy. It was the last time he or anyone at Markington saw her.

For precisely what happened over the next few days – and indeed most of the next three and half years – there are few independent witnesses. According to Sophia and Susan, Lady Illingworth had suggested accompanying Sophia, who was giving up her job, back to Docklow for a short holiday, perhaps a few weeks, with her niece Susan, whom she had not seen for so many years. According to Sophia, Aunt Puss seemed unconcerned that this was the niece with whom she had fallen out some years previously. 'I don't think it occurred to her. Cathy used to say snide things about my mother, but Aunt Puss did not say anything. She was the kind of person where you would fall in and out of favour with her.'

Susan apparently rejected the initial idea – unsurprisingly perhaps because there was no spare money to care for her ageing aunt and Docklow was cramped. Michael was often forced to sleep in a tent in the garden and Sophia would be sharing a room with Marcus and Simon. But Susan, said Sophia, was persuaded to change her mind after remembering that Aunt Puss had lived in a small cottage at Markington and therefore might not mind Docklow. She told Sophia that Aunt Puss could come for a short holiday. Cathy and Irene were told; a bag was packed. On 29 February 1984, Sophia and her Aunt Puss, clutching the minimum of her possessions, took a taxi to Paddington and the train to Hereford, where they were met by Susan, who took them to Docklow. According to Sophia, there was no doubt that Aunt Puss knew where she was, no suggestion, despite the earlier incidents, that she was confused about why she was going there. The reunion with her niece, Sophia said, was rapturous.

Five days later, Susan wrote to the branch of Lloyds Bank in Hereford where she had had an account for several years. She had, she wrote, been 'on a bit of a spending spree on behalf of an elderly relative' who had recently come to live with her and had mislaid her own cheque card. Susan assured the bank that she hoped to be 'fully reimbursed' within the next few days for all the things she had bought. She was.

6
Going Liquid

Just over twelve months after Susan had written to Lloyds Bank in Hereford, the Department of Health and Social Security offices in Hereford received the following letter:

> Forresters Hall,
> Nr Leominster
> Herefordshire,
> HR6 0RX

Dear Sir,

    Ref: 6909/239375 M Illingworth

Thank you for your letter of the 21st March. I am so sorry to have taken so long to help you in the matter of my aunt but I have had a chapter of accidents, first breaking three fingers and nearly losing the top of another, followed by pneumonia, followed by pleurisy in one lung, then the other.

Unfortunately, I am not in a position to act as appointee for my aunt, having very little money of my own and five children to cope with alone.

My aunt has had a very difficult time over the last few years. As you may know, she had been a widow for over forty years. She sold a very small house she had in about 1946 and lived off the proceeds for the next few years. Then it was all invested in Australian (?) mines, the whole of which went bust and she lost the lot. Had she been properly advised about this she could have got out in time but she was not advised and consequently lost everything. As far as I can gather she then lived with a series of friends, all of whom are now dead, until I heard about her plight and brought her to live with me. She has no property of any kind as far as I know and no family living except myself. The state she was in

when she came to me can only be described as pitiable.
Her pension was paid into a local bank, the account
there having been closed some time ago as there was
no point in keeping it open. When my aunt came to
me, she gave me her pension to use for her general
living. She has no bank account or Post Office account
or premium bonds as far as I know.

I hope this information will help you and please do
not hesitate to contact me should I be able to help you
further.

> Yours faithfully,
> S.C. Wilberforce

Lady Illingworth had indeed been having a difficult time.
Probably at the very moment the Social Security officials were
reading the letter, she was sitting in the brightly lit lounge of
Langford House, a home for the old-age pensioners of Hereford,
tucked away in a side road on the outskirts of the city. Once
a solid, Edwardian villa, it has been extended with the kind
of cheap structures that spell a state-run home, clinic or penal
establishment. One of the additions is a sort of sun lounge which
allows plenty of light into the room, where the residents can sit
enjoying the sunshine without getting chilly. If they are lucky,
they can see the cars drive past or children walking home from
school. When visitors call or deliveries arrive, there is always a
stir of excitement.

Like many of the other residents, Lady Illingworth was
wearing largely second-hand clothes, donated or bought from
charity shops, plus the rather well-worn clothes she had had
with her when she had first arrived from Hereford Hospital.
The routine at the home was kindly and caring but by its very
nature institutionalised and unvarying.

Between meals, along with the other sixty or so residents, she
would sit staring into space, occasionally exchanging desultory
remarks with her neighbours. Since she was now suffering
from the latter stages of Alzheimer's disease, she was completely unaware of her surroundings. She knew she had been
somebody, but could not remember quite who, and she knew
she should have been somewhere else, but could not say where.
Her husband, she said, had once been a peer. The staff knew her

name, but little else about her. There was not much to mark her out from their other charges. Like them, she waited for regular meals and death. Staff told enquiring visitors that she had been rich once but had now lost all her money. Some of them wondered what circumstances had brought her to this place.

When Lady Illingworth arrived at Docklow, her overall financial affairs were well organised and their administration was improved by Elizabeth Gregg-Smith. She was still receiving her income of about £50,000 a year from the stocks and shares placed in trust for her by her late husband, then worth just under £1 million. She had shares and bonds of her own; her six bank accounts – a current, a deposit and a dividend at the National Westminster Bank near York House, a current and a deposit at Ripon, in Yorkshire, and an account in Monte Carlo – were logically organised and, apart from a slight overdraft on the Kensington current account, generously in credit, largely because her own living expenses had been diminished by circumstances over the years. The will was with Theodore Goddard. In the unlikely event that she needed any money, she could have sold some of her jewellery, shares, bonds or even furniture.

But it was at this point, after so many years, that Lady Illingworth embarked on an unprecedented upheaval of her finances, which she began to carry out with a level of energy, determination and clarity of thought that belied her age and, to many, encroaching senility. It was explained to anyone who enquired that her rejection by the Markington branch had persuaded her to throw in her lot with her relatives and her dear old friend Michael at Docklow. She would live with them, help buy them all a house, ask them to organise her affairs and give them all her property, including her jewellery, silverware and furniture; and, furthermore, she would reward them for all this help by changing the chief beneficiary of her 1975 will from her nephew John to his sister, with whom she was now so joyfully reunited: Susan.

Twelve days after arriving at Docklow, Lady Illingworth wrote to the manager of the Midland Bank at Ripon, requesting an autobank card so that she would be able to make withdrawals, using High Street cashpoints, from her current account, then in credit to the tune of about £6000. The card, the first she had ever requested, was issued without question a few days later, but was not used for another eleven days. On 27 March, she withdrew £480 from a Midland Bank cashpoint in Hereford. Shortly afterwards, the same sum was paid into Susan's account at Lloyds, to cover the 'spending spree'.

About this time, Michael began to take a helping hand in the affairs of Lady Illingworth. He went to see his old friend and solicitor, Lord Coleraine, grandson of Bonar Law, whom he had known since Oxford. He told him that his friend Lady Illingworth, aunt of his other friend, Susan Wilberforce, needed someone to draft a new will and help sort out her affairs. 'Fine,' Lord Coleraine is reported to have said, 'when can I see her?' Shortly afterwards, Robert Patten, a senior partner in the Twickenham firm of Mackenzie Patten and Co., and another old friend of Michael's, was on the receiving end of an identical request. 'Fine,' he is believed to have said. 'What do you want me to do?' Instructions were sent to him and a draft of the new will was prepared. Theodore Goddard were not consulted.

Also about this time, Lady Illingworth decided that she wanted to retrieve her clothes and possessions, having made up her mind to remain at Docklow. Susan rang Cathy and told her to get Aunt Puss's clothes ready. Sophia and Marcus went to York House, but Cathy, protective as ever, said they were not ready. She refused them access to their aunt's room and a row ensued. Susan was telephoned and there was a further argument; Susan and Michael both telephoned Lord Coleraine asking him to intercede. He refused. Sophia and Marcus left empty-handed.

A few days later, on 3 April, Lady Illingworth wrote the first of a series of authorisations empowering those named and acting on her behalf to handle her affairs. 'I hereby authorise', she typed, 'my solicitor Mr Robert Patten JP to collect immediately all my belongings and possessions at 2 York House, London W8, including all papers, documents, cheque books, bank statements and bank cards, etc. Margaret Illingworth (The Lady Illingworth).' The signature was the spidery scrawl of an elderly person. She wrote a similar authorisation enabling Patten to collect 'all documents, share certificates, jewellery and any other items', held by the National Westminster Bank in Kensington High Street.

Later the same day, Patten, Marcus and Michael, armed with the authority, arrived at York House. Cathy and Irene had no option but to allow them access. They spent all day at the flat sorting through Lady Illingworth's possessions and took away boxes, suitcases and crates, loading them on to a hired van. Marcus himself took care of the four bulky accordion files, which had been carefully organised by Elizabeth Gregg-Smith. He took it all to Paddington and loaded it on to a train to Hereford, where he was met by his mother. There was so much that some of it had to stay overnight at the station.

Throughout the following month, Lady Illingworth made extensive use of her new autobank card in Hereford. At intervals over the rest of the month, she made four withdrawals, each of £500. One was on 16 April. The same day, Susan and Sophia, accompanied by Aunt Puss, went into a travel agent, where Susan paid £800 in cash for an air ticket to Japan, for Sophia, who had longed to have a holiday with her brother Alexander, then living in Tokyo.

At the beginning of the month, Lady Illingworth received a draft of the new will from Patten. Unfortunately, a few days later, Patten was taken ill and subsequently had to go to the United States to recover and has not returned. Preparation of the will was taken over by his former partner Richard Sexton, who took the file with him when he began a new company. At the end of the month, he received two typewritten letters from Forresters Hall, both dated 30 April:

Dear Mr Sexton,

Just before Mr Patten was taken ill he drew up a draft copy of my will. If you could please go ahead with the engrossment, just adding that in the event of my niece, Mrs Susan Wilberforce, predeceasing me, I should like the residue of my estate to be shared equally between her five children, William Alexander Wilberforce, Ilgerus Sebastian Wilberforce, Xenophon Marcus Wilberforce, Georgine Sophia Wilberforce and Simon Quintin Wilberforce.

I hope Mr Patten will soon be recovered and back at work. In the meanwhile I look forward to hearing from you.

> Yours sincerely,
> Margaret Illingworth
> (The Lady Illingworth)

The second read:

Dear Mr Sexton,

I would be very grateful if you could be so kind as to go ahead with my aunt's Will as it is very much on her mind. It would be very helpful if you could do it on thin paper as opposed to anything thick. She has two phobias in life, one is the telephone, the other documents on very thick paper. I do not know why this is, but she becomes very distressed when confronted with the latter.

I do hope the news of Mr Patten is good – how very awkward for you all, especially as I gather it was so sudden.

> Yours sincerely,
> Susan Wilberforce
> (Mrs S.C. Wilberforce)

Clearly deciding that there was no longer any need to spread her bank accounts between London and Ripon, Lady Illingworth transferred all her money to Hereford, opening three new accounts at the National Westminster Bank branch in Broad Street. A couple of weeks later, she moved the Ripon current and deposit accounts to a Midland branch at Hereford. Although she had been using it freely, drawing out a total of £6200 in the past ten weeks, there was still £5500 when she authorised its transfer to the new current account. Later, Lady Illingworth made both accounts joint ones with Susan, enabling her niece to withdraw money easily to assist in her keep without bothering her aunt; it was all so much more convenient.

Susan was anxious to help. She telephoned Sexton and asked

him to prepare another draft of the will, this time on ordinary paper, since thin paper was unsuitable. She urged him to pursue the bank-vault questions with the National Westminster, who were raising queries about insurance cover. She stressed that the packages contained only 'domestic items, old china and papers'. Her aunt's jewellery, she said, had long been sold to pay gambling debts, leaving poor paste copies. About this time, Susan asked for all mail to Forresters Hall to be delivered to a bin outside, so that her aunt would not be troubled by too much paper. It was also necessary to make telephone calls from a nearby box, so that Aunt Puss would not be distressed.

Michael, meanwhile, continued his efforts on behalf of Lady Illingworth, writing and telephoning solicitors, banks and financial organisations. On 17 May, from Forresters Hall, he wrote to Richard Ellis, manager of the Midland Bank Trust (Corporation) in Guernsey: 'Dear Richard, I repeat, for the record, my request that, if a joint account (in a very large sum of moneys) was opened by an eighty-four-year-old woman and her only niece with your branch, both resident and domiciled in the United Kingdom – the niece being, to the best of my knowledge, her aunt's principal legatee, what, in view of Guernsey's banking secrecy laws, would happen, in the normal actuarial course of events, if the older woman dies – presumably, the surviving account holder would continue to uniquely operate, and be entitled, under Guernsey law, to operate the account. My solicitor, Lord Coleraine, is extremely interested in yr reply. He would be equally pleased if you were to recommend that the liquid funds, believed by us both to be in excess of £1,000,000, were deposited with Midland Bank Trust Corporation (Guernsey) Ltd, in a joint account.' The word 'joint' was underline on both occasions it was used.

The will to which he referred had not yet, of course, been signed. A few days before writing to Ellis, Michael wrote to Sexton, asking him to give 'maximum and urgent priority' to the preparation of the will. Michael had also written to Father Joseph Dooley, then sixty-four and a teacher at Stonyhurst, who had taught Andrew, Michael's son by his first marriage, asking him for 'a small service'. Father Dooley, who had met Michael two or three times and had spoken to him at length only once, wrote back immediately, asking Michael to come and see him.

On 15 June, Michael hastened to Stonyhurst, where he explained that the small service involved witnessing the will of his old friend, Lady Illingworth. It was implied that she, as a Catholic, particularly wanted a priest. Michael stayed the night in the college hostel. The following morning, they went south by train and were met at Leominster station by Susan. Father Dooley did not see Lady Illingworth that evening – the highlight of which was supper eaten off the small kitchen table, up against the wall. The following day, after church in Hereford and lunch, he spent a few minutes alone with Lady Illingworth, when they talked 'about priests she had known many years before'. He thought how slowly and carefully she spoke, as if searching for the right words.

The other witness arrived during the afternoon. Anne Simeon, Susan's old friend from London, now Mrs Devey-Smith, whom she had not seen since Anne had visited Heath House in the 1960s, and recently moved to nearby Tenbury Wells. By June 1984, they had seen each other several times, including once when Aunt Puss accompanied Susan and Sophia to tea there. Susan also told her that she had rescued her aunt from neglect and decay and would now care for her until the end. Mrs Devey-Smith noted that Aunt Puss was somewhat vague and confused in her manner, only speaking when addressed directly. Now, Susan had asked her old friend to witness Aunt Puss's new will. Neither she nor Father Dooley had ever witnessed a will before.

That Sunday afternoon, they all sat around drinking tea in the small living room at Docklow: Susan, Sophia (just returned from her long holiday in Japan), the priest, the old friend, Aunt Puss. 'Michael paced the room,' said Mrs Devey-Smith. No one mentioned the will. Sophia asked her aunt several times if she wanted to go out for a walk in the garden. Aunt Puss said no thank you. Sophia asked again. Her aunt said no, she was perfectly all right where she was. According to Mrs Devey-Smith, Sophia asked: 'Would you like a glass of sherry in the kitchen?' Aunt Puss agreed and followed Sophia out of the room.

Susan exited, reappearing with a red folder. Without ceremony, she asked first Mrs Devey-Smith and then Father Dooley to sign at the bottom of each of the four pages and to include their addresses on the last. Afterwards, there was

some small-talk and Mrs Devey-Smith left. Susan then asked
Father Dooley to witness a passport application for her aunt.
Susan took him to catch the train home. It was only later that
Anne Devey-Smith thought how curious it was to sign the will
when Lady Illingworth was elsewhere.

The will represented a considerable simplification by Aunt Puss
of her affairs. It began conventionally, appointing the National
Westminster Bank as trustees and executors and Turner Sexton
and Co, as solicitors in all matters in relation to the estate. Lady
Illingworth then made three bequests:

> To my nephew, William John Anthony Wilberforce,
> CMG, The British High Commissioner to the Republic
> of Cyprus the sum of Twenty-Five Thousand Pounds
> (£25,000.00).
> To my cousin Colonel Michael Wilberforce RM,
> of 5 East Terrace Budleigh Salterton in the county
> of Devon the sum of Twenty-Five Thousand Pounds
> (£25,000.00).
> To the Right Honorable Richard Orme, Baron
> Wilberforce of Kingston Upon Hull PC., CMG, OBE,
> of 8 Cambridge Place London W8, the sum of Ten
> Thousand Pounds (£10,000.00) in recognition of
> his having added lustre to the family name in this
> generation.

Lady Illingworth bequeathed all her remaining property to the
bank to convert into a trust to be held 'for my niece Susan Cecilia
Wilberforce of Forresters Hall aforesaid absolutely provided that
if my niece shall predecease me then such gift to her shall not
have effect and my trustees shall hold my residuary estate upon
trust for such of my said niece's children William Alexander
Wilberforce, Ilgerus Sebastian Wilberforce, Xenophon Marcus
Wilberforce, Georgina Sophia Wilberforce and Simon Quintin
Wilberforce as are living at the date of my death and if more
than one in equal shares absolutely.'

This done, Lady Illingworth had a busy few weeks. She made
her Hereford account a joint one with Susan and applied for an
autobank card; she approved the encashment of £3000 worth

of National Savings Certificates and £300 worth of premium bonds; she decided to begin selling her shares and cast around for a suitable broker. Michael, acting on her behalf and writing on Stonyhurst College headed notepaper, wrote to a Major Ward, addressed on as 'Dear Ward', a partner in a firm of stockbrokers, E.F. Matthews, recommended by 'Martin Coleraine, my great friend and solicitor'. Michael said Lady Illingworth was anxious to emigrate and 'go liquid' as soon as possible; she would be writing to him soon and had requested that the firm exercise 'maximum confidentiality' in the matter. In a perfect de Stempel flourish he added: 'I am [underlined] glad that you had a grandfather who was a Faugh!' Over the next few weeks, the firm sold almost £18,000 worth of shares for Lady Illingworth, including 540 shares in the firm of Illingworth, Morris plc, which realised £159.70.

On 3 July, Michael, accompanied by the luckless and apologetic Sexton, created a scene at the National Westminster Bank branch at Royal Gardens in Kensington. Michael, banging on a table in the foyer, complained they were obstructing 'an officer of the court' (Sexton) in refusing to hand over all of Lady Illingworth's valuables kept in their vaults. Ignoring their protestations, already pointed out in a letter to Lady Illingworth, that the authority they had received – a photocopy with parts blanked out – was unsuitable, he began shouting and throwing his weight about, threatening to raise the matter in the House of Lords through Lord Wilberforce, 'the first Lord of Appeal in Ordinary', and Lord Boardman, then chairman of the Bank. Sexton had never seen anything like it before. They spent an hour in the office of the manager, who helped Sexton calm Michael down; Michael kept referring to Sexton as 'a solicitor of the Supreme Court of England' and accusing officials of being 'Jewish'.

As a result, Lady Illingworth wrote a further authorisation for Sexton to show the bank, curiously dated 2 July.

> I, Margaret Illingworth, of Denton, request and require the Manager of the National Westminster Bank, Royal Garden Branch, 55 Kensington High Street, to hand over immediately to my lawyer, Mr Richard Sexton, solicitor of the Supreme Court of England and senior

partner of Turner, Sexton and Company, solicitors,
all documents, share certificates, deeds etc., plus any
other documents held by them on my behalf. At the
same time, I formally authorise the Bank to place in
Mr Sexton's possession the items marked on my copy
of your list of my possessions held by you on my behalf.
All this is to be done totally at my own risk. I am
advised that failure to comply with these instructions
would constitute a criminal offence under the laws of
England.

Armed with this and a further authority approving the hand-
over of the goods from him to Michael, Sexton returned two
days later to oversee the loading of thirty-seven packages, each
sealed by the bank. They were loaded into a hired van and taken
to Docklow.

During the next few weeks Lady Illingworth opened two new
joint deposit accounts with Susan, in Jersey and Guernsey; she
asked her jewellers, Hennell's, to send her a list of all the property they held on her behalf; she authorised two sales of a total
of £17,000 worth of shares by Matthews and £2800 worth of
savings certificates; she paid the rent, electricity and telephone
bills for Docklow; she also asked Susan to arrange for the sale
of some of the contents of the bank vault, now overflowing into
a rented workshop at Wickton Court in the nearby village of
Stoke Prior.

Susan and Marcus took the silverware to Phillips and Jolley's,
an auction house in Bath. On 6 August, the first sale, mainly
silverware and jewellery, realised £4650, the money paid into
an account of Susan's in the Midland Bank in Guernsey. Over
the next few months, the auctioneers conducted a series of
sales from the Illingworth vaults. Most sales, of books, furniture and china, realised just a few hundred pounds but
there were two successful ones of more silverware and jewellery: on 15 October, which realised £21,475, and the last,
in December, which raised £5402. Shortly afterwards, Susan
and Sophia opened a new joint account at the Royal Bank
of Canada in Guernsey, into which Susan deposited both
cheques.

*

Susan was now very keen to marry Michael, despite a growing reluctance on his part, based on a mixture of incompatibility and fears that Simon Dale, with whom Susan was still locked in a protracted legal battle, would somehow get access to his money. He had always been rather moody and unpredictable. Now, he would occasionally throw tantrums, threatening not to find a house for them both unless Susan slept with him before their wedding, or so Susan told Sophia.

They were talking about living either in Wales, at a house in Tal-y-Bont, or in the Channel Islands, in both cases taking Aunt Puss with them. They entered into negotiations for the purchase of a large house on Alderney, priced at £120,000, assuring the estate agent that their elderly and wealthy relative would be helping with the payments. The venue of their marriage was also debated: Michael was keen on Gibraltar, presumably for obscure financial reasons; they settled on Jersey.

They made more than one trip to the Channel Islands before their wedding. Towards the end of August they walked into Hettich's, a jewellers in St Helier recommended by a bank, carrying thirteen items of jewellery, including a diamond necklace, a gold ring, a diamond and emerald snake ring and a ruby and diamond brooch, which they asked the jewellers to sell for them. Susan returned to Hettich's twice during the next three weeks, bringing a total of more than 120 pieces of silver plate bearing the Illingworth family crest. Hettich's paid £13,392 for the plate; most of it was later sold through Sotheby's for more than £28,000.

They were married on 11 September, at the registry office in St Helier, after a courtship lasting more than thirty years. After such a time, it was a remarkably low-key ceremony: none of their total of nine children from three previous marriages were present; the witnesses were strangers off the street. Susan became the third Baroness de Stempel and celebrated by opening another bank account in Hereford.

Sophia believes that her mother's desire to marry Michael was based solely on the wish to prevent him leaving. 'Mother was quite happy living with Michael at Docklow and only married him because she did not want him to leave her.' For some months, Michael had taunted Susan with talk of an old friend, Mrs Jane Mackay, who lived in Kent and who, he implied, was both wealthy and needed his assistance to sort out her finances.

There is some truth in this. The previous June, he had asked Mr Ellis of the Midland Bank, Guernsey, for help in sorting out some of the financial affairs of Mrs Mackay, although there is no suggestion of anything untoward about the involvement with Mrs Mackay. She would later tell police her renewed friendship with Michael was a casual, platonic one. But Sophia believes Michael's use of her name affected Susan. 'Michael would drone on and on about Jane needing help with this account or that investment and then go on about how poor we were at Docklow and the mistakes my mother had made over Simon. I think it all made my mother very jealous and anxious to keep Michael.' Why Michael allowed himself to be dragged to the altar at this point is unclear: perhaps it really was the mixture of threats and bribery that he would later say was responsible. Perhaps it was the need to keep an eye on Aunt Puss's affairs.

Life had improved for Sophia and Marcus, although neither was particularly keen on Michael as a stepfather. 'He was okay to have around, but he was too unreliable to be a father,' said Marcus. The food got better: they would buy from Marks and Spencer and delicatessens in Hereford. Sophia was promised £100 a week to stay at home and care for her aunt – more than she had been getting working in London and for a considerably less arduous duty: essentially walking her aunt around the garden. Between July and the end of the year, Susan paid Sophia about £2800 for looking after her aunt, in cash. What annoyed Sophia was being asked to unpack all the crates from the bank vaults.

Since shortly after Aunt Puss's arrival, Marcus had been spending several nights a week at Heath House with his father, returning to Docklow at weekends when it was less crowded because Michael was in London with his son. Marcus was working as a gardener, travelling around on his bicycle. He might have resented being used as something of a messenger boy: at York House, taking the silverware to auction and arranging the Stoke Prior storage. Matters took a turn for the better at the end of August when Aunt Puss paid £5000 for a new car for him; that was what Mother said Aunt Puss had wanted to do, although he said he never got around to thanking her himself.

In fact, neither Sophia nor Marcus had much opportunity to thank Aunt Puss for her largesse. Their aunt was often cloistered in her room with Susan, presumably organising her finances. The children, as Susan referred to them, were excluded from these discussions and sometimes Susan would lock herself in the bedroom and they could hear her typing, the machine propped up on the windowsill. To show their gratitude, the family had bought Aunt Puss a long-haired Peruvian cat called Oats.

Although Aunt Puss was keeping a steady hand on her finances, her condition deteriorated. Even before the will had been signed, Susan herself had written to Sophia in Japan, describing how her aunt became 'ultra panty' and 'thrashed about the house with her eyes bulging', although afterwards she was as 'sweet as pie'. In June, Anne Devey-Smith had noticed her inability to remember visitors and the fact that she spoke only when prompted. Now, as the year wore on, Susan told visitors how confused her aunt had become. The dentist in Hereford to whom they took her also said how absent-minded she seemed; Susan told him that her aunt had an 'unhealthy attraction to young men'. Marcus later claimed that he had stopped her from wandering down the road, trying to hitch lifts from passing motorists.

Shortly before twelve noon on 6 December, Hereford and Worcester ambulance service received a 999 call from Docklow to say that an elderly woman was behaving aggressively and smashing windows with a hammer. The ambulancemen were met by Susan and Sophia, who ushered them into the cottage. Neither saw broken windows, a hammer or any serious signs of damage; an upstairs window which might or might not have been broken was pointed out to them. Even if it was, they did not know who was responsible. It might have been the very confused elderly lady, who was apparently refusing to leave the house, despite much encouragement from the two women.

Susan explained to them that, since Lady Illingworth was only visiting, she did not have a local doctor. The ambulancemen said they would take Lady Illingworth to Hereford General Hospital. Neither woman attempted to accompany her, although the men gained the impression that they intended to follow. Lady Illingworth, after asking the ambulancemen to drive her to Edinburgh, was taken to the hospital and examined by a doctor:

she told him she was forty years old and that her husband was a peer in the House of Lords. He concluded she was suffering from senile dementia. Neither Susan nor Sophia came to visit for several days.

For the next few weeks, hospital staff were unsure what to do with this charming but potty lady. Normal policy is for such individuals, perhaps after a short break for both sides to rest, to be returned to their families, since geriatric beds are costly and in short supply: far cheaper and more humane for them to be cared for by their own. Susan, when she could be contacted, was having none of this. She told the hospital her aunt was an 'alcoholic' and 'sex-mad' and had a 'passion for hitch-hiking'. Susan said that she was incapable of looking after her because Docklow was too small; she implied that she had no money, and added that her aunt's only means of support was her pension. Susan had clearly forgotten the £1500 withdrawn from the joint account she held with Aunt Puss the day after she went to Hereford. Despite her confinement in hospital, Aunt Puss wrote to the Midland Bank in Guernsey asking them to open another joint account with Susan and request two further autobank cards. About this time, the hospital found Lady Illingworth a place at Langford House and she was transferred there on 28 January. Susan had been to see her once, two days after filling in a social security form stating that her aunt had only her old-age pension for support.

According to visitors, Docklow was like 'some kind of antiques saleroom', it was so full of good furniture. Three days before entering hospital, Lady Illingworth wrote to Giltspur Bullens, the removal and storage company which looked after her goods, asking for an inventory. When this arrived, she asked for it all to be delivered to Stoke Prior. Each load was met by Marcus and often his mother, sometimes accompanied by Sophia. Their mother, who had always provided for them, directed the sorting and unloading with a kind of military precision: some into storage in the two workshops they now rented and some into a £10,000 Mercedes van bought for the purpose, to be taken to Docklow, some for cleaning and polishing, some for daily use.

But among the antiques and treasures was evidence that the

storage eighteen years before had originally been intended as temporary. There were unwrapped presents of scent and talcum powder, boxes and boxes of letters dating back to the 1920s, masses of wrapping paper, sacks of preserving sugar and even the now solidified jam which had been made from it. It was all, remembers Marcus, incredibly dusty. He also remembers Susan burning all the letters in the orchard at Docklow in a fire that went on for days. 'My mother knew more about Aunt Puss than anybody after that,' he said.

Phillips and Jolley's in Bath were again delighted to be pressed into service and the goods were progressively shipped there in the van. The first sale, on 25 February, of 'Victorian reproduction furniture and effects' achieved only £164, but 'antique furniture and works of art' a week later did much better: £15,789. Over the next year the sales continued, some raised little, one a mere £2.55, but this was amply compensated for by the successes: a sale of 'antique furniture, clocks and works of art' on 1 April raised £11,125, a similar sale on the 29th of the month raised £7463. In June, the best of all, 'oil paintings, watercolours and prints', raised £20,588. A smaller auction house, Russell Baldwin and Bright, in Leominster, carried out a number of sales of minor items, raising £2603 on 21 March and £1458 on 11 April.

Lady Illingworth meanwhile, not content with disposing of all this property, sold the last of her shares for £1184. It was the following day that Susan wrote to the Department of Health and Social Security, outlining both her own tale of woes and those of her aunt. Although she was correct in saying that Aunt Puss no longer had any premium bonds or Post Office savings, she still had several bank accounts shared with Susan, which she was using vigorously, including the one they had opened together in January. It must have slipped Susan's mind again.

As the money flowed in, relations between Susan and Michael broke down completely, largely because Michael was reluctant to commit himself full-time to Susan. In December, just after Aunt Puss went into hospital, Susan had begun annulment proceedings on the grounds that the marriage had not been consummated. Michael, becoming increasingly agitated, had kept telling her she had committed an illegal act, in fact 'a crime', by marrying him, since she was still 'fiscally married' to Dale. That she could even begin to accept this was odd, but she stopped the proceedings within a few weeks. 'Mother realised Michael was wrong and she stopped because it would have been convenient for him to be free,' said Sophia. For instance, he claimed it was all a figment of Susan's imagination, saying that when he was in London he stayed with Francesca. 'He was rather put out when I went to see Francesca to see if he was telling the truth. She said she had not seen him for months. He had probably been with another woman,' said Sophia.

During the first part of 1985, as the auctioneers' hammers were falling in Bath and Leominster, there were arguments about money – Susan claimed Michael never contributed to the bills – or his impotence. Sophia later said: 'Michael would come down in the mornings and claim he was impotent. That's not a nice thing to have anyone say over breakfast, is it?' Susan even telephoned her brother John, in Cyprus, and asked him to intercede, claiming that they had not been properly married. John, who had not seen his former undergraduate friend for at least thirty years, refused to become involved.

Michael would later claim that Susan had blackmailed him into marriage by threatening to report him for mistreating Alexander. He promised to sue *The Times* if it published an announcement of their wedding, declaring that the whole thing was a hoax. Susan said this was because he was telling Mrs Mackay he was not married; she went ahead and arranged for an announcement in the *Daily Telegraph*. He insisted they had never consummated their marriage.

According to Sophia, Michael became 'mentally sadistic' to her mother after their wedding: 'He just turned on her and developed an attitude of "Now I am married I can do anything." His general attitude was awful and overbearing – he just changed overnight. Michael kept claiming his life would have been different if only she had married him in the 1950s and what a huge mistake she had made in marrying my father because of all the trouble he had caused her. He used to go on and on about this, incessantly, and Mother would not say anything. Eventually I just told him that she had obviously married my father because she had wanted to, she knew what she was doing. That shut him up for a bit.'

Susan's response to Michael became progressively more distraught. The fraud trial would later hear that she sent him strange telegrams. 'Keep looking over your shoulder big brother. Sandwich carrot to be withdrawn on matrimony. Massive financial aid re borstal changing sides. Jilters ruin.' ('Sandwich carrot' it was speculated in court, referred to Mrs Mackay, 'borstal' to Alex and 'Jilters' to Michael.) Some letters implied they were sent by a young woman who believed herself to be engaged to Michael and referred to an ex-wife called Susan, who had died of cancer; others declared that this woman was glad he was not homosexual.

Perhaps as a gesture to encourage him to remain with her, Susan anonymously transferred £20,000 into his account to help ease the pressure from his own bankers, who were demanding that he settle a £50,000 overdraft. He told his solicitor that the money was part of the £150,000 inheritance he had received when his father died in 1983, although most had been spent. A few weeks later, he put a deposit on a flat in London for himself and Alex.

In February 1985, following the withdrawal before Christmas from the Alderney house purchase because of Michael's behaviour, Susan found time to detach herself from Aunt Puss's affairs and to reopen proceedings with Simon over Heath House. Two years previously – and largely as a result of constant nagging by Michael to do something about Heath House – she had resumed negotiations for the first time since 1977. Richard Sax, her solicitor, had obtained a legal opinion that, if Heath House were sold, half the proceeds should go to Susan and the rest held by solicitors for a court judgement on how it should be apportioned between them. Sax told Susan that a court would want her ex-husband to receive enough for a small house and something on trust to provide an income, which would revert to her on his death and then to the children. But negotiations with Simon's solicitors on this solution foundered. Now, with Aunt Puss safely in Langford House and some money in the bank, Susan was determined to have Simon removed. In words that would return to haunt her, she wrote to Sax: 'Desperate situations require desperate remedies.' And, despite the healthy cashflow, Susan must also have felt impoverished herself. She wrote: 'Yours, frozen, broken bones, starved, almost destitute, disillusioned, in need of a quick removal of a husband, painlessly, cheaply and above all speedily.'

This somewhat agonised image was not quite the face presented to favoured strangers, to whom she could be all charm. Simon Verdun, a young chartered surveyor, painted an interesting picture of life at Docklow, as seen by one of the few outsiders. Early in 1984, the £80-a-month rent was often being paid late and Verdun, who worked for the managing agents, was asked to collect it in person. She clearly took a liking to a pleasant, gregarious man; they became friendly and would indulge in gossipy chats, sometimes over a drink (gin and tonic, no ice) when he called. 'She was quite the most incredibly positive woman I have met. A lot of women of that type and era tend to be under the thumb of the men. She was very different, she was in charge. I felt she could have been a successful and dynamic businesswoman or politician if she had been given the opportunities.'

Verdun went on: 'I picked up the feeling she wanted me to stay, that she liked having someone different to talk to. Perhaps she was a bit lonely. We would talk about various Herefordshire families and people we both knew. Susan was always incredibly polite, charming and interesting; very well dressed and properly made up, she had been a stunner in her youth. I remember these very piercing eyes and she would look you right in the eyes when she spoke. Although Susan was very formal, calling me "Mr Verdun", she could have been flirting, but I tend to think she just liked someone to have a chat with.'

Susan confided in him that she was fed up with living in Docklow, 'a little cottage on the main road' as she described it. He wondered what a woman who was obviously from a landed background was doing living in such a small home, albeit one crammed with antiques. As 1984 went on, the rent at Docklow began to be paid on time, sometimes from accounts in the Channel Islands.

Verdun met the Baron and saw a lot of Marcus and Sophia. 'She was quiet and pretty – I thought Sophia could have been a real fun girl. She had a bit of a sparkle in her eyes, like her mother. But she dressed rather oddly, sort of 1960s-era tweeds, not like a modern girl at all, no Benetton.' Marcus, he said, was less likeable. 'I never really trusted Marcus, he never looked you straight in the eye. I think they both had a rough deal from their father.'

In July 1985, Michael made his last trip to Docklow, bringing for Susan, as one last favour he said, a miniature statue of William Wilberforce which she had asked him to buy. They spent most of the time arguing, reaching a pitch on the second night. Early the following morning, Susan went into Sophia's bedroom. Michael, she said, was refusing to leave and threatening to smash up everything. To give him a chance to calm down, they drove to Anne Devey-Smith's for breakfast. According to Sophia, 'Simon rang up to say that Michael was acting in a bizarre fashion and threatening to smash his way out of the [glass] rear door of the house with a champagne bottle.' On their return, accompanied by Mrs Devey-Smith, they found that Michael had abandoned the idea of smashing his way out and was locked in the bathroom, drinking the champagne. Mrs Devey-Smith tried to reason with him, but he proved impossible and they called the police.

Michael said he woke up to find the house empty, his clothes strewn over the floor and his chequebooks down the toilet bowl. He claimed that Susan had hit him in the face, had begged him to hit her back and had threatened him with compulsory confinement under the Mental Health Act. 'She said I was a dangerous maniac and locked us all in the house.'

A policeman and woman arrived to find Susan outside, the rest inside, Michael fuming. They called a doctor, who suggested a psychiatrist might be the answer for Michael. According to Sophia, the doctor advised Susan to lock Michael inside the cottage, which she did. They pretended to depart, but merely moved their car out of sight of the cottage. Thinking he was alone, Michael smashed his way through a downstairs rear window and vaulted over the fence directly into the arms of the police, still wearing his pyjamas and dressing gown. He was taken to Leominster, charged with a breach of the peace and left to cool his heels in the cells for a few hours. When he was released, he returned, argued again with Susan, packed his things and flounced off. A week later he filed for divorce.

All this flung Susan into greater despair and she began

furiously writing melodramatic letters to anyone she thought might help. As the court would later hear, she wrote to Father Dooley at Stonyhurst: 'My life is in shreds. Michael and I were married in September in Jersey. Almost immediately afterwards he became mesmerised by a wretched rich widow and has been living with her ever since. Every word he says about everything is a lie. He has always been a pathological liar but now things seem to have got completely out of hand.' And: 'I love Michael so much and have done for years. I am so worried about him because I think he is mentally ill.' She wrote to Richard Sax: 'He is terrified of being thought barmy, which of course he is.' She wrote many times to Michael: 'My heart aches at the thought of being apart from you during the summer, but I understand that you cannot leave your sister Jane for the moment.'

Somewhere among all this she found time to send to Richard Sexton the new will made by her aunt a year previously, together with 'her funeral arrangements' on a typewritten little note, on which Susan did not elaborate. It read: 'In the event of my death I no longer wish to be buried near my husband Albert. Certain facts having come to light after his death make this impossible for me, so I now wish to be cremated privately as soon as possible wherever I die and for no announcement to be made in the press. I also do not wish any members of my family from Markington to be present at my funeral, nor any of my late husband's relations. My ashes are to remain wherever I am cremated.' Underneath was a date: June 1982.

Michael found it impossible to serve divorce papers on his wife. When agents acting for his solicitor arrived at Docklow, Susan made everyone keep still and pretend there was no one at home. He later claimed that a private investigator had been forced to chase her on a motorcycle up the platform at Paddington. It was about this time that Sophia, fed up with her mother's mood of near hysteria and endless hours shifting dusty furniture, decided it would be a good idea to go and work as a nanny in New York for a spell. Her brother Alexander arranged for her to go and stay with distant relatives in the city. Aunt Puss, still gazing out of the windows at Langford House, paid and Sophia flew out in the first week of September. Marcus, who had tended to stay at

Heath House, began to spend more time at Docklow following Michael's departure.

Susan told everyone that she had cancer, or at least she implied as much. She wrote to Sax: 'The medical profession think the end is nigh, weeks rather than months.' She wrote to Michael, saying she was dying and imploring him to come and nurse her. He refused. In November, not long after Phillips and Jolley's sold for £5231 the silver galleons which dinner guests of Lady Illingworth at Grosvenor Square had once so much admired, Susan went into the Princess Grace Hospital for an operation on her varicose veins. She left after four days and comforted herself with a £5500 pair of pearl and diamond earrings from Asprey's.

As the year neared its end, Susan's ardour for Michael increased, so did his enthusiasm for divorce. She sent him half-pleading, half-threatening letters, at the same time anonymously transferring substantial sums of money into his accounts. She changed the name of one of her Guernsey bank accounts from Wilberforce to de Stempel.

Sophia had returned from New York to discover her mother distraught over Michael and her 'cancer'. Susan also claimed to Sophia that she had become pregnant by Michael and implied she had miscarried. (She would later write to Sax saying that Michael had told 'the whole of London' that the baby she had conceived in May was not his.) The truth of the pregnancy episode is impossible to establish.

Susan decided she needed a holiday and a few days before Christmas, accompanied by Sophia, left for a rented flat at La Manga del Mar Menor, a resort near Cartagena in Spain. They stayed for three months. According to Sophia, it was an unhappy time: 'The weather was cold and Mother was depressed.' She was unable to engage in normal holiday pursuits; her mother was disconsolate and they spent much of their time playing backgammon or cards. By way of consolation, they decided to purchase a flat near to the one in which they had been staying. Susan transferred £41,000 from her accounts in the United Kingdom and decided that to help in these financial transactions it would be a good idea to open a couple of accounts in Spain, both jointly with Sophia, through which the monies were subsequently moved. They were not alone for the entire time; Marcus made two visits to see them, Alexander flew in for a short stay and a boyfriend of Sophia's joined her for a week, during which they went away to explore Spain on their own.

When they returned towards the end of March, Susan was feeling much better. She had got over Michael's departure and was not about to die of cancer. Thanks to Aunt Puss, still in Langford House, she was more financially secure than she had been since her marriage to Simon Dale: she had a flat in Spain and she and her three youngest children had a number of healthy bank accounts. There was still one major unresolved problem on the horizon: she decided to turn her attentions to Heath House.

7
Total War

As Susan's fortunes had changed during the first half of the 1980s, so had her those of her ex-husband. And Simon Dale's improved quality of life was also due to the sudden arrival of an elderly woman.

Veronica Bowater is one of those middle-class Englishwomen whose virtues have grown rather than receded with age. Somewhere, someone like her is always serving tea to cricketers on the village green. Englishwomen like this wear gumboots to potter around the garden in the rain and serve tea by the fireside, her little dog at her side, her silver hair impeccable.

Her first husband was a bomber pilot whose aircraft was shot down in 1940. She spent the war in Cairo with Special Operations Executive; afterward she was in the Voluntary Aid Detachment, like Lady Illingworth. In the 1960s she moved to Shropshire when her second husband, Geoffrey, an engineer, retired. They divorced several years ago but remain inseparable, living in adjoining cottages, communicating by intercom, parking their Morris Traveller cars in the field opposite. The relationship causes gentle amusement among friends and confusion to outsiders. She writes and talks, mostly on the history of the borders: 'It was all very violent then – it's all much more tranquil now,' she says, sitting in the kitchen, overlooking what remains of Hopton Castle, where the ditches once ran with blood.

One day in 1980 she knocked on the door of Heath House. In such a sparsely populated rural area, where people know each other by the names of their houses, she had not met Simon before, although the house was a familiar sight. 'I'm very keen on local history and had seen this most interesting-looking house many times. When this man answered, I said it was very rude of us – I was with Rupert, my son – to call and he said not a bit, do come in, and that was it really.' Simon, starved of human company and flattered at the interest in the house, was guaranteed to offer a warm welcome.

And so Simon, now in his early sixties, entered the circle of which she and Geoffrey were the centre. In her own way, Veronica ('Vicky' to her friends) is every bit as much a social animal as was Lady Illingworth: the day seems incomplete without some kind of function. She and the affable, whiskery Geoffrey were (and still are) part of a loose circle of middle-class, elderly people with time, energy and an enthusiasm for regular socialising. There was the Brigadier and his wife down at Bodenham, the widowed Lady so-and-so at Bucknell, the gentleman farmer and his wife, a couple of other elderly ladies in Leintwardine and so forth. For Simon, this untroubled, middle-class life must have seemed a welcome echo from the world he had largely left behind in the 1950s. After so long, it must have seemed blissful to be able to make new friends.

All this came on top of another beneficial development. In 1979, Simon had been officially registered as a blind person. This qualified him for a small grant to employ a reader/secretary and a home help which improved the quality of his life and increased his ability to communicate with the outside world. The correspondence on his theories and with his solicitors flowed thick and fast.

'Eccentric? Yes, oh absolutely,' says Veronica. 'But charmingly so. He was wonderful as long as you could keep him off Arthurian legends and Armenian loos.' Kenneth Davison, a farmer and landowner, admits: 'Well, frankly, Simon could be a bit of a bore when he got on to all that stuff. One would sort of sense it coming and try and divert him away from it beforehand, in case he got into full flow. It was fine, really. I know he understood.'

The group took turns holding lunches and dinners, afternoon tea ('Cucumber sandwiches', says Veronica, deliberately and without embarrassment, 'were de rigueur') and evening cocktails. Some meals would take place at Heath House. Simon provided the wine and perhaps vegetables and the rest would bring the other component parts: Veronica would make a quiche, someone else the pudding. 'We never did anything wildly exciting. I would just ring up somebody and say "Let's go and cheer Simon up," and we would all go round there.'

He was welcomed for his humorous, gentle, cultivated manners and his active mind. Veronica recalls: 'He was a great big benign teddy bear of a man. Perfectly charming, a lovely man, a spare man for parties. You would put his hands around a drink and he would be perfectly happy. His blindness was never a problem, he would know where everything was.' Suggestions, then and subsequently, that Dale was some kind of recluse, are hotly disputed. 'Oh, he was a very friendly man. He just hadn't had the opportunities before, since his wife left him.' He would spend Christmas with the Bowaters, sometimes in the company of Marcus and Sebastian.

Veronica Bowater also provided an outlet for his theories about Heath House, through contact with the organisers of tourist parties from the United States, anxious to learn more about the history of the borders. Several times, small groups staying in Ludlow, soaking up the medieval atmosphere, were taken to Heath House, where Veronica would show them around and Simon would talk about the Armenians and the Arthurians. 'They adored it,' says Veronica. And Simon enjoyed the company and attention.

In the early 1980s Simon remained in contact with four of his children, still on the basis that nothing was said about the legal wrangles with Susan. Although Sebastian was living in London, initially working as a researcher for Conservative MPs and then studying law, he would return regularly to Heath House for holidays and some weekends. Alexander would visit when in the country, Sophia when she felt like it. Significantly, from early 1984, Marcus, who had failed his landscape-architecture course at Thames Polytechnic in London, resumed his habit of spending a good deal of time at Heath House, returning at weekends to Docklow, then full of Michael, Aunt Puss and, eventually, the bank-vault goods, where he was pressed into various services by his mother. He wanted to be a gardener and the Bowaters assisted by finding him regular work among their friends. He spent some time working in Germany, arranged through a German lawyer they knew.

According to his children, Simon enjoyed the attentions of the Bowaters and their ilk, although aware that it was possible he was being patronised. Said one son: 'I think my father was much happier during this period. He was a little taken aback when Veronica first called at the door, but not for long. He welcomed the company because up until then he did not have many friends in the area. But he was an extremely intelligent man and I am not sure he felt they were always up to his intellectual level. We had our own family name for Veronica: "Knickers" on account of her frilly personality.'

There were rumours, following her divorce, of more than pure friendship in the relationship between Simon and Veronica. 'Oh no, it was never like that. Close friends, yes, but never anything more. Besides, the idea was impossible because for some of the time I was engaged to Major B———.' His children also consider it highly unlikely. Susan may have felt differently.

'Hah!' snorted Susan contemptuously at the mention of Veronica. 'She didn't like it at all because she had been queening it around Heath House and suddenly there was I back on the scene as the other woman.' In April 1986, Susan, assisted by Sophia, Marcus and sometimes Simon, returned to Heath House, which now became the focus of her obsessive behaviour, as well as Simon's. It would once again become the backdrop to their war of wills, this time the final battle. There was money in the bank; why not spend it on the house? Rising property values put its price at more than £300,000. It was a prize worth fighting for.

In the years since Susan had left, little had been done to the outside of the house – the woodwork needed painting and the roof repairing – and, although Simon had mowed the lawns, the rest of the grounds and gardens were untended. It was hardly surprising, considering Simon's poverty and blindness. Susan's plan was simple: work on improving the appearance of the house would boost its value when it was eventually sold. The children, who had no other jobs, were encouraged to assist because they were told it would, in the long term, increase the amount of money for their father and help to provide a decent place for him to live. They seem to have genuinely believed in this. But a more objective assessment might be that their personalities rendered them unable or unwilling to refuse to help their mother. However Simon junior, a much stronger character, felt able to spend little time at the Heath. He took a job as a lorry driver.

It was not as though they just suddenly turned up one day after many years' absence. Marcus had been living at Heath

House for most of the time until returning to Docklow the previous summer and Sophia had been back to see her father occasionally. Susan had seen Simon less frequently – only when she had been back there to collect furniture, by prearrangement. This time, Simon was warned by Marcus that Susan was coming to do some work on the house. However, the first meeting between Susan and Simon, given her suddenly formed intention, can only have been traumatic. It is a pity there were no witnesses.

Susan tackled the job with the same enthusiasm and energy she had brought to all her activities over the past couple of years. She and her children drove to Heath House from Docklow just about every day: tidying, sweeping and clearing the grounds and repairing, cleaning, mending and painting the outside of the house itself. They bought a self-assembly scaffolding tower for work on the upper floors and a leaf blower to help with the gardens. Duties divided neatly: Sophia cleaned and painted the window frames; Marcus, naturally, looked after the grounds; Susan would weed, help clear up and direct operations, as she had done with the furniture shipments to the rented workshops at Wickton Court. They used the little cottage at the side of the house as a store and a place to rest. They worked long days, arriving about 10 a.m. and leaving at dusk; in the summer they were there until late evening.

Meanwhile, inside, Simon continued his life of visits from secretaries and friends. For a few weeks, at least, the arrangement worked and relationships were cordial, if not actually warm. It could hardly be expected to last. As one lawyer was later to describe it, 'total war' eventually broke out.

The screw of confrontation turned slowly. Susan later claimed that Simon had allowed her to go into the kitchen to refill her watering can. But then, she said, he turned 'nasty and hostile' and objected, ordering them to leave. It cannot have been easy for him, for so long the master of the house, to find his position being subverted in such a fashion, and with the connivance of his children, who were in his eyes totally under the spell of their dominant mother.

So, when he objected to them coming into the house through the kitchen door, they began entering through the cloakroom window or using the scaffolding tower to reach the upper floors. Simon eventually took counter-measures: asking Kenneth Davison to nail up windows and changing the lock on the door outside the kitchen. Sophia subsequently claimed that her father knew they were going in and out. She still believes he was encouraged to nail up the windows by his friends; later she took them out so that she could paint more easily.

Simon's visitors would drive up, see all this activity and find Simon pottering about as usual inside, 'under siege' as they described it. Susan would ask them who they were and what their business was. In various ways, she would tell them: 'It is my property and you should not be here. Simon Dale should not be in my house. He will soon be out and you are wasting your time.' In an encounter with Davison, who had referred to 'Simon's kitchen garden', she is said to have angrily retorted: 'That garden's mine. Every bloody thing is mine: house, garden, furniture, the lot!'

It was inevitable that physical confrontation would occur, as before. In July 1986, according to Susan's account, she was alone outside the kitchen, sitting in a chair reading during a break from work. She said he came around the corner and was 'thoroughly obnoxious', claiming she had been clearing too much of the undergrowth. There was a pile of old ashes from the Aga nearby and she threw a piece of clinker at him. 'I went away and he stopped screaming and went into the house.' Simon suffered a swollen lip and small cuts to his face.

Later, she claimed she attempted to kick him. Marcus had gone into the house at Simon's request to mend something. Susan heard shouting and argument: 'I thought Simon was going to attack my child.' In the kitchen, she said, she saw Simon arguing with Marcus. 'He came to the kitchen door and I tried to kick him in the balls. I missed, but it pulled Simon up in surprise. He shouted at me and I walked out.' It was shortly after this, Susan said, that she began carrying a crowbar in case he attacked her.

Simon would later imply that Susan was now opening his post – which was entirely possible – and tapping his telephone – which was less likely. It is possible that simply by listening outside to his booming voice on the telephone, in the echoing house, Susan and her children could get a fair impression of his movements. She would later accept they had been entering the house to remove furniture which she claimed was hers.

It was during this period that one of the most curious strands of the whole affair developed. Sophia, while painting window frames, saw her father sitting at his desk wearing brown, open-toed ladies' high-heeled shoes. 'I was a bit shocked, you know, and asked him why he was wearing them.' According to Sophia, they had a long conversation in which her father said he had been advised to wear them by a doctor who said they were a good if unorthodox method of treating a troublesome Achilles tendon. 'I said people might think it a bit odd and he eventually saw my point. I don't think it had occurred to him.' But this was not the last time the question of Simon Dale and women's shoes cropped up.

The uneasy tension continued during 1986. Eventually, Simon allowed in valuers to survey the house, and an agreement was being prepared under which he would move out two weeks after exchange of contracts. Purely by coincidence, the valuers chosen were the same estate agents who managed Docklow, and Simon Verdun, the surveyor whom Susan had befriended, was asked to carry out the survey. 'I didn't realise who it was at first. She had sort of mentioned this husband, and suddenly it all fell into place.'

Verdun conducted the survey. 'He [Dale] was always polite and civilised with us, but I can see how he might have acted in a fairly bloody-minded and cantankerous way. I got the feeling he really was like one of those members of the landed classes, still living in complete cloud-cuckoo land, with no idea of how other people lived and never any thought of living anywhere else, even if he doesn't have an uncracked glass in the place. It was a very sad house, there were still children's clothes and books in the bedrooms.'

He remained very friendly with Susan. 'She would send me letters with the rent and ring me up at the office and tell me enthusiastically about what she was doing at Heath House, what work was needed on the garden and so forth.' Verdun remembers that she would also ask about Simon's attitude to some things; in reality, her contact with Verdun may simply have been another way of monitoring her ex-husband's activities, making sure he had not found a way of hanging on.

Although some potential purchasers went to look around Heath House, at least one was greeted with a 'Get off my land!' from Simon, who the visitor believed might have been drinking. It was not surprising no one was keen to purchase. His solicitors then rejected the valuation. This increased Susan's bitterness and Simon's stubbornness. For the children, it was a matter of gritting their teeth and getting on with the work. Verdun says: 'Every time I went to Heath House, [Susan] was in the grounds with Sophia and Marcus, supervising the work. She usually wore country tweeds, gardening gloves and wellington boots. She never wore trousers and was always wearing carefully applied make-up.'

At the end of September, Susan and Sophia flew to Spain for their first holiday in the new flat. A few weeks later, while Susan and Sophia after their return were at Heath House working, Marcus arrived with a message from Docklow. There had been a telephone call to say Aunt Puss was fading fast.

Margaret, Baroness Illingworth of Denton, died at Langford House on 9 November 1986, from the progressive effects of Alzheimer's disease, two weeks short of her eighty-sixth birthday. She had been visited every month or so by Susan, sometimes with Marcus. Sophia went less frequently; she found it 'terribly depressing'. She hated going because her aunt was so different from the vigorous woman she had known. 'She looked so vacant. There came a point where I could not go again. I didn't feel guilty about it because I knew she would have understood.'

The hearse had a journey of a few hundred yards up the hill to Hereford Crematorium. This is not an Undercliffe, a monument to Victorian enterprise, where the lords of the city's commerce could overlook their domain even in death. It lies between the edge of the city and farmland, with a distant horizon of grey hills, and can be bleak and windswept. There are pleasant gardens of remembrance, sheltered by hedges of laurel and small silver birch trees, and bordered by stones topped with small brass plaques engraved with the barest details of those whose ashes are scattered there. The brighter ones are the recent deaths. To the left of the low, modern building that houses the furnaces, the gardens are almost full, with few spare places. To the right, new gardens are being carved out of rough ground. Here the plaques shine brightest of all, the roses and shrubs are younger, the flowers fresher, the earth richer. Aunt Puss did not even get a plaque. It was the most simple ceremony, attended only by Susan, Sophia, Marcus and Simon. The bill of £389 was never paid.

Within a few days, Susan had informed banks and the Public Trustees. She wrote to Richard Sexton: 'Laura, my sister-in-law, will have a heart attack when she discovers that my aunt made a Will AFTER the one Laura knows about!!! . . . she did not seem to understand that everything goes back to the loathsome Illingworths.' Three of the crates from the vault had 'nothing but soap in them, scrubbing soap at that'. Four contained nothing but 'unopened Christmas presents; endless sets of scent and talcum powder which had gone off'. The cutlery boxes, said Susan, were mainly empty. 'Such cutlery as there was was what I would call medium kitchen and was disposed of. And so on.' The 'And so on' implied that nothing of any value was in the thirty or so remaining crates, which Susan did not mention to Sexton.

The first member of the family to know of the death was Everilda Wilberforce, then eighty-two, a cousin of Aunt Puss and granddaughter of Henry Wilberforce, youngest son of William. A spinster, she lived alone in Cirencester, and was telephoned by Susan, although precisely when is not clear. Everilda telephoned another cousin from her branch of the family, Robert Wilberforce, then ninety-eight, a distinguished former barrister and diplomat, who lived near Bath. Aunt Puss had now been dead for a while, possibly several weeks. He rang Sebastian in London asking if it were true. Sebastian rang Docklow, spoke to his brothers and sister and, eventually, his mother. He rang his cousins at Markington to tell them.

On the last day of the year, Lord Wilberforce received a letter from Susan, full of half-truths and disinformation, coupled with a bit of deliberate flattery, but seeming to show that she was aware that the awkward questions had begun: 'Just to tell you that Aunt Puss died on the 9th November. She went into a nursing home at the end of October [Susan failed to mention that it was two Octobers previously] where she was very happy and beautifully looked after.' She described the funeral arrangements, saying how Lady Illingworth had decreed that 'no members of the Markington branch of the family should be at the funeral and no Illingworths, who she always loathed'. Her aunt had clearly had 'one hell of a tiff' with her nephew John's wing of the family. 'In her will, which she re-made a few months after she came here, she left John £25,000, Michael Wilberforce the same, you £10,000 and me the rest. I do not think anyone will actually get any money because I do not think there really was any, the income coming from the money Uncle Albert left in trust.'

Then the flattery: 'Aunt Puss was so proud of you, Richard, as a person and for what you have achieved in your profession, as was Uncle Wee. I have so often been asked if I am related to you, in various parts of the world.' Then there were some references to the terrible state of Aunt Puss when she arrived at Docklow: 'It was remarkable watching her gradually come back to life as the weeks went by.' When taken to Hereford hospital to have a cut stiched, doctors had 'marvelled at her mental state and general condition'. 'That she regained her peace of mind was the greatest triumph of all. To retain one's dignity in old age is so important, don't you think?' People had been to see her in Docklow, including Everilda Wilberforce and Father Dooley. 'He and A.P. had long talks together. In fact he was one of the witnesses of the will.'

Getting all her possessions out of store gave Aunt Puss 'great pleasure', said Susan. 'I found it an absolute nightmare, in fact I got pleurisy from the dust and dirt, but A.P. was blissfully happy.' Then the usual points about the crates being full of rubbish, scent, sugar and jam. Most of the things from Grosvenor Square had been disposed of at the time the house was vacated, two tallboys that remained were 'quite unusable. . . . And so it went on.' She said it was her aunt's dying wish that 'Laura would not get her hands on anything, in particular the portrait of herself by de László, which is here. I well remember being told it would be mine when I was about twelve, after the war, at the White House . . . she was enormously loving, always saying how she wished I was her daughter.'

Then, the punchline: 'I am telling you all these things so that you will know the true state of affairs. There is bound to be a lot of chat and things get so distorted in the telling. I am quite aware that various people think Aunt Puss should not have been removed from York House, but someone had to do something. She was being treated worse than an animal, so we had her here. I know how very much Aunt Puss appreciated your visits and how kind Yvette was taking her flowers. Everyone else just sneered.'

It was another month before the obituaries. *The Times* of 2 February 1987 read:

> Lady Illingworth, second wife of the first Baron Illingworth, died recently. She was thought to be 86.
> Lord Wilberforce writes: Lady Illingworth (Margaret Wilberforce) made a host of friends for herself and for this country through her hospitality at her house at Grosvenor Square and, after its demolition, at Claridge's.
> Her generous personality supported by remarkable good looks (English style) never left her.
> She was always at home to the Diplomatic Corps and travelled widely. She was also a supporter of the Red Cross and of anti-slavery causes.

The *Evening Standard* diary column, later the same day, was more colourful and inaccurate, saying that, although there were 'few people alive to remember them', for many years Lady Illingworth had thrown some of the best parties in London on 21 June. It said that she had never listed her age in *Debrett's* and the guesses varied from eighty-four to ninety-three. (In fact, her birthday – 23 November 1900 – appears among the three pages devoted to the Wilberforces in *Burke's Landed Gentry*, the standard reference work on such families.) The item described her as 'one of the great beauties of her generation' who, after declining to enter a nunnery, preferred to 'spend her last days in a suite in Claridge's'. Either this was bad journalism or someone was not being entirely frank about what had happened to Aunt Puss.

A few days later, the *Daily Telegraph* was considerably more fulsome; someone had clearly consulted the files. It described her as an 'indefatigable hostess' at Grosvenor Square, which was 'disgracefully demolished' to make way for the Britannia Hotel. It gave a summary of her life and times, not forgetting the balls, the wall painting, the convent clause in the will. She and her late husband, it said, were of 'sound Yorkshire stock'. But its conclusion rather fudged the last two decades of her life: 'Following the destruction of 44 Grosvenor Square, Lady Illingworth migrated down the road to Claridge's where she continued her legendary hospitality.'

The degree of concern among the family outside Docklow about the circumstances of Aunt Puss's death is difficult to estimate. As far as they knew, she had left specific instructions about her funeral with Susan, which clearly countered the 1975 will, when eventually unearthed. Although it might have seemed unusual, by going to Susan's care Aunt Puss may have been making clear her feelings about the relative merits of Docklow, where she was wanted, and Markington, where she might have felt the opposite was the case. No one had spent long enough with her to be able to say whether there were genuine reasons, as Susan suggested, for all this. But had she been well enough to be aware of what she was doing? Who could say? Communication within the family was difficult: Uncle Wee was dead and Aunt Marion very old, other relatives were of a similar age and were dispersed around the country. John and Laura were in Cyprus and their children were leading their own lives around England; Lord Wilberforce was in London; Sebastian barely on speaking terms with his mother, who was out at Heath House every day. For some time yet, the questions were unanswered.

In May, John Wilberforce received a letter from Richard Sexton's firm, along with a copy of Aunt Puss's 1984 will. He said later that it was the first time he had known that his sister was the principal beneficiary of a will from which he had assumed he would also substantially benefit. Since he had some idea of the size of his aunt's trust plus her own personal estate, the contents of the letter shook him. The letter read: 'As you see, you are a beneficiary under the will. Unfortunately, there would appear to be very little money in the estate.' The letter said there might be sufficient to discharge all the pecuniary bequests.

Susan knew that the estate was limited; she had been forced to transfer money from her own account in Guernsey to the joint account she still had with her aunt, to cover a £9000 overdraft. She was able to do so by raising another £10,000 through a couple of auction sales. Shortly afterwards, as part of the legal battle over Heath House, she swore an affidavit which declared that her only income was £2000 a year from family trusts.

As the family wondered what had happened in those last years of Aunt Puss's life, Simon Dale, sensing that a final stand against Susan over the house was imminent, redoubled his efforts to establish its significance as a site of historical importance. Following some excavations he had conducted in the walled garden in the late 1970s, he had become convinced that Heath House stood directly above a 'lost town', the centre of a pagan cult destroyed in about the seventh century AD. Simon claimed that the site was referred to in early Welsh and English legends and poems, linking it convincingly with Camelot, the legendary court of King Arthur. He also suggested, supported by a combination of place names and literary references, that the site had been the home of the ancient Armenians, who, according to classical records, were moved to Gaul by the Romans in the fourth century AD. Two books were being written: one a serious historical work called 'The Sleep of Arthur', drawing upon the Arthurian legends, and the second, 'The Staircase', a fictional romance set in the Civil War based on the house; neither was ever published. All of this involved a good deal of research in the local studies department of Shrewsbury public library. It was typical of his attitude towards such matters that he had been referring to Leintwardine by its old Roman name of Branogenium for some time.

His physical evidence for his theories was a combination of what he believed were ancient ruins visible in the extensive cellars of Heath House – including the sewerage pipes of the Armenians – and specimens from his own excavations in the garden. A single brick from the garden, professionally dated as being from AD 600 plus or minus 200, was, he claimed, confirmation. He also compiled a map of the city by dowsing, the technique of searching for water using two wires which move together when above damp ground.

'The whole idea', he told a *Manchester Evening News* reporter, 'could be a figment of my imagination. But I don't think so. What I appear to have found in this area are streets, 40 feet wide and up to 200 yards long. They appear to be typical Ministry of Works jobs, standardised shops, houses and things.' Dale, said the article, believed that the house, backed by some trust, could serve as a residential archaeological centre, with himself as the curator. The article kept a straight face, but added a footnote: 'Simon Dale telephoned as we were going to press to say he had found King Arthur's Round Table – under a clump of laurel bushes in the garden. "It's becoming more and more far-fetched," he said, "but the thing down there is just the right shape and size for the table."'

During the early 1980s Simon wrote to different archaeological experts, academics and organisations such as the Council of British Archaeology, the Royal Commission on Historical Monuments and English Heritage, seeking support for an excavation to prove his theories once and for all. The possibility, he wrote, was that the truth about the sub-Roman period had been 'deliberately expunged from record'. 'As a result, I have some 120,000 words on this, completely rewriting three hundred years of British history.' Most responded with words of approval and encouragement; no one committed themselves to accepting or publishing his theories or even subjecting them to closer scrutiny.

How much of this was due to a desire somehow to halt Susan's attentions is difficult to estimate. It is clear that Simon had a genuine belief in the importance of the site, which could be determined only by an archaeological dig. If this subsequently proved its worth, it could just about – and probably only after considerable legal argument – come between Susan and repossession, possibly ensuring his residence. Professionals who encountered Simon and those among his family who talked to him about his theories, particularly Sebastian, certainly considered him sincere, if misguided. It just so happened that pursuance of them appeared to help conveniently to frustrate his ex-wife.

Simon's greatest argument was with the department of archaeology at Hereford–Worcester County Council. In 1983, he persuaded them to conduct a small excavation in the walled garden. When it failed to support his expectations, he claimed that he was being deliberately ignored and that officials were behaving as if 'in the Soviet Union'. He threatened legal action. His formal complaint about the actions of the department was rejected. In late 1986 and early 1987, with Susan now working on the house, the letters took on a fresh tone of insistence, accusing officials of deliberate negligence and irresponsibility. He warned them, darkly, that they were being left 'progressively out on a limb'. He told his friends that the establishment were conspiring against him again.

Adrian Tindall, appointed as the new archaeologist for Hereford and Worcester in January 1987, became caught between the two protagonists. Simon, helped by a local councillor, persuaded Tindall to look at what his predecessors had dismissed. Reluctantly, he agreed to see Simon. A few days later, he received a telephone call from a solicitor claiming to represent Susan, asking him about the planned visit. It occurred to Tindall that the only way Susan could have known about the visit was if she had some knowledge of what had been in Simon's post.

The following month, he visited Heath House. He was taken on a tour of the house and cellars and incurred Simon's anger when he expressed his scepticism. 'Dale said to me, words to the effect "You'll be hearing more of this" and made clear he was unhappy with my views.' As he was driving away, a woman, who he realised was Susan, leapt out of the undergrowth by the drive and flagged him down. When he pulled up, she asked what he was doing there; he explained that he was the county archaeologist.

'She knew what I was doing there because she implied her son would go into the house and read his letters and that was her way of finding out what was going on.' Tindall explained that he felt this was only a call of duty and there was no chance he would be doing anything about it, particularly since he felt there was a suggestion that he was being used as a pawn in the game. Susan, he said, appeared relieved.

'She then started all this stuff about how he was dangerous, how he had tried to kill her on several occasions, how he had dug a grave for her in the grounds and how he kept lots of poisons in the house. She certainly looked frightened to me, always looking around furtively. All in all it was a spooky experience.' Susan told him that she always carried something with which to defend herself and pointed to this thing on her arm, which only registered with him as 'a walking stick or object like that'.

Susan began regularly to harangue visitors to the house, showing anger towards Veronica Bowater and her friends. Veronica claims objects were deliberately placed in her path: 'The first time I saw them there, Marcus was on the roof. I came down the drive, which was in a ghastly mess. Marcus shot behind a chimney. She appears, eyes blazing, holding this flame-gun affair in her hands, and makes for me, clearly intent on a head-on confrontation. I knew she had changed her name but could only think of Wilberforce. So I said, "Hello Mrs Wilberforce", or something like that, and she just gave me this look and said, "I am the Baroness de Stempel. I suppose you have brought your friends to visit my house."'

Later, the two German friends of hers who had found work for Marcus in Germany visited England. Veronica took them to meet Simon and, hopefully, Marcus. 'The drive was covered with logs and bricks and Marcus kept bobbing up and down behind the hedge. We could not get down to the arch on the right-hand side, so we drove across the lawn.' They went in to see Simon, had a meal, at which Marcus did not appear, and were driving away when Susan appeared again with what Veronica describes as 'a flame-thrower' but was actually a flame-gun that Susan used to clear weeds. According to Veronica, Susan looked angry and began screaming something they could not understand, before kicking the car radiator several times. 'It was all rather hysterical, actually, with Marcus frantically bobbing up and down behind this hedge.'

According to Sophia, Veronica Bowater would become very angry when she arrived to discover them working, and her father would become more aggressive and antagonistic after her visits. 'She would get mortally offended if she was unable to park the car where she wanted or was prevented from walking through the arch.' Susan and the children blamed much of the confrontational atmosphere on what they saw as Veronica's over-emotional reactions, which only served to stoke up Simon's anger against his normal instincts. Much to their amusement, members of the Bowater group took to arriving in pairs or even in convoy with friends, but never alone.

Susan may have talked in a curious fashion to other visitors, but there were few similar confrontations. Giselle Wall, Simon's secretary until July 1987, would talk normally to Susan, 'always very polite', outside before going in to hear Simon's version of events. A man who accompanied his wife for an interview as Wall's replacement was told by Susan that it was not much use his wife taking the job because Simon, 'squatting in the house', would not be living there in fifteen days' time. She said she had stopped his excavations by instituting legal proceedings. When Susan was joined by Sophia, she explained how Simon had used to beat her. Sophia, at her side, agreed.

A few weeks later, John Miller, from Devon, who had also met Simon when a friend had been for a job interview, went to discuss the conference-centre idea. Simon wanted Miller to put money into the scheme and become manager, an offer Miller subsequently declined. When Miller left, the driveway was obstructed by a wheelbarrow and Susan emerged from behind a rhododendron bush on the lawn. When Miller explained the purpose of his visit, Susan, joined by Marcus, said Simon had ill-treated her. Miller thought they both looked 'quite frightened'. He was one of a number of visitors whose departure was obstructed by some object, allowing Susan the opportunity (at the very least) to establish who they were.

His friends marvelled at the stoic fashion in which Simon took all this, despite occasionally appearing with the odd bruise on his face and having his impromptu dinner parties interrupted by the roar of Susan's car, apparently deliberately revving up outside. He told them that wires and obstacles had been placed around the house in his path; that familiar objects, such as pens, would go missing; that he was sure he could hear someone following him around the house. He spoke rarely of Susan, but when he did, according to one secretary, it was 'as a parent might speak of a wayward child', good-naturedly complaining about 'my bloody wife trying to put me out on to the streets again'. Despite this casual demeanour, his attempts to win support for an excavation or to arouse interest in his ideas became increasingly desperate. He must have felt some sense of panic.

Simon did appeal to Sebastian for help, by telephone. But Sebastian, then working hard in London for his final law examinations, firmly refused to become involved, as always. The fact that Sebastian only made one other telephone call to

Heath House in the last nine months of his father's life and did not visit him again after Christmas 1986 was probably due in equal measures to his determination not to become embroiled and to his important examinations. It is symptomatic of the anguished nature of communication within the family that it was only during that last time he saw his father that Sebastian made it fully clear how he had striven over the years to avoid taking sides and that the desire to see his father had cost him his relationship with his mother.

According to Susan and her children, it was not really so bad at Heath House. She said her ex-husband often confided in her that he would mischievously start rumours about attacks upon him, only to watch the gossip run through the Bowater circle. Their children say that, while the relationship between their parents still had many argumentative echoes of the old days, it did also occasionally extend to civilised conversation. Simon would also happily spend time talking with Sophia and Marcus.

By September 1987, solicitors were trying to agree an independent valuer whose decision would be binding on both sides. Susan suggested a name and Sax was confident a court hearing could be arranged for early in 1988. 'Towards the end, my mother and father were talking and getting on much better. I really did think it would work out okay,' said Marcus. 'I would discuss with my father where he was going to live and how much nicer and better it would be in a small house or cottage somewhere. I think he accepted it. The house was a cancer that had been hanging over them for fourteen years and needed to be dealt with.' Susan wrote to Simon Verdun: 'We have got Simon Dale on the run.' The end seemed imminent.

Friday, 11 September 1987 was the third anniversary of Susan's perfunctory wedding to Michael in the Channel Islands. It was also the day Simon Dale was murdered. Simon rose about 9 a.m. and dressed in a much repaired shirt, dark jumper, a brown tweed suit and brogues. That morning he had to go to Leominster to see his osteopath, who was treating him for his eyesight. Geoffrey Bowater had offered to give Simon a lift and, driving his nineteen-year-old Morris Traveller, picked him up at the top of the drive of Heath House at about 10 a.m. He remembers it as a perfectly normal morning; there was no sign of anyone around Heath House.

Returning, the car developed a problem in the fuel pump, which meant that every two miles or so Geoffrey had to get out and 'give it a good kick'. When they reached Leintwardine, Geoffrey decided to go to the village garage and Simon telephoned Jo Corfield, his current secretary, who lived nearby and was due to visit him that afternoon. She agreed to pick him up and take him to Heath House. The last time Geoffrey Bowater saw his friend Simon was out of his rear window, as he pulled away and Ms Corfield arrived.

She drove him to Heath House, arriving about 1.30. He had his lunch – two slices of bread, Cheddar cheese and two tomatoes, and Ms Corfield heated up the rest of his breakfast coffee for him in a saucepan. She refused his offer of food because she knew how poor he was. They spent the afternoon working. She left about 5.10 or 5.15, with instructions to buy bread on her way in on Monday. Simon was going to walk up to Hopton Heath to buy green beans and tomatoes from a friend and regular supplier near the railway station. As she left, she saw Marcus cleaning the windscreen of a car and Sophia pushing a wheelbarrow.

Minutes after returning from Hopton Heath, Simon had his next visitors: Su Evans and Ben Scott. Mrs Evans, a talkative woman from a village near Shrewsbury, had worked as a reader for Simon in 1985 and 1986 and, having become fond of him, had kept in touch, feeling that he needed people to look after him and enjoying his sense of humour. She would visit whenever she was in the area and would sometimes cook him Sunday lunch. Ben Scott, a white-haired man in his early seventies, who is, he says, 'very into New Age things', was also an enthusiast for historical and archaeological theories and often visited Glastonbury, another supposed site of Camelot. He was working in Shrewsbury at a centre for alternative medicine when he met Mrs Evans through the estate agents by whom she was then employed. Mrs Evans suggested it would be good for him to meet her friend Simon, so they could discuss matters of mutual interest.

They arrived in Scott's Volkswagen Caravanette, accompanied by the two young sons of Mrs Evans, Matthew, seven, and Dominic, ten. She had not been for some months and was surprised to see that the outside of the house had been cleaned and tidied up. As they drove down the path, they saw what appeared to be a boy tending a bonfire. They were prevented from driving through the arch to the front of the house by a water butt placed in its middle. When the van stopped, Susan appeared. 'Who are you?' she said. 'Are you the famous visitors?' Susan told Ben: 'He thinks I'm mad, but he is mad. What do you want to go there for? The upstairs rooms are full of fleas and the kitchen is filthy.' She added something which is important in retrospect: 'He'll be out by the end of the month.' Scott switched on the alarm of his camper van, then they walked around to the front of the house. Simon had appeared at the door and they went inside.

Dale greeted them all warmly and offered sherry, so Mrs Evans knew she was being honoured. They sat in front of the fire in the big lounge on the right-hand side of the house. It was dusk and a fine autumn drizzle had begun, so Simon put on the lights. Scott had checked his watch when Simon offered sherry and it was just before 6 p.m.

Scott and Dale began discussing Camelot, so Mrs Evans showed the boys the house. Looking out of a window, she saw a younger version of Simon's ex-wife walk by. She took her sons up the great staircase in the middle. On the half landing, she looked out of the window to see Sophia on a scaffolding tower handling up a pot of paint on a rope. 'I let her get on with whatever she was up to. It just seemed like a lunatic thing to be doing at that time of night in the dark and rain.' She showed the boys the passageways and concealed doors, the dusty bookcases full of works on the Wilberforces and a room with two rocking horses.

At one point, Simon also took Scott around the house. They went outside and Scott had the distinct recollection of seeing three figures in a huddle in the middle of the lawn. A few minutes later, rounding a corner, two figures were moving the scaffolding tower. The gloom and drizzle made it difficult to see exactly what was going on. Inside, the two men, together with Dominic and Matthew, went to the cellars, Mrs Evans remaining at the door because of the uneasy feeling they gave her. In one cellar a small window high up the wall, on a level with the ground outside, was open. Simon shut it. It was immediately pushed open again from the outside. An angry voice was heard to say: 'I've left the window open because it is damp and smells musty.' Scott could not see the source of the voice, but recognised it as that of the woman they had encountered outside. 'Dale's attitude was extremely phlegmatic, sort of "Oh, it is the usual thing, ignore her,"' says Scott. 'He was more interested in talking about what he termed the bloody-fool academics who were not taking him seriously.'

Simon did not seem to want them to go; he talked enthusiastically about his plans for an archaeological centre. He was unperturbed by Susan. They recounted the conversation they had had with her outside. He said she always talked like that; it was in the hands of the solicitors, a compromise would be reached. Scott felt it was difficult to break away, but eventually they took their leave at, he later estimated, about 8.45.

It was now dark and raining. They were getting into the Caravanette when Mrs Evans stopped and went back to Simon, standing in the door. She briefly held his arm, apologised for not having visited for so long and promised to return soon. Her last memory of Simon is of a tall figure silhouetted in the doorway, waving. She returned to the van, her boys and Scott. Scott turned to her and said, 'I'm never going back there again.' Of Susan and her children there was no sign. Scott swears there was a light in the little cottage.

After bidding them farewell, Simon Dale went inside and carried the sherry glasses back into the kitchen. With well-practised movements which needed little sight, he set about making his evening meal. He poured batter over some sausages in a baking dish. He turned on the electric oven, not the Aga, and placed his toad-in-the-hole inside. He filled a saucepan with water and put it on to the cooker to boil. He turned back to the table and began to prepare the green beans. It was then he had his last visitor of the day.

8
Paper Trails and Pokers

At 6 a.m., on the following Monday morning, Detective Super-intendent Ian Bullock was awoken by the screech of the telephone at his bedside in Wellington. Through rapidly receding sleep, the voice from the Worcester operations room passed on a message from Detective Chief Superintendent David Cole: there had been a murder in the Clun area; could he get there right away? Like so many others the previous evening, Bullock reached for his map.

A craggy-faced individual, whose hair is swept back in a tight crinkle, Bullock has a blunt Midlands manner which serves as a nice counterpoint to the more suave Cole – a good man to make sure the operation was running smoothly, who could mastermind the details and knock heads together if things went wrong. Cole wanted him to run the day-to-day enquiry.

When Bullock arrived at 8.30 a.m. he found nothing to command. Those who had been up half the previous night were still making their way to Heath House. He sat in the incident caravan at the back of the house, talking to a bobby who had been on early duty. Eventually, they trickled along: Cole, Matthews, bearing the poker and news of his meeting with the Baroness, other detectives, the various scientific teams. Soon, the house swarmed with a range of people going about their duties: fingerprint officers, scenes-of-crime officers, forensic scientists, photographers: dusting, brushing, sampling, scraping, snapping. Hundreds of small plastic bags were filling up with hairs, dust, fibres, food, paint, blood; larger ones for the sherry glasses, a cardboard box soaked in blood, a broken basin smeared with traces of batter and the black, crusted, carbonised remains of the toad-in-the-hole that Simon Dale never ate.

A decision was taken to search the whole house, the grounds and the cottage. A massive undertaking, they knew it would be the only way to be confident that nothing was overlooked. They had also to be certain that the signs of entry by the kitchen door were being read correctly. The search would also confirm that nothing was missing from the house, ruling out burglary as a possible motive. It would include Simon's personal paperwork, helping them trace friends and contacts and construct the picture of his lifestyle.

Cole and Bullock conferred. Obvious steps were being taken: Giselle Wall and the Spencers were being questioned in depth, not only about the weekend, but on everything they knew about Simon Dale, his former wife and their relationship; Bullock set about the practicalities of a murder enquiry: the allocation of enough officers, the routine house-to-house enquiries, recruitment of catering and administrative staff, a suitable incident room from where it would all be handled.

First there was this tight-lipped Baroness woman and her children Matthews had visited the night before. Matthews explained that he was, putting it mildly, extremely unhappy about their response to Dale's death. 'It was unusual,' he told his superiors, 'they just didn't act like any other family might. I was waiting for them to, but they didn't.'

At Docklow, they rose early. After Matthews and Clarke had left, Sophia and Simon had returned to bed, leaving their mother and Marcus downstairs talking. Sophia was in a state of shock, the rest numb. There was no crying – that was not their style. 'I had great difficulty believing it was true. There was nothing we could do – the police were only telling us so much. What could we do? I wanted to work it all out, but they were not giving me enough information.' The first time the world 'murder' was used was on the breakfast news on television, reporting that their father had been battered to death in his kitchen. It was, said Sophia, just unbelievable. 'There was a great sense of loss. And I felt so angry at my father for getting killed just when we were getting on better.'

At midday, the police were back, staggering their arrivals. Detective Inspector David Borthwick and Detective Constable Michael O'Keefe arrived first and took Susan away to Bishop's Castle. After a few minutes, Matthews and Clarke arrived for Marcus, then Detective Chief Inspector Peter Parry and Constable Trudy Radcliffe for Sophia, and lastly Detective Sergeant Jim Lucas and Detective Constable David Roberts for Simon. Naturally, the police took the opportunity to have a little look around the premises. In the room used as a bedroom by the children, Matthews, the kind of sharp-eyed little man who misses nothing, saw an envelope on the bed, addressed to Margaret, Lady Illingworth. 'Who's this Lady Illingworth then?' he asked Marcus. 'Oh, that's Aunt Puss, she used to live with us until last year. She's dead now.' Matthews thought no more of it, at least for a short while.

All four were taken to different police stations to be questioned, although not as suspects, merely witnesses. The questioning would last many hours. That may have had more to do with the particular style of the Wilberforces.

As Matthews had already discovered, the latter-day Wilberforces have developed an ability to turn tight-lipped, British upper-class diffidence into something approaching an art form. This control of the emotions is at its most resolute when faced with challenge and adversity. When detectives question most people, whether sex offenders or city fraudsters, there is usually some play of the emotions or chink in the armour. There may at least be common points of reference. Here, there was almost nothing for the police to grasp. A group of orthodox, decent detectives, who went home each night to their comfortable homes in Hereford or Leominster, rather than to crumbling mansions and the accumulated weight of family history, struggled to describe what they faced, resorting to barely adequate stock descriptions: 'cool and calculating' or 'hard' or, used in a derogatory fashion, 'highly intelligent'. In police terms, this generally means someone capable of schemes more devious than those they have previously encountered.

Faced with awkward questions, Susan shrugs her shoulders and looks away or gives a small, inward laugh and says something irrelevant; alternatively, by manner and body language, she disdains involvement, and sometimes she will put it into words: 'It doesn't matter one bit what you say or do to me. I know my position and everything else is irrelevant. Do what you will, you cannot hurt me.' That would be delivered quietly, without visible emotion or variance of pitch, but in an accent that carves words like a diamond cuts glass.

If anything, Marcus is more controlled. The small blue eyes go blank, rather than piercing. The voice is muted and precise. But he almost always answers, in some fashion. Sophia is more talkative and brighter, more responsive than her brother and mother. Sometimes she talks too much and then, like all of them, resorts to a favourite weapon of defence: a reflective, non-committal 'hmmm'.

They all acknowledge this lack of emotion. Susan says that, as a child, she was taught to sit upright and perfectly still for long periods, to teach self-control and discipline. Marcus and Sophia have a more immediate explanation: 'We were caught so much between Mother and Father trying to get us to take sides that we simply learnt not to show any emotion one way or the other. We learnt that it saved a lot of trouble.'

Where there is a complex net of family relationships, police proceed cautiously, noting everything which might become relevant later. And in the case of the Wilberforce/Dale/de Stempel relationships, there was a lot to disentangle. Where had they been on the Friday night and over the weekend? What had they seen, heard, thought, said, both to themselves and to each other? By now, as a result of Dr Acland's post-mortem in the early hours of Monday morning and the obvious evidence in the kitchen, police knew that Simon had died as a result of a strong blow to the throat, probably on Friday evening. Matthews had been told that Susan and her children had been around Heath House at the relevant time and they were almost certainly the last people to see Simon alive.

All four related essentially the same story, which they were to repeat many times. At Bishop's Castle police station, Susan explained to Borthwick and O'Keefe that they had all been working at Heath House on Friday and saw various visitors come and go. Sophia left early – about 7 p.m. – complaining of tiredness and returned to Docklow to cook. Susan and Marcus remained until 7.55 p.m., when they too returned. During the evening, they watched an Agatha Christie drama on the television.

On Saturday, Sophia and Marcus rose early and travelled to the wedding of a friend in Kent, returning late at night. In the morning, Susan made the first of two visits that day to Heath House, driving the Peugeot estate and accompanied by Simon junior driving the Mercedes van, which carried a saw bench. After it had been unloaded, Simon junior, who rarely visited Heath House, departed. Susan went to the walled garden to check the beehives Marcus kept there, placing a brick on one. The chainsaw did not work and, after failing to repair it, she returned to Docklow and went to Hereford to shop. She returned to Docklow later, again accompanied by Simon junior, to take some ladders she had forgotten earlier and because she wanted to place a weight on another beehive, to stop it moving in the wind.

Saturday evening was spent at Docklow washing working clothes and doing housework. On Sunday, with Sophia and Marcus, they had swept the chimney at Docklow for the first time and also cleaned a number of fireside tools, including the poker Matthews had found in the car. Then they visited some gardens open to the public near Worcester. No, Susan had not seen Simon during those trips; no she had not gone into the house; no, she had not seen anything suspicious. But, yes, she had hit her former husband twice during the period she had been working at Heath House. She told them about these incidents.

It was very late when Susan and her children were driven back to Docklow, exhausted.

Earlier that evening, Ben Scott had been for a stroll and a pint in Shrewsbury. The police were waiting for him at the natural-health centre where he had been staying. He had been traced through the number Susan had given them of the vehicle belonging to the 'famous visitors'. He was taken to Shrewsbury station where he was fingerprinted; his Caravanette and room were searched thoroughly. In Kent, his wife had been questioned. The detectives swiftly decided that this seventy-year-old man was not a suspect, but they found Scott's account of his eerie visit to Heath House extremely interesting – particularly his accurate recall of certain timings.

By Tuesday morning, an incident room had been established in Bedstone village hall, two miles down the road from Heath House, which would become the focus of the enquiry for the first month. At 9 a.m., Cole called a debriefing to assess the state of play. There was no privacy or peace inside the incident room, so they sought refuge in the tea wagon, parked in the neighbouring farmyard. For much of the day, Cole, Bullock,

Matthews and the other detectives sat in the back of the wagon, farm mud on their shoes, poring over every aspect of the case.

Although a vast number of enquiries were being conducted, it all came back to this Susan de Stempel and her children. By now, they had ascertained the basic circumstances of Simon's life and were hearing of the confrontational atmosphere at Heath House, during the last few months and on the night of his death. Susan and her children were on the verge of becoming suspects, not simply because of their unusual behaviour on Sunday night and inconsistencies in their stories.

Against this, the detectives had nothing to link Susan or the others directly to the murder: no smoking gun. Results from scientific samples from the search of Heath House and their cars would take time; fingerprints inside the house would mean nothing; there was no immediate sign of blood on the pokers they had seized. If it was true that Susan was reaching the end of her legal battle to get the house, an obvious motive evaporated. Perhaps, they wondered, there was another, less obvious reason, or a combination of motives and long-term resentment and frustration, which had led to a violent confrontation.

Other aspects intrigued them. Here were four people surrounded by luxurious antiques and furniture, driving good-quality cars, yet living in a little rented cottage. They had explained how poor they had been and none of them, apart from Simon junior, had jobs. There might be evidence of a motive there, perhaps to do with the financial circumstances of the children. And who was this Aunt Puss whom Marcus said had given them money and property? Someone should find out about her. In the meantime, said Cole, let's have them in again, as witnesses.

On Wednesday, there was little change to the overall story. Sophia told them she had 'a theory', which just happened, the detectives noted, to dovetail with what they privately believed but had not disclosed to the family. Simon, said Sophia, had returned to the kitchen after waving goodbye to his visitors, and had begun preparing food; someone he knew had arrived; there had been a row and Simon had been struck, hard. But not her mother, oh no, never her mother. This caused consternation among the police. She said afterwards: 'It's only natural to speculate about who killed your father, isn't it? What I was saying was very close to what they thought.' Later, she named, in a speculative fashion, a friend of her father's. Naturally, the police examined that person's background and motives in detail. It never stood up.

Back at Heath House, a scenes-of-crime officer exploring the little cottage found a crowbar, hanging inside a cupboard. Later detectives established that this was the object that Adrian Tindall, the archeologist, had seen on Susan's arm during his encounter with her in the drive of Heath House. Dr Acland would be asked whether he believed the blows on Dale's head had been caused by this. It was 'possible', he said, only 'possible'.

In the early hours of Thursday morning, Susan's interrogators, almost as a matter of routine, asked her how many bank accounts she had. Two, she replied, one at Lloyds in Hereford, another at Barclays at the Old Brompton Road in London. 'Can we have a written authority to examine them, please?' 'Certainly.' At Bromyard police station, Sophia was asked the same questions and signed a blanket authority for the inspection of all her accounts. 'Oh yes,' she told detectives, 'I have several bank accounts and some joint ones with Mummy, including one in Spain.' Marcus, at Ludlow, also began talking about accounts his mother had not mentioned. When, by telephone, the detectives compared notes, alarm bells rang. Susan had clearly misled police. They went back to Susan: 'Just how many accounts do you have?' they asked. She told them about the Banco de Bilbao in Spain and the London branch of the Banque Nationale de Paris in Knightsbridge. She signed authorities for their inspection.

The interviews were ultimately inconclusive as far as any prospect of a swift success was concerned; the pressure of the first few days was leaving the police exhausted. This was obviously not going to be one of those quick, two-to-three-day jobs and chummy in custody. This was going to be a long haul. They were going to have to find out a lot more about this strange family they had encountered. They had to find a motive. Perhaps it might lie in this money business.

*

'You cannot move money about the banking system without leaving some kind of record,' says Detective Constable Robin Longmore, a typically smart fraud detective, perfectly interchangeable with the bank managers and accountants with whom he regularly deals. 'It is impossible, unless you have a corrupt bank, which in this case they did not. And so one account leads to another and so on . . . We call it the paper trail.'

A team of fraud detectives, headed by Detective Inspector Mike Cowley, like Cole the possessor of a fine West Country burr and an engagingly crafty smile, were called in at the beginning of the second week to follow the trail. What began as a standard examination of Susan's finances, as they might relate to the murder, gradually transformed itself into something else entirely.

Anne Devey-Smith had by now contacted police. They might be interested in what she had to say, she told them. They certainly were. In a series of interviews during October, she described the doubtful mental condition of Lady Illingworth, the antiques at Docklow and, because she was on the receiving end of telephone conversations from Susan and Michael during the break-up of their relationship, much about the emotional backdrop. She told them how Lady Illingworth had been 'enticed' or 'coaxed' out of the room by Sophia before the will she had been asked to witness was signed. That single fact was enough to invalidate the will – the first solid evidence of a crime likely to stand up in court. Michael had informed her that Susan 'used to place blank pieces of paper in front of Lady Illingworth and ask her to sign them'.

Mrs Devey-Smith explained Susan's attitude to cashcards. '[Susan] told me quite shamelessly that she was using her aunt's bank cashcards. She said something like, 'You just pop them in the wall and take money out.' I understood she was using the cards quite often.' Mrs Devey-Smith said she had 'numerous conversations' with Susan about the cards. 'She was quite dispassionate and almost jocular when she recounted these incidents to me. She told me how she had erected a large fence at Docklow to prevent her aunt escaping or others viewing her.' Susan also told her about the house they had planned to buy on Alderney. 'Susan had stated her intention of putting bars on the windows and having a woman at the house in order that she could look after Lady Illingworth in the absence of Susan.' Aunt Puss, said Anne Devey-Smith, behaved 'like a well-trained child'.

Meanwhile, Matthews, investigating the murder, but curious about how this Lady Illingworth fitted in, had been to Hereford Hospital, where he was told how this confused elderly lady had been left in care because her niece clearly did not want her back, saying she was a drunk. They showed him a form completed by Susan indicating that her aunt's only source of income was her state pension. This was completely at odds which what Matthews had already and easily established: that Lady Illingworth had been a woman of some substance. Later, at Langford House, Detective Constable Kevin Bayliss heard how Lady Illingworth had had no money and had rarely been visited by her relatives. A few hundred yards up the road, he discovered an unpaid crematorium bill.

The fraud enquiry gained its own momentum, running away from the murder. Cowley's team set about examining the history and circumstances of Lady Illingworth. Her husband had been a rich man, she the principal beneficiary of his will. Yet Matthews and Bayliss had discovered that she had died a senile pauper; Marcus said she had given them money and furniture. Where had it all gone? the police asked themselves. Had Lady Illingworth known what she was doing? They went back to the paper trail.

It took them to auction houses and removals companies; to Turner Sexton in Twickenham and E.F. Matthews, the Essex stockbrokers; it took them to the original 1975 will at Theodore Goddard and Co.; and it took them to York House, Markington Hall and Spain. It would eventually take them to Cyprus, where John Wilberforce, said yes, he had been surprised to learn that his aunt had changed her will after moving to Docklow to live with Susan. It took them to Elizabeth Gregg-Smith and Albert Oslar, who told them of Lady Illingworth's wealth and her mental condition a few days before she went to Docklow. At Giltspur Bullens, the managing director, Aubrey Appleton, caused great, if temporary, excitement when he began talking about the gold bars he believed he had seen in the bowels of Grosvenor Square. Police were never able to find any supporting evidence; no one else had seen or heard of them, including those former members of Lady Illingworth's Grosvenor Square staff who had been traced. Despite extensive enquiries through the Bank of England and the various Wilberforce relatives, no further evidence of their existence was found.

There were other dead ends. They went to see Michael, living on his own in London, but spending time with his second ex-wife, Francesca. 'My code of honour as a gentleman', he informed them, 'would preclude me from giving you any information about Susan de Stempel. Even if I had any to give.'

When they reached York House, Irene was dead and Cathy Whelan ageing and waiting for a council flat. Cathy would be too infirm to give evidence in court but she told them how close Lady Illingworth had been to Sophia, how Mr John would stay there when in London, how his wife and children visited as Lady Illingworth's favourite nieces. She said Susan had never visited in the fourteen years she had been there. She spoke of the visit of Sophia and Marcus and of the angry scene, and of how, two days later, Michael and Marcus brought a solicitor called Patten, who threatened her with arrest if she did not let them into Lady Illingworth's room. Cathy told police: 'The solicitor rummaged in the cardboard box [which contained Lady Illingworth's financial papers] and said this was what they were looking for.'

The Docklow will, retrieved from the National Westminster Bank trustees department at Hereford, was sent to Dr David Baxendale, a documentation expert at Birmingham forensic science laboratory: the signature of Lady Illingworth was a forgery, a good one. By now, Cowley's team had collected a large amount of paperwork purportedly signed by Lady Illingworth: cheques, letters of authority, letters to stockbrokers and the trustees' office, bank mandates, applications for autobank cards and for the repayment of Premium Bonds and saving certificates. More than sixty contained the forged signature of Lady Illingworth.

It would take months to complete the details, but within a few weeks the shape of the fraud was clear: the will had been forged to give the estate to Susan and her children. Either it had been an insurance policy in case Aunt Puss died before the assets were stripped, or the original intention had been overtaken by greed. The assets had been obtained by prodigious forging of her signature backed by widespread lying and disinformation about Lady Illingworth's character, movements and intentions. There was no obvious grand plan or system; in fraud terms it was a simple crime, if extensively executed. Because there was so much paper evidence, it was also relatively easy to solve. Cowley reported that they had a clear case of asset-stripping and money-laundering, but no evidence of motive for murder. It was an entirely separate crime. Whether it would have been discovered if it were not for the murder, no one would ever know.

A number of matters would be irrefutably established. When Lady Illingworth arrived at Docklow in February 1984, Susan had five bank accounts on the margins between overdraft and credit. Her annual income was about £2000, from dividends and family trust money. After Aunt Puss had arrived, four of her accounts swelled with cheques and cash payments. Susan opened thirteen more accounts: five new joint accounts with her aunt and a sixth obtained by adding her name to an existing account of her aunt's in Monte Carlo. Lady Illingworth opened eight new accounts in Hereford or the Channel Islands, closing those in Ripon and London. Susan opened four accounts with Sophia: one in Guernsey, one at the London branch of the Royal Bank of Canada and two Spanish accounts. Susan also opened three accounts with Simon, in Guernsey. Before February 1984, Sophia had one account, her first, opened in later 1982. By late 1987, she had eight more: four with her mother, two with Marcus in Guernsey and two of her own in Hereford. She had two building society accounts. There were a total of twenty-three accounts used to launder the money.

After the autobank card had been requested on Lady Illingworth's Ripon account within just two weeks of her arrival at Docklow, £6000 was withdrawn by cashpoint. When the account was transferred to Hereford in June 1984, a further £11,000 was withdrawn, mainly the trust income. Four more cards were issued to Lady Illingworth, three after she had entered hospital. Susan received three cards on the joint accounts. All Lady Illingworth's trust income of more than £40,000 had disappeared, almost all of it in cashpoint withdrawals or cheques made to cash, many of them containing the forged signature of Lady Illingworth. Unfortunately, many of the earliest cheques drawn on Lady Illingworth's Ripon account and the first joint account at Hereford had been innocently destroyed by the banks. All the accounts had been made possible, like the will, on the basis of forged letters and authorities. The trust itself, containing about £1 million, was untouchable; Lady Illingworth herself could not have gained access to it.

Also as a result of forged authorities, the National Westminster Bank handed over thirty-seven separate items from its bank vault; Giltspur Bullens moved eleven lorry-loads containing 459 separate items from their warehouse to Wickton Court Workshops; E.F. Matthews, the stockbrokers, conducted four separate share sales, realising £20,000, and nearly £6000 worth of saving certificates and £300 of premium bonds were cashed.

Most of the goods were sold at Phillips and Jolley's auction house in Bath between August 1984 and February 1986, raising £130,000 at forty-eight separate sales of about 500 different items of furniture, carpets, pictures, china, silverware and jewellery. Russell, Baldwin and Bright in Leominster also conducted seven sales, which raised just under £25,000. In the Channel Islands, Hettich's bought jewellery and silver plate for £45,000. Among £15,000 of cheques forged in Lady Illingworth's name were ones to pay the rent, rates, gas and telephone bills at Docklow, all happily accepted.

A further £150,000 worth of property from Wickton Court and Forresters Hall and paintings worth around £27,000, left with an art restorer, were also recovered. In two briefcases deposited by Susan at Lloyds Bank in Hereford, detectives found a substantial quantity of jewellery, including pearls, diamonds and gold rings, which had belonged to Aunt Puss; they also found some miniature paintings, several silver toast-tracks from Heath House, the Asprey's earrings she had bought herself and the brass plate from the de László portrait of Lady Illingworth. A massive exercise was undertaken to identify, trace and recover every piece of property; members of the Wilberforce family at Markington were shown videos of the furniture to see if they could identify what they remembered as belonging to Aunt Puss; police even traced Francis Barnett, then seventy-three, Lady Illingworth's former butler at Grosvenor Square, a pall-bearer at Lord Illingworth's funeral, who was taken to identify property he had not seen for more than twenty years.

When Mike Cowley eventually told Susan what they had discovered, she denied ever forging anything, denied the contrary claims about her aunt's mental condition and replied blithely: 'Aunt Puss wanted to give it all to me. Families always give things to each other.'

The fraud investigation was conducted discreetly, away from the public spotlight. Not so the murder enquiry: everyone in the borders was talking about the horrific death of this eccentric old man who lived alone in a crumbling mansion. But only one face of the enquiry was made public: the appeals for witnesses, the house-by-house interviews of everyone in the surrounding area, the search for cars and a mysterious hitchhiker, seen on the road outside Heath House. A massive exercise examined the background and possible motives of everyone who knew or who had met Simon Dale.

The incident room moved to more spacious surroundings at Kidderminster police station. There, a computer recorded 700 witness interviews; 1700 different lines of enquiry; 3200 doorstep interviews in 800 homes, which took twenty-two officers three weeks to complete; a seven-day road check outside Heath House in which 900 vehicles were identified and eliminated; a three-week search by ten police dogs of an area of one-mile radius around Heath House; and a seven-week search of the house and its grounds by fourteen scenes-of-crime officers and forensic scientists.

A range of people from friends of Sebastian to cleaners who had been inside Heath House were given close scrutiny because they had left either fingermarks or footprints inside the house. Many were undatable because such marks can remain for months. Some belonged to Marcus and Sophia; a few to Susan. 'This meant nothing,' said a detective, 'because everyone accepted they had been inside the house at various points over the previous months. The only one which would have interested us were any in blood. And there were not.'

The inward-looking face of the enquiry was a question: what was the strength of the case against Susan, Sophia and Marcus? The factors which went to support the case against Susan, somehow assisted by Sophia and Marcus, never quite locked together. The best possible evidence of a single motive – Simon's reluctance to leave – was weak. The solicitors made it obvious that, although Simon's eviction might not have been imminent, it was a definite possibility.

There was certainly independent evidence of a confrontational atmosphere and some support for the claim that Simon had used violence against Susan. Also, the police had substantial circumstantial evidence surrounding Susan's movements over the Friday night and weekend: she had confronted Scott and Evans, argued with Simon and, she conceded, had watched him walk back through the house to the kitchen, staying later at the house than normal. There were serious inconsistencies in her movements on the Saturday: she had remained at Heath House alone despite stressing how afraid she was of him; she had denied, until Simon junior confirmed it, that she had walked directly past the kitchen, with the shutters drawn and the light on; she had twice parked in the courtyard of the cottage, though she and her children had always previously parked in the garage so that Simon would not know they were there; and she had denied this until her youngest son had told police, which prompted her retraction. And why had they not gone to Heath House on the Sunday, when the weather was good and when they had hardly missed a day there in months; moreover, why had they chosen that day to clean pokers and the chimney?

But police knew that a decent defence barrister could tear much of that apart in court, since there was little other concrete evidence to back it up. Despite the sterling work of Dr Norman Weston and his colleagues at the Home Office foreign science laboratory in Birmingham, none of the scientific samples provided a positive link to anyone from Docklow; neither was there anything further of consequence – relating to the murder at least – found at Docklow or in any of the cars. Much time was spent on the sherry glasses: it was established that Simon had drunk a sherry with Mrs Evans and Scott at about 6 p.m. on the Friday evening. In the kitchen, he had taken out one more glass, either then or later, which he had put aside because it was cracked. But had the fifth, half-full, sherry glass been poured for a later guest? The only prints upon it were Simon's, and the detectives assumed he had poured a second sherry while cooking. It had never been finished.

Crucially, the precise timing of the murder was in doubt. The kitchen scene, the accounts of Scott and Evans, the lack of sightings of Simon over the weekend and the unanswered telephone calls from Giselle Wall and others firmly pointed towards Friday night. But the heat in the kitchen had made it impossible for Dr Acland to state the time with the certainty that pathologists can normally employ. Police attempted an estimate by cooking toad-in-the-hole. Three samples of the dish, made in the police canteen at Worcester, were solemnly cooked in the kitchen at Heath House for different lengths of time to observe the changes they went through after being burnt black. The answer was inconclusive: after six hours the dish was a crusted black lump. It did not matter how much longer it was kept there, it remained a crusted black lump. And Simon Dale had been dead longer than six hours. It was all deeply frustrating.

Immediately after the second interviews, Susan and the children had been left alone, apart from one brief contact when Susan was asked to give permission to search all her accounts. Then silence again. 'We all felt ill. We walked around like zombies doing nothing, not even eating.' A few days afterwards, life improved when the cars were returned. Then the police returned to Docklow to search the house and garden thoroughly.

While the police agonised over the lack of evidence against their chosen suspects, Susan and the children began to have a more pleasant time. 'In some ways it was one of the most enjoyable spells we had together, in our bubble, the four of us again,' said Marcus. 'It brought us all back together for the first time in several years. We would drive out for a spin and explore Wales or the Malverns. My mother later wrote from prison saying she was glad we had the time together. And so was I.' Sophia thought visiting gardens was better than being up scaffolding.

But all was not well, as Susan implied when writing to Michael at the beginning of October. Dating her letter 'Feast of St Chaotica', she wrote:

Darling, it was so kind of you to have telephoned
Richard about Anne's extraordinary malicious
behaviour. I feel we all, you included, need protecting
from her. This is going to add greatly to our problems
I am afraid. You may be interested to know that
yesterday I've had a very nasty letter from N.W.B. in
Hereford, acting as executors, saying how they knew
some things had been delivered elsewhere, in the way
of furniture and they had a list of it and where was it
etc. I am going to say that what A.P. did with her things
before her death was her own affair, as you suggested
when you were here.

The police will also discover that I gave you some
money (for your overdraft, do you remember?) which
I consider none of their business and totally irrelevant
to Simon's death. If they ask me why I shall say the
truth, that I loved you and it was natural to help one's
husband and that I would continue always to help you
in any way possible. The fact that someone else came
between us and wrecked our marriage is neither here
nor there and I feel just the same about you as I have
always done. You may not particularly want to be loved
by me anymore, but you will have to lump it, as it is
not something I can just turn off. Richard thinks it quite
all right for us to speak, so why don't you give it a try.
After all, we know each other's lives so well and some
things can be alluded to and no one listening would be
any the wiser. But it is no good if you make things up.

The letter continued: 'The children were very touched that you
took the trouble to warn us about Anne; Sophia in particular.
Strange to say, we all miss you like mad. Sophia has been asked
to Roy Jenkins' do and he is installed at Oxford (as Chancellor
of the University) in two weeks' time. King B will be there and
various interesting people. . . . I suppose the next thing is to sell
the house and start again. Someone is coming for drinks this
evening to discuss it, when those damn police let us go home.
Must rush to Here-pom-pom. All my love, darling, S.'

In November, the police left Heath House, their job done. After so many years, Susan was able to return. Strangely, she did not immediately move in. 'There was still a lot of work to do: cleaning and tidying. We just spent time there working on it. I suppose we would have moved back in the end.' They did not have the opportunity.

Eventually, Cole and Bullock knew they had gone as far down the road as they could; a vast amount of information about the affair had been accumulated. It was time to see their responses to what police knew. On the fraud, it was a question, one detective said, of 'topping and tailing' an already detailed investigation, using the clear evidence from the paper trail, as a lever to elicit further information, fill in gaps, put it all together. The murder was more difficult. The case could stand or fall by the detailed responses in the interviews. Unfortunately, the detectives already knew most of these from the witness interviews. Given the now familiar demeanour of the Wilberforces, no one felt that a few robust questions would lead to a tearful confession.

The detectives paired off: one from the fraud side, one from the murder enquiry, would conduct the four interviews. They worked long days reading the paperwork and drawing up questions. At Hereford police station a special suite was prepared. Each interview would be recorded on both audio and video tape; one officer would watch and listen from a control room, so that inconsistencies and contradictions could be identified immediately, instead of afterwards. The interviews would be the only ones admissible in court, and solicitors would be present. They had to get it right.

At 7.30 a.m. on the morning of Monday, 7 December, they arrived at Docklow. Marcus let them in again. Susan, Sophia and Marcus were arrested on suspicion of conspiring to murder Simon Dale and to defraud Lady Illingworth. 'They took us off rather like lambs to the slaughter,' Marcus said. Michael was arrested in London at the same time, over the fraud.

Sophia was interrogated for fifteen hours of alternating sessions on the murder and fraud. On the murder, she repeated her theories and her own account of her movements. That got them nowhere. On the fraud, the position was unchanged: Aunt Puss had not been on good terms with the Markington wing; once at Docklow she had wanted to give her belongings to Susan. Mother handled all that. Aunt Puss had gone senile only just before she was taken into hospital; then she went to a home and died. End of story. So, when Robin Longmore showed Sophia the bank accounts, she had what she later called 'a revelation'. She told them: 'I didn't know about all these accounts or the amounts of money going through them. Mother spent all her time in the room with Aunt Puss. I just signed wherever I was asked.'

The police concur. 'She was visibly shaken at the large amounts of money which passed through the accounts. It took her breath away,' said one. But police did not see this as evidence of innocence of the entire fraud since they had considerable evidence to contradict her assertions, some of which were, they said, complete lies. And they saw no mitigation in her demeanour. 'There were certain lines of enquiry where Sophia would get a little weepy and you would feel she was going to come out with it all. But she would bite her tongue, pull herself together and, when you had a break or changed a tape, it would be "Well, isn't it a nice day?" or "I do like your suit." She was very hard, we were dealing with a very hard young woman.'

So the buttoned-up emotions of the Wilberforces, the determination never to let go, was seen simply as an act of deliberately suppressed confession or the inability to admit guilt – evidence either way, in fact, of true criminality. This was one-dimensional thinking: the police should have understood that none of the Wilberforces would ever say things like 'It's a fair cop, guv.' Sophia claimed that her shock was prompted by learning something for the first time, rather than, as the police would have it, learning that they knew what she knew . . .

Marcus was interviewed by his old friends DI Matthews and DC Clarke. Two-thirds of his questioning involved the murder and it was clear that police suspected him, as the strong male, of assisting his mother in the physical assault. Asked about the poker, he said it had come from Heath House about eighteen months previously and they had taken it to Docklow. When told that Simon's cleaner had seen a full three-piece set at Heath House two weeks before the death, Marcus said he must have been confused and and must have been referring to a poker from the set the police found at Docklow. When it came to the fraud, Marcus took the family line: there was nothing wrong with Aunt Puss, she gave her money and property to their mother freely. Or, at least, that is what his mother had told him. No, he had never asked Aunt Puss about it directly. No, he knew nothing about any forgeries.

While they had firm opinions and some inverted respect for Susan and Sophia, Marcus remained a slight enigma to the detectives. 'They were a very close unit, but Marcus was even more under her thumb than Sophia,' said one, who added: 'I didn't dislike Marcus, he is a bit of an odd one, but I think he was quite straightforward and told us a lot of things that were very useful in building up the case.' Nevertheless, they felt his answers in many areas were suspicious enough to justify a charge: he denied any knowledge of payments into his account; denied paying for the Stoke Prior workshops; and claimed, as his mother had told him, that Aunt Puss had to sell property to pay off tax debts. On each of these counts, police had directly contrary evidence from the paper trail.

DI Cowley, DC O'Keefe and DI Borthwick spent seventeen hours interrogating Susan. She repeated her accounts about leaving Heath House on the Friday and returning twice on the Saturday. 'If you think I killed the man the previous evening and then went back there to saw wood, you must think I have nerves of steel.' They did, actually. The poker, she thought, had come from Heath House and had been taken to Heath Cottage for cleaning. As for the crowbar, she had needed it for picking up pieces of glass out of the driveway and for self-protection.

Of course she had all the money, furniture and stocks and shares of Aunt Puss: that was what her aunt had wanted, and she had been in a fit state to know what she was doing. It was as simple as that. As to the evidence of her aunt's mental condition and the forgeries, Susan flatly denied any knowledge of what they were talking about. The detectives were not unduly worried; they had enough paper evidence from the accounts and forgeries, from the statements from the hospital and her own relatives, on which to charge her. Later, Cowley would scratch his head in bewilderment and give one of his rueful smiles: 'There was just this complete switch-off from what she had done. A total, utter lack of emotion and an ability to distance herself from any problem, just like that . . . She is quite an amazing woman. Anyone else, you or me, faced with all that incriminating evidence, would have been scared by it all, would have some kind of emotional response. Wouldn't they?'

The police, with their stereotypical visions of good or bad, guilt and innocence, cops and robbers, were unprepared for what they faced: not just a blue-black-eyed woman, but a whole historical backdrop. Besides, Susan did try and develop a relationship with her interrogators. She asked: 'Have you seen the Heath from the west side? It looks so beautiful that way, don't you think?'

Michael was not seen until the second day because he had been brought up from London after being arrested. While he was certainly more forthcoming than the others, Detective Inspector Eamon Croft and Detective Constable Andy McVicar knew they had trouble when he started explaining that, well, yes, he only been 'technically married' to Susan; that some of the financial dealings were because she was still 'fiscally married' to Simon Dale. Lady Illingworth, he said, was 'life rented' through her trust.

Interviewing him was complicated by his insistence on adding superfluous detail, such as informing them that Major Ward had 'commanded the King's Troop of the Royal Horse Artillery', and by his inability to refer to any solicitor without adding his full company name and address. But they sat up when he referred to Sexton as 'a solicitor of the Supreme Court of England'. It was precisely the ornate phrase used in one of Lady Illingworth's supposed authorities. Coming on top of the other letters they had discovered, the dealings with Sexton and his behaviour at the bank and York House, they knew they had enough to bring a case against him.

The questioning went on all day. At 6 p.m., Michael joined the others to be taken before a magistrate in Hereford who granted the police an extension to the time they were allowed before charging or releasing anyone. Just before 10.30 p.m. Michael was charged with conspiracy to defraud Margaret, Lady Illingworth of Denton.

Later that night, Marcus broke down when questioned about

his father. 'I was just so exhausted. They kept saying, "You must have helped out, Marcus, you must have known what was going on. C'mon, Marcus, tell us the truth and you will be all right, it will all be all right." But I know what our story was and I just kept repeating it. Funnily enough, I felt quite safe because I knew I had not done anything.'

The next morning, a subdued Michael was taken before a special sitting of Hereford Magistrates' Court and remanded in custody. As he was being taken back to the cells to await transfer to Gloucester prison, he asked to see DI Croft and made a further statement about the murder which greatly excited detectives. Michael said that on the Saturday morning after Simon had been murdered, he was staying at Francesca's and had received a telephone call from Susan. 'Michael,' she had said, 'the inevitable has happened. Simon has been killed.' She could have known this only if she had seen the body before it was discovered by Giselle Wall. The implications were obvious.

As Michael was unburdening himself to DI Croft, it was clear that the police were not going to make any further progress on the fraud. The positions were clear; no one was going to confess. It was time to charge them. At 5.40 p.m., Susan was taken from her cell to the custody area at Hereford police station and charged with conspiracy to defraud her aunt, Lady Illingworth, together with Michael, Marcus and Sophia. The children were both charged within minutes of each other just after 7 p.m. At 12.30 the next morning, they and their mother were taken to Hereford Magistrates' Court and remanded in custody.

Later that day, all three Wilberforces were questioned in detail on Michael's allegations about the murder. What about the telephone call, DI Cowley asked Susan? 'You cannot prove I called him,' she said. 'I don't know the telephone number.' They would never be able to confirm that she did. Sophia, according to Michael, had also made a telephone call that morning while on her way to the wedding in Kent. Questioned, she also denied it. The murder charge would have to wait. Bullock set about writing what became a 340-page report on the murder for the Crown Prosecution Service (CPS), which had to decide whether they should be charged.

*

In the middle of the night of her arrival at Pucklechurch remand centre in Gloucestershire, Sophia broke. Unable to cope with the remorse over her father's murder and with her mother's level of dishonesty, Sophia entered a state of shock from which she may not yet have fully recovered. 'I went completely off my trolley. It was my freak-out.' Going through her head was a minor mugging which she had endured during her Spanish holiday and which had not troubled her since – at least not until the police had kept asking her to go through it, repeatedly saying 'You will understand why . . .' She heard the voices of her mother, her solicitor, she demanded to see a police officer. She began screaming. 'I just cracked up. I started to hear voices at three in the morning. I heard my own voice and it sounded different. I thought the world had gone mad.' She stopped eating and lost a lot of weight.

Marcus was in Shrewsbury and Susan all the way up at Risley remand centre in Cheshire. The ensuing weeks were interrupted by their remand appearances in court rather than by Christmas and the New Year.

The return journeys from court to prison allowed the detectives, who had now become well known to Sophia and Marcus, the opportunity to have a few unofficial words. And they made it clear they were talking about the murder, not the fraud. According to Sophia and Marcus, they would say things like 'You know, it's best to make a clean breast of it . . .' or 'We know you went back to the house, Sophia, and cleared up after the murder. Why don't you tell us about it?' And 'If you tell us everything, it won't be so bad.' Sophia said: 'They must have thought I was the weak link or something, but I told them not to bother trying. I told them I was being totally straight and honest with them and could not say any more.' Unlike his sister, Marcus would not engage them in conversation. They gave up trying.

On 6 January, Susan, Marcus and Sophia were taken to Hereford police station and charged with the murder of Simon Dale. Marcus remembers: 'There were loads of police around and I knew something was going on. I saw Mother at the desk and although they hustled me past and into a corner, I could hear. Then they charged me.' Sophia: 'They were all really excited, it was like they were all hyped up about something, like they were on drugs. They were hoping to shock us into confession. I didn't know what was going on, but as my mother was taken past me, she mouthed something about a murder charge and then I knew.'

The casual conversations in the cars continued. 'Anything you want to talk to me about today, Sophia?' her interrogators would ask. It was fruitless. Meanwhile, the enquiries into the allegations by Michael about the telephone call had reached a dead end. They could never prove the call had been made when he said it had been made; his own account was liable to variation; there was no proof Susan knew the number he was on. It was clear that the hoped-for evidence to seal the case was not going to be forthcoming.

Towards the end of January, Cole and Bullock met with senior CPS lawyers who, from the first, had been reluctant to bring the murder charges against anyone. It was decided to continue with the case against Susan – there was enough evidence to let a jury decide. The charge against Sophia and Marcus would be dropped. For them, the relief was immense. Marcus: 'It was an absolute bloody farce. There was damn-all evidence. They hadn't a leg to stand on.' Sophia: 'Well, the charge should never have been brought in the first place. It was only right. We didn't kill our father.' And neither, they said, did their mother.

Susan arrived at Pucklechurch. She had been allowed her request to move from Risley to 'look after my daughter', now a deeply confused person, shortly to begin psychiatric counselling. Sophia did not know how to react to her mother, except that she had questions to ask. 'I said to her that if she had really loved me, she would not have put me in this position and done it so calmly. When I started asking her about the bank accounts or why I spent all the time up that scaffold when we were supposed to have this money, she would pretend she hadn't heard or say things like "Oh don't go on about it" or "Stop being so bitchy" and simply change the subject.'

From then on, she blocked things out. 'I still felt deeply fond of my mother. I mean, if you have loved somebody more than anybody else and everything falls apart, you just don't lose it straightaway. You just become rather disillusioned, don't you? Things went back to normal after a while. Everybody said how nice it was for mother and daughter to be locked up together.'

Marcus had been in Winson Green prison, with 'a wing full of murderers'. ('I felt quite safe – they seemed quite nice people.') Then to Gloucester, where Michael avoided him.

A few weeks later, Marcus and Sophia returned to Hereford Crematorium, each accompanied by two prison officers. The same ovens that consumed Aunt Puss now despatched Simon Dale, his body released by police to Sebastian, who took the ashes away in a casket. About twenty people braved the February cold. Alexander was in Japan and could not come; Simon gave Sebastian a lift and would not stay. There were Dale's two elderly sisters and some old friends from Oxford. The Bowaters and friends were not asked; Susan declined her invitation. It would have been hypocritical, she said.

9
Bollocks, Mr Palmer

Within a few sentences of the start of his opening speech to the jury at Worcester Crown Court on a sweltering July day in 1989, Anthony Palmer QC had reached a point where he could summarise the prosecution case quite simply: 'This killing was the culmination and high point of a long history of bitter discord between this woman and her husband.' That, essentially, was what it was all about.

Susan stood composed and aloof in the dock, twenty months since that traumatic winter. If she had chosen to display such involvement – and she did not – she could have turned and looked upwards to see the crowded public gallery above the large, Victorian courtroom. The affair had attracted considerable interest, even in an area which had seen more than its fair share of strange and interesting murder cases. Many of Simon Dale's friends were in the public gallery; she might have seen Sebastian and Simon; she would not have spotted Sophia and Marcus.

By now, they were taking a different view of their mother. In the spring after Simon's funeral, Sophia and Marcus had been released on bail. Sophia went back to Docklow and to Oats, the cat, to 'blank out' before moving to stay with Sebastian in London and work as a temporary secretary again. Marcus went to Heath House, alone, as caretaker. He had suffered the same kind of shock, but with less effect, when told about his mother's activities. That shock was reinforced dramatically when, in paperwork disclosed to their lawyers, they saw the evidence from the police investigations: columns of figures, the bank accounts, the money transfers and the forgeries. They had known nothing about all this, they said; Mother always provided.

This prompted them to change solicitors from the Worcester firm which represented their mother to a Birmingham company, Glaisyers, which specialised in difficult and contentious cases. It was a critical psychological break: they were doing something of their own accord, for themselves, and not, as so often had been the case, in the service of their mother. It was also a necessary break: their paths had diverged and they would need to mount their own defence, at odds with their mother's account of events. But that was still months away. First their mother would be tried for murdering their father; even if they had wanted to, they could not attend because of the possibility that they might be called as witnesses. However, Michael, freed on bail only after his application to a High Court judge and the offer of sureties of £240,000, would not now give evidence against Susan. He had appeared at the committal, but his testimony added little and appeared confused on a number of key points. It was decided to make do without him.

The law dictated that the media had been unable to report what most people with any interest in the affair knew anyway: after Worcester there would be another trial later over the defrauding of Lady Illingworth. That would have been good enough in its own right, but coupled with the accusation that Susan had murdered her ex-husband, the eccentric, half-blind Simon Dale, and in a lonely mansion, it was enough to fuel the gossips of the villages and market towns of the borders for months. The media were not far behind, eager to see the crime-fiction cliché of the country-house murder actually brought to life. The public gallery and the press box were packed to see the 'The Baroness' on trial.

The British system of adversarial justice, in which an advocate will attempt to prove the guilt of the accused, who is defended by another advocate, both armed with a set of rules and precedents, has been much criticised for turning justice into a game whereby both sides attempt to catch each other out, while sometimes actually failing to get at the truth. But time and time again, the courts, with their ritualised opportunities for conflict and oratory, have shown their capability for turning this contest into great theatre. The public came to Worcester expecting a show; they were not to be disappointed.

Susan's trial achieved theatricality simply: there were no smoking guns, no giveaway bloodstains, no witnesses to the crime. It was a case based entirely on circumstantial evidence: the jury would simply have to decide whether, given what they were told about the background circumstances of these rather odd people and lacking any direct piece of evidence, this woman, for the reasons outlined, picked up a crowbar and bludgeoned her former husband to death. In essence, it was to be a single-issue trial and the issue was Susan; Anthony Palmer made that clear in his opening of the case for the prosecution.

Palmer is a short, bespectacled man, formal and precise; highly respected both as prosecution and defence advocate, he had been selected as one of the best cross-examiners in the country, who would have to fight a courtroom duel with Susan, this extraordinary woman of little emotion.

The prosecutor outlined to the judge, Mr Justice Owen, and the jury of eight men and four women how Susan and Simon had met and married, and he described the breakdown of their relationship and the divorce settlement. He spoke of Simon's resistance to being moved from Heath House and of Susan's life at Docklow and her brief marriage to the Baron. He told the jury how she and the three children had returned to Heath House to work on the gardens and exterior of the house and how they had watched his movements, intercepted his mail, harassed his visitors and removed items from the house.

He said it was clear that Dale had been murdered on the evening of Friday, 11 September, after he had put his toad-in-the-hole into the oven. Palmer then turned to Susan's movements over the weekend and the implications drawn from them by police. He finished his opening: 'The accused had every motive for wanting to see Mr Dale off the face of the earth, and she had a hatred for him that had built up over the years and festered.' It was an effective beginning.

The rest of the prosecution case was an amplification of this thesis. The essential problem for the police and prosecutors was that all of their evidence was circumstantial. Over the next two days a succession of witnesses, including all of Simon Dale's recent secretaries and visitors, gave evidence as to his blindness, his relationship with Susan, the fact that he would not let anyone into the house he did not know, the fact that Susan appeared to have entered the house several times without his knowledge and removed furniture. Lynne Williams, his cleaner for two hours every week, said he was very security-conscious and kept doors locked: 'I do not recollect any occasion on which he let anyone he did not know into the house.' She said that she believed someone else was also trying to clean the house because once she had found that someone had polished the floor and spilt Brasso, the cleaning agent.

Adrian Tindall, the former Hereford and Worcester archaeological officer, was one of a number of witnesses who spoke of strange meetings with Susan in the grounds of Heath House. And he told the jury of the jemmy or crowbar she had been carrying. Tindall told Palmer that the next time he had seen the object was when he was asked by police to examine a variety of implements at Kidderminster police station. He said: 'None of them had any significance until I came to the crowbar and I realised that was the item she had had over her arm with which to defend herself.' It was the one recovered from the cottage.

Dr Acland, the Home Office pathologist, told how he had examined the body at the scene and described the positions of the blows on the head and throat. 'In my opinion, the jemmy of all the implements I saw was most likely to have caused the wounds. If it had been wielded by a man I would have expected a skull fracture.' When compared against the wounds, it had the best fit. But under cross-examination from Susan's counsel, Anthony Arlidge QC, he conceded that it was impossible to draw any firm conclusion about the sex, size and weight of the attacker. He could not say the murder weapon definitely was the crowbar. It was the first real point to the defence.

The next day the court heard of the events on the day of the murder. Jo Corfield, Susan Evans and Ben Scott, Simon's visitors, recounted their recollections, Scott in particular describing his encounter with Susan in the cellar. With the image fresh in the minds of the jury, of Scott's and Evans's departure in the mist and drizzle, as Susan lurked in the grounds of Heath House, Palmer performed his equivalent of the film director's single dramatic cut. The court was to adjourn, he said, to the old law library upstairs to see a video of the murder scene with the body still in place.

Everyone filed upstairs to see the carefully edited highlights of the hours of film taken by the video crew on that September afternoon and evening nearly two years previously. The film showed Dale lying on his back with his eyes screwed up and his mouth open. His hands were on his chest with his fingers clutching his jumper. A pool of blood had flowed away from his head and had dried on the blue-and-white tiled floor. A broken basin was on the floor near by. The camera panned across the big refectory table: papers neatly arranged in piles, a Welsh railway timetable and a cardboard box into which Dale had bled profusely. On the working surface were five sherry glasses – one with sherry still in it. For fifteen minutes, Susan sat at the front between two women prison officers, watching the video. She was expressionless.

The following day began with Dr Norman Weston, the jovial Yorkshire-born forensic scientist, whose evidence was crucial to both sides. For the prosecution, it had to be suggested to the jury that the absence of any scientific evidence – such as bloodstains or fingerprints – linking Susan with the crime suggested her guilt rather than innocence, by implying that she had thoroughly cleaned up behind her in the two days available. The defence would seize upon the thoroughness of the scientific investigation and its failure to find anything linking her to the murder as conclusive proof of her innocence.

Dr Weston, veteran of the courtroom as well as the murder scene, explained how he had concluded that Dale had been struck on the head or face while standing just in front of the door. He believed Dale had been pushed into the room from the door and had struck the heavy table, moving it slightly. Dr Weston believed Dale could then have received a heavy blow across the throat causing a substantial injury, which made blood rush through the nose and mouth. It appeared that he had pivoted round towards the kitchen door and ended by falling backwards so that his head struck the floor with some force.

Cross-examined by Arlidge, Dr Weston said there were also bloodstains on the plant stand, the legs of a chair, the skirting board and the back of the door itself. The blows to the head and one to the throat had occurred over a period of time; there could also have been a struggle near the fridge. Dr Weston explained to the jury how he had taken hair samples from everyone who might have been in the kitchen, including Susan. He had positively identified hairs from Dale. One hair could not be matched with any of the controls, he said, although this was not unusual. Dr Weston told Arlidge that he could not exclude the possibility that some hairs found at the scene might have come from someone else.

He also described how he had recovered some red fibres from the frame and jamb of the door and had tried unsuccessfully to match them with everything in Dale's house and with clothing and a wool car-rug which belonged to Susan. Yes, he said, he had also examined her car thoroughly for blood and other clues; but no, nothing that could connect it with Dale had been found. He took swabs from the sinks of Heath Cottage, but found no signs of blood. There was no blood on her shoes and gumboots. He had found turquoise carpet fibres in the kitchen, but had failed to match them with anything connected with the Baroness or Dale. After this litany, Arlidge waited until the last moment to deliver his punchline: 'The upshot of all this is that you could find absolutely nothing to connect the Baroness with the scene of the crime?' Dr Weston replied: 'I found no positive connection.' Shortly afterwards the trial adjourned for the weekend.

On the Monday, DI Matthews described his encounter with Susan on the night of the discovery of the body. Under cross-examination, he admitted that at one stage police had wanted to find a man – the so-called hitchhiker – with long hair and an anorak seen twice on the road outside Heath House on the night of the murder. Despite public appeals, he had never been traced or eliminated.

When DC O'Keefe, one of Susan's interrogators, entered the box, he casually introduced one of the more bizarre moments of the trial. Susan, he said, had described to police how once during that summer she had seen a woman banging on the door of Heath House shouting, 'Let me in, you bastard!' The woman left and Susan claimed she had then seen Dale through a window, wearing lipstick, tatty trousers and grey ladies' high-heeled shoes. He was making faces at himself in a mirror, imitating the woman. She also told O'Keefe, he said, that she had seen Dale wear high-heeled shoes on numerous occasions and that he had asked her to put ladies' face cream on him. She added that during their marriage he had been interested in anal sex and that, when she had refused to satisfy that interest, he had said she was inhibited. The press scribbled away furiously. The half-blind, dotty architect who believed his mansion to be Camelot was now revealed as a putative cross-dresser with a penchant for buggery.

It is not entirely clear why the prosecution sought to introduce this element, except as further evidence of motive by stressing his unpleasant side. The question of cross-dressing was certainly completely inconsistent with Simon's character, which appeared to be thoroughly heterosexual right up until his death. Although the suggestion sounded implausible – he was a large man with feet seemingly too bulky to cram into even the biggest pair of women's shoes – Sophia said she had seen him wearing them and he had provided a possible, if odd, explanation. But this might just have been seized upon by Susan to discredit Simon, and the fact that he could hardly see would seem to rule out any sense of satisfaction from looking at himself in the mirror. Police certainly found two pairs of women's shoes in the house; they never found the woman at the door.

O'Keefe said that Susan had told her interrogators about Dale's changing moods, his demands for sex and the deterioration of the relationship after the birth of Marcus, which had led to her great fear of him. The jury also heard the story about the grave he was said to have dug for her and then her explanation of the jemmy. Her statements to police contained a number of inconsistencies and some of her replies were evasive, said DC O'Keefe. And that was the end of the prosecution case.

The task for the defence counsel Anthony Arlidge was simply to present Susan's side of the story with enough vigour to counter the rather weak prosecution case. Where Palmer had presented a straightforward, conventional case, the younger, more easy-going Arlidge aimed to show the other side of the coin. He began by telling the jury that the reason for calling Susan to the witness box was quite simply so that she could tell them herself that she was not the person who had murdered Simon Dale. From her innocent behaviour at Heath House, he said, suspicion had been drawn to her. Susan had gone home that evening and watched Agatha Christie's famous detective,

Miss Marple, on the television. 'Perhaps,' suggested Arlidge, 'the Baroness could do with Miss Marple's assistance now.'

When Susan took the stand the following morning she was wearing her characteristic colours: a blue flower-pattern pleated skirt, a white high-necked blouse and light-blue jacket. Throughout the proceedings she had been poker-faced and distant, almost indifferent to these discussions taking place around her. Her manner suggested that they might all relate to someone else, not her. Generations of Wilberforces ensured that there were no shows of emotion on her face, no tell-tale body language. The only breaks in the façade came when she occupied herself by writing music on a piece of paper or when, because of the stifling temperatures, she took her shoes off in the dock.

Everyone knew that this could be the pivotal point of the trial. Susan was nervous and wiped the palms of her hands before taking the oath, but she managed to summon-up a firm, clear voice and a polished accent. Her testimony was, and remains, her only public defence of her actions throughout both the murder and fraud cases. The first part would be the easy bit; her own counsel would not give her a rough ride. At the beginning, she spoke very quietly and the judge was forced to ask her to go and sit next to him, closer to the jury. When her voice gained in power and confidence, she was moved back.

Susan was carefully taken through her story by Arlidge, emphasising Simon's aggressive behaviour towards her and the children, his obsessions, his intransigence over the sale of Heath House. She explained how all her money had been spent on the renovations; how they had no social life because he would shut himself away; and how her back had suffered permanent damage because of his blows.

She explained her attitude to Simon's visitors: 'I wanted the house to be sold very much, but I was thwarted by Simon. He would make excuses such as his grandmother dying to break arrangements with people coming to view the house. This went on for years and years and years. His solicitor sent a letter saying he would not agree to the property being put on the market and any agreement from 1973 was now void. He had expressed interest in buying the house himself, but it was one of the many delaying tactics which he carried out for years. Simon was wasting a lot of people's time telling them it was his house and that I had nothing to do with it. That was why I told his visitors not to go to the house.

'Simon had arranged for archaeological digs to take place at the property. I objected very much because professionals had told him there was nothing of interest there. Nobody would want to buy a house when the garden looked like a bomb site. He was trying to get everybody to believe it was the seat of the Arthurian legends, and he was determined to stay there. He wanted to make it the biggest archaeological site in the country.'

Before she and the children had begun work on Heath House in March 1986, 'absolutely nothing whatever' had been done to maintain the house and gardens. 'The grounds were very overgrown, the drives were clogged up with young trees, there were brambles and nettles everywhere and it was appalling. I started working on the house because things were progressing quite nicely on the legal front to get him out, and something had to be done before the house fell down because it had not been painted for years.'

She said that at first Simon had let them in through the front door, but then had become nasty. 'We used to get in through the cloakroom window.' She added: 'We went into the house mainly for painting, but he turned nasty and would not let us in about a month after we started working there. There was one occasion when I went to warn him about some chemicals we had put in a water pot, and he was hostile and aggressive. He was extremely abusive and told me to get out all the time. He did not want to know. I was frightened of Simon. I was frightened he would do what he used to do when he beat me up.' Susan said that on both occasions when she had admitted attacking him it was in response to his aggression.

Under careful encouragement from Arlidge, Susan explained that she had bought the case opener (the crowbar) when she had needed something strong to hack down the undergrowth in the grounds of Heath House. Yes, she said, as Adrian Tindall suggested, she had walked around the garden with it hooked over her arm. 'I hoped he [Simon] would think twice about attacking me if he saw the case opener over my arm. I used to keep it hanging on the door of what we used as the tool cupboard in the kitchen [of Heath Cottage]. Everybody knew where it was.'

It was 'utter nonsense', she said, to suggest she was hanging around Heath House on the Friday night because she had decided to kill him or confront him. When Arlidge asked if she knew he was dead when she set off for Heath House the following day, Susan replied: 'No, of course not. I didn't think he would attack me with a chainsaw in my hand.'

After taking Susan through the explanation she had given police of her movements over the weekend, Arlidge asked about the visit from Matthews and Clarke on the Sunday night. This, he said, had led the police to allege that she showed no reaction because she knew Dale was dead. Susan said she had always been brought up not to show emotion. 'I used to be sat on a chair for ten minutes when I was six and I had to keep absolutely still and not bat an eyelid. I did not ask how he died because I assumed that, if they wanted to tell me, they would do so. They adopted such an extraordinarily furtive manner that I thought there was no point in asking anybody anything.'

Arlidge concluded: 'Were you the person who went into the lobby and struck Simon Dale with a weapon causing his death?' Susan: 'No, I was not. That is utter nonsense. After I saw the visitors go on the Friday evening, I saw Simon Dale walk through the Rocking Horse Room in the house, continue along the glass passageway, check the front door and walk across the hall. That was the last time I saw him. My son and I then went back to the cottage, collected some things and drove to Docklow.' Arlidge sat down.

The whole courtroom knew that the real test would come in the cross-examination, which began in the afternoon. Palmer knew that his fundamental lack of a smoking gun among the evidence made this his best chance of convincing the jury of her guilt. For several hours, in a model of incisive cross-examination, he relentlessly probed and prodded, hoping for a fatal slip or indiscretion. The questions came rapidly and fluently, occasionally changing tack completely, prowling around the edges and sometimes sweeping in for the kill. Or what he believed to be the kill. By now Susan had told her side of the story many times and was entirely confident. As their duel continued, she gained in strength, winning many of the exchanges and using manner and voice firmly to put down Palmer, unfortunately already at a physical disadvantage because of his height and the relative position of the witness box. Even the judge would later refer to her calmness under persistent questioning. The public gallery and press box were packed.

Palmer, looking up at Susan over the top of his glasses, began by asking: 'The object was to watch his every move and try and outwit him. There was a war of wills between you.'

Susan: 'Yes, I think you are right in that.'

'Would you agree that you were both obsessed characters? You had an obsession that he was going to stay there as long as he could.'

'No, I was not obsessed with it. I was just fed up with the situation.'

'Would you regard yourself as a strong-willed woman?'

'Yes.'

'There was not a glimmer of love between you by 1987?'

'Yes.'

'He had treated you and the children badly.'

'Yes.'

'The love had gone out of the marriage by 1962.'

'Yes – earlier than that.'

'Do you think he was mad?'

'Yes.'

'Since when?'

'About a year and a half before I started the divorce proceedings.'

These exchanges continued for some time. As Palmer grew more insistent, Susan's replies became more robust. Courtroom observers noted that she spoke as if to a family retainer. When Palmer suggested again and again that Susan had been angry with Dale on the night of his death she eventually replied: 'Bollocks, Mr Palmer, that's absolute nonsense.' (During his summing up, the judge took care to remind the jury that this type of word was now in everyday use and no particular inference should be drawn from it.) 'It was just a great nuisance and a waste of energy, but I was not angry and bitter.'

'You hated him, didn't you?'

'No, I did not. I was exasperated by him, but I did not hate him. I did not feel anything particularly.'

'The evidence is that on the Friday night you were angry.'

'I suggest the evidence is wrong – that is the truth.'

As Palmer persisted, she summoned her full aristocratic weight and countered, with some sharpness: 'I wish you'd get it into your head, Mr Palmer, that I was not angry.' The vehemence of her tone showed that she could at least become angry with him. One of the best criminal advocates in the country was now on the defensive.

Susan made it abundantly clear that she had harboured an intense dislike for her former husband's visitors, including one particular close friend: 'There was this woman, Mrs Bowater, who was the bane of my life and used to insist on taking visitors round my house when it was in a most appalling state. I am all for visitors going round a house when it is clean and tidy, but not when it is a complete slum. I think it sets an awfully bad example of how people live.'

Palmer then tried to deal with the events of 11 September. He said: 'I do not suggest you planned to kill Mr Dale over any length of time. I am suggesting that on Friday, 11 September, things were so building up in your mind that you went to have a confrontation with him and that is when you killed him. You were very pent up indeed.'

'No. At no time that day was I pent up.'

'You were sad when the marriage with the Baron ended. You loved him very much.'

'Yes,' said Susan. She replied in a different, quieter voice.

'On 11 September 1987, no doubt you thought back to your marriage with the Baron – exactly three years before.'

'No. I didn't realise it was my wedding anniversary.'

'Sophia drove herself home early because she was fed up and tired. That left you and Marcus to move the scaffolding.'

'Yes. We chose to move it.'

'You realised that with two people each regarding the other as mad, one was going to be injured by the other. That was why you carried this jemmy.'

'No – it was not. He was more and more determined never to get out. I regarded him as becoming more mad than I had regarded him in the past. On the Friday night, I was waiting for the visitors to go, but not so I would know that Simon Dale was alone. I was waiting for them to go so I could walk through the arch without interrupting their conversation. Marcus and I stayed out there. We were just going for a little walk to admire the work we had done on the house.'

'There was no reason for you to be there save to watch Mr Dale to make sure he was alone in the house. Marcus went across to feed a colony of bees – do you recollect this?'

'No, I don't remember it.'

'Before 1973, Simon Dale struck you many times. You were apart from 1973 to 1986. After you started working in the grounds of Heath House, did he strike you at all?'

'No.'

'But in 1986 you were willing to show violence to him.'

'It has been blown up out of all proportion.'

'You went to confront him, didn't you?'

'No, I didn't, Mr Palmer. I have never confronted him verbally – it has been handled through solicitors. There would not have been any point because he would just have become abusive.'

Later, Palmer said: 'You went there on Saturday because you knew Simon Dale was dead.'

'No, I didn't.'

'You were walking with impunity past the house and into the walled garden – breaking the habit of several months.'

'He would not have known I was there.'

'You twice went to that house when he lay dead on the Saturday morning.'

'Yes – but I think you forget I am a woman. This is a case against a woman made up by men.' Palmer, who had obviously been somewhat disconcerted by the vigour of Susan's replies, was again taken aback. It was clear that neither enjoyed being spoken to in this fashion.

Palmer began the next morning by suggesting that after her first interview on the Monday after the murder, Susan had talked with Sophia and Marcus about what they had told police and had amended her second statement accordingly. As a result, there were inconsistencies in her evidence about the route she had walked in the garden of Heath House when she went to put the brick on the beehive.

She replied sharply and imperiously: 'There seems to be no inconsistency no matter how much you twist it. Now stop it, Mr Palmer.' The court stirred at such impertinence. Palmer attempted to regain control. He said: 'You will please confine yourself to the question.' But by now Susan would not be broken. 'When I was interviewed,' she insisted, 'my children were interviewed at the same time and were taken off to different parts of the country. When we got back in the morning, we did not speak to each other because we were just too tired.'

'You added these facts between Monday and Wednesday.'

'So what?'

'I suggest you went there to see what had been found out and to take the case opener back.'

'You can suggest that until you are blue in the face, but it is not true.'

'You are very cunning and clever at being able to say what suits you, aren't you?'

'No.'

'It was the first time you had swept the chimney at Docklow. You were trying to make sure that every bit of evidence you had burnt on the fire had been destroyed.'

'No.'

'What you blurted out [about Dale burning down Heath House] was a self-conscious thought about the oven and cooker. You thought the house had caught fire, didn't you?'

'I had no such thought.'

'It would have taken you a moment to get the jemmy and go round to his kitchen door for a verbal confrontation. You realised the leopard would never change his spots and he would never leave.'

'It doesn't make sense for me to have killed him. The courts were going to get him out cleanly and legally. I believed it for the first time in fifteen years.'

'Having watched the visitors go and him lock up, you used that weapon on him.'

'No, I didn't. As far as I can remember, I was together with Marcus the whole time after the visitors left.'

'Has Marcus anything to hide about this matter?'

'Certainly not. He was given a grilling for hours on end, and if he had anything to hide the police would have discovered it.

I know perfectly well none of my children would have hidden anything if I had done it. They would not have approved of that. They were grilled for hours and hours, and never once did they incriminate me.'

She went on: 'This was a crime I had nothing to do with, and I didn't even have a motive. There was no point in my killing him when the courts were going to get him out. I agree I had the opportunity and the weapon, but there are millions of jemmies in the world. Why should I have killed him? Think of all the hassle I have had since. It would have been much easier to have let the courts deal with him. I was amazed when they arrested me because I knew I had not done it.'

It was her closing speech. Most felt she had won on points.

Anthony Palmer summoned his most grave demeanour to begin his final address. He would have to regain the ground many believed he had lost during the cross-examination.

Five questions faced the jury, he said. First, when was Dale killed? All the indications were that it was on the Friday night. Secondly, who was at Heath House when he was killed? The Baroness and Marcus. 'Why was she watching the visitors? Was it to see them go? There was plenty of time for her, if she was angry and uptight, to get the jemmy in order to go round and have a verbal confrontation with him.' Thirdly, how was Simon Dale killed? The size, shape and angle of the injuries accorded with a jemmy; Susan always carried one. 'Have you any doubt that it [the murder weapon] was this?'

Fourthly, who had the motive for frustration and explosion? 'This was not a premeditated murder. This happened like a domestic killing with a build-up and then an explosion. There was loveless marriage, a settlement Simon Dale would not stick to and a valuable house as the battleground for total war. She agreed with me that this was war and in a war someone is likely to get injured or killed. She knew the leopard would never change his spots. There was no other visitor that night. The only visitor he received was his ex-wife.'

Fifthly, who benefited from Dale's death? 'After Dale's killing, she was back in possession of her own house.'

*

Arlidge rose again. From the start he had adopted a relaxed approach. Now he addressed the jury in his most chatty fashion: 'If you have an ex-wife whose husband is killed and who has been advertising to all and sundry her animosity towards him, a wife who stands to gain by his death, it is all too easy not to look any further.' The mystery man, the hitchhiker, seen nearby had never been located; there was no reason to suggest that, simply because Dale opened the door, it was to someone he knew; the jemmy was not the only type of object that could have caused the wounds.

Most of the evidence, he said, had been revealed to the police by the Baroness herself. Apart from a few minor details, her story had been consistent and the Crown had emphasised the trivial. 'Only one trace of blood and her story would have been exposed.' This woman, he said, had been grilled by the police and cross-examined at length by Palmer. 'Not once had she given herself away.'

Mr Justice Owen began summing up on the morning of 31 July, the tenth day of the trial. Until then, he had kept silent, rarely interrupting proceedings. Now, when it was most important, he came into his own to deliver a crisply efficient summing up. It would be a particularly critical one. Susan's trial was straightforward but finely balanced: only a small amount of material was disputed: One hint from the judge on one point rather than another, delivered consciously or not, could lead the jury in either direction. Mr Justice Owen was impeccably balanced.

Looking directly at the jury, he first explained the difference between murder and manslaughter. Murder, he said, was committed when the accused had a deliberate intent to kill; a manslaughter verdict could arise only if the jury agreed that the accused had committed the crime, but believed that the provocation was so great that a reasonable person might have acted in the same way. He then outlined the most vital issue on which the question of Susan's motivation rested, a question which the jury would need to have foremost in their minds: 'She says she did not hate her husband, but there had been no love between them for twenty-five years. She thought he was mad. How much further it went, you will have to judge. Although Simon Dale had thwarted her wishes for fourteen years, there was a procedure, which might or might not have been successful, to lead to the eviction of Simon Dale from that house. It must have ultimately been successful because nobody could go on denying the law forever.'

If the jurors were satisfied that Susan did commit the murder, said the judge, they would have to consider the issue of provocation. 'Firstly, did his conduct cause her to lose her self-control? It is correct to say he was awkward in the extreme and may well have provoked some people. Secondly, would that conduct have caused any reasonable person to lose their self-control and do this to him?'

Of Susan's reference to Dale dressing up in women's shoes, the judge cautioned the jury that they must decide whether it was relevant. On Susan's statements to police, so carefully extracted with so much preparation in that interview suite at Hereford, the judge was dismissive: 'An awful lot of it does not carry the case forward one little tiny bit.' So ended the first day of the summing up.

The following morning, Mr Justice Owen continued: 'The prosecution case is that of course the Baroness knew it was the anniversary of her wedding to the Baron, whom she still loved. When she contemplated Simon Dale, who was living still in her house, it was too much for her. They say it had a significance in her mind that was far deeper. It is a suggestion, but I say to you that suggestions are not evidence. You have to ask what her true feelings were at the time for Simon Dale. She says she did not hate him and you have to bear in mind whether that is a true answer.

'The accused has said that this was a war of wills. He was not frightened of her, indeed she says that she was frightened of him. Was she frightened, however, if she was armed? The prosecution say she must have attacked him and, if Dr Acland is right, it was a woman wielding the weapon. The suggestion is that there was blood on her clothes and eventually she burned them, and they [the prosecution] draw attention to the cleaning of the chimney flue at Docklow.'

The judge posed a series of questions for the jury: were they sure that Susan killed Simon Dale? If she had done so, was it by a deliberate or unlawful act? If the answer was yes, said the judge, were they sure that, at the time, she intended either to kill him or to cause him serious physical harm? Might she, continued the judge, have been provoked by things said and done? If the answer to that was no, then Susan was guilty of murder; if the answer was yes, the jurors would have to ask themselves one final question: was the provocation such that a reasonable person might have acted in the same way? If the answer was yes, then Susan was guilty of manslaughter; if the answer was no, then she was guilty of murder.

The jury were led from the courtroom.

Four hours later, in mid-afternoon, the verdict came. 'Not guilty,' said the foreman. Susan stared, as blankly and aloofly as she had done from the start. The court erupted. Someone threw her flowers. Downstairs, Susan was allowed a few minutes with Sophia, Marcus and Sebastian. She told them it had taken a second or two to realise she had been cleared; she had hardly heard the verdict because of a slight ear infection.

The meeting was, according to their account, as subdued as that when they were first told of Simon's murder: 'Full of relief, but no elation. The charge should never have been brought.' For about thirty seconds, she broke. 'It was the closest I have ever seen her to tears. Then she brought herself back under control,' said Marcus. Asked about it later, she gave a characteristic little dismissive shrug of the shoulders, as if to say it was really all rather trivial, gone, forgotten. 'Before I went on trial,' she said, 'they [the police] asked me if I would plead guilty to manslaughter. They said I would get a light sentence. I knew I was innocent so I was not going to plead guilty just so that they could clear up the murder.'

Another period of limbo. Susan was back at Pucklechurch. Michael, who had lurked in the background throughout the trial, was with his second wife, Francesca Tesi, in St John's Wood.

Once a week, Marcus and Sophia travelled to Birmingham to spend several hours with Ewen Smith, their new lawyer, working their way through dozens of volumes of evidence and statements gathered by the police. Smith's firm had to clear space in a special office for it all; the second trial would be held in the city. Sophia was having trouble coming to terms with what was on the pages in front of her – often her mind just refused to accept any of it. Instead, she would volunteer to make coffee for everyone.

Marcus, at Heath House, led a melancholy existence. There was still much work to be done on the grounds; the house itself had to be maintained. Weekends would see visits by his brothers and sister. Sebastian, when he had the time, was sorting out the voluminous papers of his father, attempting to put all the architectural drawings, the correspondence and the writings into some kind of order, spreading them out across the floors, pinned down by old books. Marcus took a clerical job at a transport company in Birmingham, driving there and back each day, a long way to commute. He told friends it was to give him some idea of what it was like to work in an office, something he had never done before.

Like his father, during the long evenings he was mostly alone, walking the echoing and now dusty corridors and rooms, seeing little of the neighbours; visitors were few. In the winter, even the rooms with furniture were desperately cold and he was sparing with the electricity because he had little money. There were bad storms that season: as the wind whipped through the trees and around the house, Marcus would spend much of his time in the kitchen, cooking and warming himself with the Aga. And he would eat on the long refectory table about which his father had woven his own days and on which he had been beaten to death, but which was now washed clean of his blood. Often, his only company was Oats, the cat they had bought for Aunt Puss when she lived at Docklow. He would lie at one end of the refectory table, curled up on an old nightdress of Sophia's as cats do, seemingly half-asleep, but watching and knowing everything.

Marcus and Sophia would also go and see their mother, at Pucklechurch and then at Risley. Conversation was limited by the constraints of prison. 'When I saw her, I found it very difficult to believe that anything had happened at all,' said Sophia.

Beverley Bell, Susan's solicitor, took the prosecution papers to discuss them with Susan. The evidence the police needed to support their case was all there: perhaps the bank accounts could be explained, but the handwriting evidence on the forgeries, particularly the will, was virtually undeniable; they told their own story in a way most juries would easily grasp. Evidence of the auction sales would simply support this line. And, on top of all this, police had found a considerable number of witnesses who would spell out her aunt's mental condition and her attachment to Markington, rather than to Docklow. Among them would be her own brother, John.

Susan weighed the options. She could fight it out in court in the knowledge that she would almost certainly lose and receive a longer sentence than if she pleaded guilty now. She had been in prison almost two years; a sentence of about six or eight years would mean freedom anyway with remission within another year or eighteen months. Was it worth a fight?

Proving conspiracy often stands or falls on all the conspirators acting together. If Susan were not in court, if the main conspirator were absent, it would make the case more difficult to prove. Michael, she realised, would almost certainly be blaming her to save his own skin; he would seek to minimise his role and maximise hers. Sophia and Marcus had already told police that they had been unaware of the extent of the bank accounts and the money transfers; that would be used anyway. The possibility that they could all stand fair square and deny everything was slim. If she pleaded guilty, in the face of the damning evidence, it would at least allow her guilt to support the innocence of Sophia and Marcus, giving them a substantial defence. But this would be limited if the jury were prevented from knowing that she had pleaded guilty – the normal ruling in such cases. And would she give evidence?

On 8 December 8 1989, at Birmingham Crown Court, in a hearing unreported on the judge's orders, Susan, fidgeting in the dock, which she does when she is nervous, but summoning up her most disdainful, everything-is-such-a-bore voice, pleaded guilty to seven charges. Five related to the theft of property from Lady Illingworth, each one a different strand of the asset-stripping: money, silver, jewellery, share certificates and furniture. The other two charges were of forgery: one was the will and the other the 2 July authority to the National Westminster Bank. Sentence was postponed until after the trial of those who would now be seen as her accomplices: two of her children and her ex-husband.

10
A Malign and Appalling Influence

Birmingham Crown Court is everything the entirely undistinguished but municipally respectable, pine-fitted, modern court building should be. Although few appreciated it, it might have been more appropriate to hold the second trial a few yards across Corporation Street in the old Victoria Law Courts, a red-brick gothic fantasy of spires, gargoyles, flying buttresses and stained glass, a building that would have suited the tastes of the Yorkshire families who had created the Undercliffe Cemetery.

It is impossible to know what the jury of seven men and five women, sworn in on that chilly morning in February 1990, made of the next nine weeks. As they settled into their seats in Court Twelve, they had some foretaste of what was to come when they saw in front of them a corner of the courtroom turned into an antiques shop, featuring ornately framed pictures, large statues, jewellery, silverware, china and even pieces of furniture, each carefully labelled.

Before them were brought three people charged with each other, and with Susan de Stempel, with stealing property belonging to Lady Illingworth between 1 January 1984 and 31 December 1986. Marcus and Sophia were both slim, pale and reserved, and although of a type the jury might have recognised as 'respectable' or 'well spoken' they did not quite seem like most other young people they would have known. Next to them stood the cartoon-like figure of the Baron, plummy-voiced and ornately mannered, referred to throughout as plain Mr de Stempel. Now here was really uncharted territory.

Birmingham is a working-class city, whose inhabitants are inward-looking and parochial, devoted mostly to the production and use of the motor car in a city built in its honour. The majority do not send their children to expensive public schools or have them 'come out'; nor do they live in Grosvenor Square or country mansions; nor are they on familiar terms with barons from the more obscure European lineages. Their money is earned and their elderly relatives are cared for and not left, some might say abandoned, in dusty old flats. And what is the disgrace in bright, state-run homes like Langford House? Much of what the jury heard must have seemed like watching a television documentary on a vanished age, full of sepia-tinted photographs and bearing little relevance to their own rather humdrum lives.

What the jury did not know, and the judge and every lawyer and journalist in the court did, was that Susan had pleaded guilty to a number of charges two months previously and would be sentenced at the end of this trial. The Recorder of Birmingham, Judge Richard Curtis QC, the leading judge on the Midland and Oxford Circuit, said the jury need not concern themselves with why the Baroness was absent. But her presence hung over the proceedings as the only missing member of the cast for the second and final act of the Wilberforce courtroom drama. The court was packed with public and journalists eager to see even more dirty linen of the upper classes displayed in public.

The defence lawyers for Sophia and Marcus were carefully chosen Birmingham advocates who could talk in familiar ways to the jury, signalling that although these Wilberforces might be odd, they at least had the good sense to pick local people as their lawyers. Richard Wakerley QC, an advocate with a dramatic, aggressive touch, would represent Sophia; Marcus would be looked after by Conrad Seagrott QC, a tall, lean, energetic-looking individual. Michael had engaged a much older man, a Londoner: Richard du Cann QC, one of the most experienced barristers in the country, a former chairman of the Bar who had appeared as a junior counsel in the *Lady Chatterley* obscenity trial in the early 1960s. 'My man Du Cann', as Michael referred to him, was by far the most polished and efficient performer in court, whose turn of phrase provided the best headlines, though not always ones sympathetic to his client.

There had been considerable discussion among the barristers and Sophia's and Marcus's solicitor, Ewen Smith, over whether to call Susan as a witness. Some argued that, by allowing the jury to see this strong character, who had faced (and some said defeated) Anthony Palmer at Worcester, it would reinforce the fundamental basis of the defence case: that both young people were totally under the spell of their mother. It was a risky strategy because the Crown could have introduced evidence, through Susan, which might have damaged their case. Caution prevailed; Smith still wonders whether they did the right thing. It would certainly have created a stir.

Timothy Barnes QC opened for the Crown. Barnes, a diligent fraud specialist, was in his element. Beginning with the life of Lady Illingworth and moving through the family history, he noted the splitting of the Wilberforce assets between Susan and John and the lack of financial support Susan had received from Simon. To emphasise his point, when describing the luxurious life Lady Illingworth had enjoyed he flourished copies of photographs of 44 Grosvenor Square, taken from *Country Life* in the 1960s, not a magazine found in most Birmingham households. He outlined how Lady Illingworth, living in reduced but familiar circumstances at York House, and suffering from a progressively deteriorating mental condition, was taken to Docklow and then to Hereford County Hospital before ending her days at Langford House.

Barnes said: 'The case for the Crown is that Susan, the two children and the Baron stole Lady Illingworth's property on a massive scale and continuing basis from the moment she arrived in Docklow – money, stocks and shares, jewellery, valuable antiques, paintings and objets d'art. Anything and everything they could lay their hands on was taken and stolen. Holidays abroad were financed, new cars, a flat in Spain, expensive jewellery was purchased.

'Susan played the dominant role and exhibited a degree of callousness. It was she who forged Lady Illingworth's signature over and over again to obtain property and finance. It was Susan whose bank accounts were most substantially boosted by the sale of Lady Illingworth's property. It was Susan who refused to have Lady Illingworth back from hospital when asked if that could be done.

'These three people were willing, ready and able fellow conspirators in stealing. They were all in it together, they enjoyed the benefits, they were all living at Forresters Hall. Lady Illingworth was wholly unable to make any rational decision about her own property. They were all well aware of the scale of the property being procured and sold, and the proceeds of sale were being used for their benefit as much as for the benefit of Susan. They all played a part in the effective stripping from Lady Illingworth of her possessions.' That certainly spelt it out for the jury.

The next morning, Barnes read out the 1984 will, passing copies to the jurors. When he came to the phrase 'recognition of his having added lustre to the family name in this genera- tion', he paused: 'That is not the kind of language that Lady Illingworth would have used – it is the language and grandiose form of expression which are the hallmark of Baron Michael de Stempel, who is so concerned with matters of that sort.' The idea behind the bequests, he said, was to disarm suspicion. But there was more: 'Not only was this old lady stripped of much of her wealth during her life, but even after death she was denied her wish to be buried with her husband.'

Barnes described how Mrs Devey-Smith and Fr Dooley were asked to witness the will. 'The family were anxious', he said, 'to get Lady Illingworth out of the room when the will was signed. It was Sophia who tried to coax her out of the room. She was out of the room when her will was signed. Mrs Wilberforce brought the will into the room and it already bore the forged signature of Lady Illingworth on it.'

Docklow, said Barnes, had become a 'forgery factory' where Lady Illingworth's signature had been repeatedly forged on a variety of documents in pursuit of the asset-stripping, proving the involvement of those in the dock. 'Any of these defendants could have come into the room and said: "What are you doing signing Aunt Puss's signature?" They were all aware of this systematic forgery.'

On day three, the first witness to enter the box was John Wilberforce, now sixty, tall, grey-haired and grey-suited. For such a desperately introverted man, the box must have been an ordeal; the fact that he was giving evidence against his sister, about intimate family matters, must have been truly agonising. His main task, for the prosecution, was to describe Lady Illingworth to the jury and recount his last visit to York House, in the November before she went to Docklow, when he realised she was 'in a very senile condition'. John Wilberforce could almost have been saved the distress: this point was later reinforced by many others and the rest of his testimony added little beyond some glimmers of the relationship with Susan. She had, he said, resented the efforts of her Uncle Robert (Uncle Wee) to look after her assets following the partition of the Markington estate. When Susan had gone to Markington after their mother's death 'it had not worked out' and she had left.

Under cross-examination he said Susan had been unhappy at Markington 'because of her passion for privacy'. He added: 'She kept things to herself very much indeed. In particular there had been this long period when she had been on her own isolated from the rest of the Wilberforce family. I do not think she liked living on top of us at Markington.' He was followed by Lord Wilberforce, now eighty-two, bespectacled and dignified, seeing a court for the first time from a witness box rather than looking down from the bench. Both Lord Wilberforce and his wife Yvette testified to the former grandeur of Lady Illingworth's lifestyle and their distress at her deterioration. Lady Wilberforce admitted that she regretted not trying to discover why her letters to Lady Illingworth at Docklow had gone unanswered.

Elizabeth Gregg-Smith took the stand. By 1983, Lady Illingworth had become 'less elegant, confused and vague', once putting on a shabby coat and odd stockings. Once, Lady Illingworth and Cathy had been unable to find her ladyship's handbag: 'We asked Sophia,' said Mrs Gregg-Smith, 'and she said it was in her room under her bed.' Sophia got the bag from her room. It contained £160 and a brooch. She was one of a large number of witnesses, from both the family, hospital and Langford House, who testified to Lady Illingworth's confused condition. Dorothy Haynes, who helped with the housework at York House, said: 'She wasn't good at signing cheques, she needed help. She wouldn't remember if she had to pay a bill.' Despite all this anecdotal evidence, the important question of whether or not Lady Illingworth was clinically senile at the point she went to Docklow was never established before the jury. The prosecution had an expert prepared to say she was, but withdrew him after the defence made it clear they were able to call another expert to say that if that was the case, so was just about every other elderly person.

The jury heard how Susan had apparently rejected Aunt Puss once she had left Docklow. In a statement read to the court, Dr John Wood, the senior consultant at Hereford, said his staff had told him: 'The niece says she is a sex maniac and no man is safe. She always asks males to encourage her.' Others were told by Susan that her aunt had a history of alcoholism and was 'weaned off' at Docklow. Particularly damning evidence came from Pamela Luke, the hospital social worker charged with arrangements for her long-term care, preferably back with her family. Lady Illingworth was unable to tell Mrs Luke anything about her own finances or whether she had a bank account.

Describing a series of telephone calls to Docklow before and after that Christmas 1986, Mrs Luke testified that Susan had said they did not want her aunt back because she sometimes tried to hitch a ride when she got out. Besides, the house was too small. Susan said Lady Illingworth had only a state pension, but agreed to come and discuss her aunt's financial position. She never made the appointment or returned the form sent by Mrs Luke which asked for financial details. Mrs Luke said she was 'fobbed off' by Susan, Marcus and then Sophia in successive telephone calls to Docklow. By the last call, on 16 January, arrangements had been made for Lady Illingworth to go to Langford House. Mrs Luke asked Sophia for some fresh clothes to replace the shabby shirt and worn jersey which were the only clothes Lady Illingworth appeared to possess. None arrived.

The case moved to the will. Father Dooley, seventy, later described by the judge as a man 'of the cloth, not the world', explained his 'very distant' relationship with Michael and the trip to Docklow. He had seen Lady Illingworth for ten minutes before lunch. 'She said she had frequently been to church and spoke about the priests who had been there in the twenties and thirties. She spoke very, very slowly, as if searching for a word with long periods of recollection. She always finished a sentence. She was very intelligent and didn't mumble.' After lunch, Susan produced a document in a red cover. Michael was in the room. She handed the document to him. 'I said "What shall I do?" She said or he said I was to sign at the bottom of each page and the last page. Possibly both said it.' Father Dooley told the court that there were no other signatures on the will. But he had not read the document and had never signed a will before. Shortly afterwards, a passport application form and a photograph of Lady Illingworth were given to him to sign as a witness as well. Under cross-examination by du Cann, for

Michael, Father Dooley said he had absolutely no recollection of his alleged co-signatory, Anne Devey-Smith.

But before Mrs Devey-Smith could take the stand, on the tenth day of the trial, the defence allowed the prosecution to let the jury finally hear the explanation for Susan's absence: Susan had pleaded guilty to the sample theft and forgery charges. This was important because it allowed full use of the argument that Sophia and Marcus were merely pawns in the game, that Susan had used them in pursuit of her own evil ends. The revelation had a flip side: to the jury the defrauding of Lady Illingworth was now a concrete reality because the key participant had admitted that something took place. The defence had to deny knowledge of, or involvement in, the plot, rather than arguing that the plot had never existed at all.

Anne Devey-Smith was a better witness than Father Dooley. Lady Illingworth, she said, was 'a very sweet old dear' who never spoke unless asked something. 'I don't think she recognised me from one visit to the next.' Susan had asked her at an earlier point if she would witness a will and had telephoned on the Saturday to say it would be tomorrow. Arriving at 3 p.m., Mrs Devey-Smith sat having tea in the living room with Lady Illingworth, Susan and Sophia on the sofa, Father Dooley in an armchair and Michael walking about the room. Michael left after the tea. 'Sophia then asked Lady Illingworth if she wanted to leave the room. Lady Illingworth said no. There were several more attempts and then Sophia asked Lady Illingworth if she wanted a glass of sherry. She said yes and they left the room. Susan then left and re-entered, she had the will in her hand. It was the first I had seen of the will. Susan pointed out to me where to sign it and then she asked Father Dooley. Lady Illingworth's name was on the will, but I cannot remember if the signature was on the will. Lady Illingworth was not present when I signed the will and I was not present when she signed the will. Susan took it out of the room and I never saw it again.'

Although her relationship with Susan had cooled the following year, Michael had telephoned her several times and stayed at her home. 'He told me that he had wondered what Susan had been doing that day.' She also recalled something Michael had said during his row at Docklow: 'He told us he had found a blank piece of paper with Lady Illingworth's signature on it and

that he had been very concerned about the implications of this.'
Although she had found it difficult to trust Susan, Mrs Devey-
Smith had not suspected anything about the will: 'One doesn't
suspect one's friends of doing something like that.'

Richard Sexton explained how he had inherited the commission to draw up Lady Illingworth's will, originally entrusted to
the senior partner, Mr Patten, now in the United States. He
had never met Lady Illingworth nor had he previously been
requested to draft a will on thin paper. Sexton had not questioned the letters ostensibly signed by Lady Illingworth, and
Susan had told him he was not to concern himself with the
bank-vault goods, which were domestic items, papers, worn
china. The jewellery, Susan had said, were paste copies; the
originals having been sold to pay gambling debts. Sexton
recounted his visit to the National Westminster Bank when
Michael had demanded the release of the belongings of Lady
Illingworth in the vault. Michael was 'beside himself with fury,
like a man possessed', in the face of the bank's reluctance to
hand over what he wanted.

The trial also heard about the attitude of William and Anne
Wilberforce. William, thirty-two, an accountancy student in
London, said that although he had told Aunt Puss there
were times when it was inconvenient for her to visit, that
did not mean she was unwelcome. William said he had not
been there when Sophia had accompanied Aunt Puss on trips
to Markington in 1982, when Sophia had said she found her
aunt's welcome cool. Anne stressed her fond memories of Lady
Illingworth, but said that she had arrived at Markington in
February 1984, confused and muttering 'Where am I?' as she
disembarked. 'You had to keep an eye on her all the time,'
she said. Under cross-examination she explained that although
Lady Illingworth had considered Markington 'her second home'
Robert and Marion had lived in one wing and in a state of
deteriorating health until late 1984. No one had told Lady
Illingworth that she could not stay or live at Markington if
she had really wanted to.

Anne Wilberforce was later recalled to be cross-examined on
a letter written to Sebastian a month after Aunt Puss went to
Docklow. She wrote: 'Your mother and Sophia have done very
well fielding Aunt Puss for what is a historically long visit. I am

sure cousin Irene and Cathy would give them a medal for the respite it has given them. Even the usual stream of postcards to both the uncle [Robert] and I, asking us to arrange transportation to the Hall, has ceased.' This was a significant point to the defence because it proved that the Markington branch of the family knew exactly where Aunt Puss was living and were expressing praise rather than concern.

A lot of time was spent reading to the court statements from those too old or infirm to attend, such as Cathy Whelan and Marion Wilberforce. The court was also presented with substantial financial evidence, mostly on paper and unchallenged by the defence: lists of the dozens of bank accounts, auction sales, share sales and cashcard withdrawals were all given to the jury to study. And there was a list of forty-seven documents containing the forged signature of Lady Illingworth, ranging from cheques to the will. Dr David Baxendale, the forensic scientist who had confirmed the forgeries, said the better ones were very well done. The different samples of the antiques and furniture, the de László painting and the china cheetahs were all paraded before the court and the wide-eyed jury.

The fourth week opened with a statement from the judge: William Wilberforce had, unprompted, referred to the murder of Simon Dale. The jury had sent a note to the judge asking why everybody was going out of their way to avoid mentioning the murder they all remembered from the newspapers. These facts, the judge told the jury, bore no relevance to the case they were trying and must be disregarded. True, but the defence could hardly have relished the disclosure.

Barbara Smith, an old schoolfriend of Sophia, then told the jury how she had visited her at Pucklechurch remand centre. Sophia had said she was astonished at the number of bank accounts and money in them and upset and mixed up about her mother and Michael. 'Sophia asked if I'd kept any of the letters she'd sent me. I said no. She said I was an angel, thank goodness.'

The prosecution case moved into its final stages: the interviews. For several days the jury watched those hours of interrogation painstakingly recorded on video and tape at Hereford police station in December 1987, more than two years previously. Although the jury were able to see the

Wilberforce manner for the first time, the videos added little to the sum of their knowledge; the real opportunity for judging Sophia, Marcus and Michael would come when they took the witness stand.

They had spent much of the preceding weeks as almost incidental bystanders. They had sat, stoically or fidgeting, staring around the courtroom. Sophia was still in 'blank-out' mode. 'I just really didn't know what was going on. A lot of it just passed me by. It was all too awful.' Marcus took a similar view. 'It was like going to work. You would just go home and forget about it, lead a normal life.' Michael, who had barely spoken to his co-defendants, was more the live wire, whispering and passing notes to his solicitor, watching with keen interest, greeting the press and the lawyers each morning. Now their time had come.

The defence opened on the morning of Friday, 23 March. Already the trial was nearing the end of its fifth week; winter was turning into spring. The case for the three was similar: Lady Illingworth had been unhappy at dismal York House because she did not get on with Irene or Cathy; she was dissatisfied with the Markington branch because they had shunned her; she had been happy to come to Docklow and be looked after by Susan and Sophia and to have them handle her financial affairs; indeed, she changed her will in their favour in gratitude for their rediscovered friendship and help, fully aware of what she was doing.

If Susan forged documents, raided bank accounts, sold Aunt Puss's furniture, valuables and shares without her permission and laundered the money, this was without their knowledge. They were mere helpers, believing that any actions, such as visiting the National Westminster Bank or York House, caring for Aunt Puss or writing to solicitors and stockbrokers, were carrying out the wishes of Lady Illingworth, for whom Susan was both carer and oracle. It was normal for wealthy members of the family to help out the less fortunate ones; Robert had helped with school fees, why should not his sister help them now? And, as far as Sophia and Marcus were concerned, had not Mother always provided?

Like or loathe Michael de Stempel, du Cann told the jury, it was irrelevant to the facts before them. Michael, dressed in his finest but sometimes threadbare suits, spent four days in the witness box, being defensive, pompous and recalcitrant. His first task was to admit to having lied to the police by claiming he had a degree from Oxford. Michael then spoke of his early relationship with Susan, his subsequent marriages, how he had begun to finance Susan during the early 1970s, how he had paid the rent at Docklow and how they had remained friendly until the early 1980s. He would visit Docklow every three or four weeks, sometimes sleeping in the garden in a tent. There had been no sexual relationship, he maintained.

He had agreed to Susan's demands to get married because she had threatened to report him to Camden Council in London over his treatment of his son Alexander. His solicitor advised him that he was 'the sort of person Camden social services would love to take your son away from'. 'I think I was very frightened. I panicked. There had been friendship before this, there was lifelong friendship. No, there was not real love, not that there should be in a marriage. But Susan was a forceful woman and I wanted someone to go to when the divorce proceedings with Francesca were going on.' He refused to consummate the marriage and his visits to Docklow had become infrequent. He had agreed to a joint Gold Card because Susan had said she wanted it just in case she and the children did not have enough to eat. He stopped it when he realised the size of the bills she was running up.

Michael told the court that he had met Jane Mackay, 'an old friend' in June 1984. Susan, he said, had not been pleased about this. She had later become hysterical, he said, which had led to strange letters and telegrams like the one referring to 'Sandwich Carrot.' and 'Jilters.' At this point the barristers spent some time attempting to decode the strange missive. Michael told them that Sandwich was probably an abusive name that Susan used for Mrs Mackay; Jilters was Susan's name for him. Susan's objection to his renewal of an old friendship, he said, had contributed to the break-up of the marriage to Susan.

He distanced himself from the defrauding. When he told the National Westminster Bank – when applying for a loan to pay off his overdraft – that he was expecting 'an inheritance', he had been referring to an expected £150,000 from his father, already in another account. He had assumed Patten would see

Lady Illingworth and receive instructions; he had no dealings with the contents of the will and certainly had not been there when it was signed. Any money Susan had came from her side of the family, he assumed.

The Channel Islands trip had been necessary because of legal procedures for their wedding; Susan had told him Lady Illingworth wanted to dispose of jewellery because she was getting old; he had assumed the silver plate Susan had was Dormer or Borwick plate; at the jewellers he had introduced Susan and left. He had carried the bags, but played no part in packing them: 'I was a porter if you like, I made the introductions and then left.'

Why payments of £20,000 and £18,000 had been made anonymously into his account he was at a loss to explain; it was not his reward. He had chalked up an overdraft of £20,000 on Susan and the children and he supposed she had sent him a repayment 'I don't think she said where the money came from,' he said. It had to be anonymous, he then suggested, because if Richard Sax, acting for Susan in her negotiations with Dale, had discovered, the money might have had to go to Dale because of his legal claims on her over Heath House. He also suggested that it was to prevent his ex-wife Francesca discovering his additional income. He spoke of the incident on 17 July when he had discovered the white papers in a drawer with Lady Illingworth's signature on them. 'It crossed my mind that maybe they were forgeries but maybe because Lady Illingworth was very old they may have been done by Lady Illingworth to avoid repeated signings.'

Cross-examined by Barnes, he said he was a 'liaison officer' who knew the right professionals. Others had told him Lady Illingworth was wealthy, but when she first came to Docklow he had subsidised her. The lifestyle at Docklow did not change beyond a mowing machine and new car for Marcus. The food got worse. There were no extra pictures on the walls. He presumed Lady Illingworth was making a contribution. By helping arrange a lawyer for the will, he was doing the best for the family; when the will had been signed, he had either been in the public house in Docklow or having a bath. He believed he was marrying a poor woman. Sometimes Susan had money, sometimes not. There were many family trusts;

she was kept by Robert (Uncle Wee). He had no idea what was in the bank vault; he was told it was largely rubbish, stale biscuits and food.

But, said Barnes, metaphorically ticking the points off on his fingers, within weeks of Lady Illingworth's arrival at Docklow, Michael had made urgent enquiries about the will, hadn't he? No, he did not think they were urgent. There had been urgent attempts to remove items from bank vaults, had there not? No, not urgent, but steps were taken, yes. Accounts were transferred to joint accounts between Susan and Lady Illingworth? 'I never knew there were joint accounts.' Large sums of money had been withdrawn by cashpoint from Lady Illingworth's account, had they not? 'I never saw Susan use a cashpoint card.' 'If Lady Illingworth was so easily persuadable,' Michael asked the jury, 'then what was the need for all these forgeries?' After confessing to du Cann that he never looked at his own bank accounts, under cross-examination he volunteered more insights into his approach to life: 'I'm sure my lifestyle costs more than my income. I live on my capital,' and 'I'm almost innumerate,' and 'I can't remember what happened an hour ago — maybe Lady Illingworth couldn't.' Susan was in turns 'dominating' and 'secretive'.

At 4 p.m. that afternoon, 28 March, the case for the Baron closed and that of Sophia Wilberforce opened. Richard Wakerley said that the defence had wanted to show the video of Sophia's interviews with police, so that the jury could see her reactions to things the police said her mother had done. 'Sophia cannot help who she is, the daughter of Susan.' 'It would be difficult', he added, 'for you to come to terms with what your mother has done, you may think.' And was it easy, he suggested, for a daughter or son to understand the intricacies of marriage and tax affairs? Sophia had been only twenty when she was at York House, twenty-one when Lady Illingworth came to Docklow.

Sophia, a small creature with a firm chin and sometimes defiant manner, took the witness stand. She said: 'My mother loved Lady Illingworth very much. Lady Illingworth was like a mother to my mother.' Explaining the long years of silence between Susan and her aunt, Sophia said that although Lady Illingworth was annoyed with her mother for marrying Dale, because she did not consider him good enough for her niece, by the time of the divorce she had suddenly turned her affections upon Dale, throwing parties on his behalf. That caused a terrible rift between them, said Sophia. Furniture? Mother got the best bits of Granny Lucas's furniture when the property was divided. 'We were always surrounded by lovely things. Sometimes things disappeared to be sold by Mother to pay for school fees.' She knew nothing about her mother's finances. She never had, partially because of the divorce arguments. Why should she?

At York House, she had shopped and eaten with Lady Illingworth and had twice accompanied her to Markington, where her welcome had been 'less than rapturous'. 'She was tolerated . . . Lady Illingworth said that for some reason they could not have her. She was very proud. She would not admit to herself that she was not welcome.' When Cathy finally made it clear to her, Aunt Puss 'just wept'. Sophia said she could not understand why William had denied being at Markington when she had visited with Aunt Puss.

When Sophia gave up her job to go home, Lady Illingworth had raised the idea of accompanying her. 'I thought it was a marvellous idea, but Docklow was not ideal. Mother did not leap at the idea, initially. Later she agreed, in theory.' After the Markington-by-taxi episode, Lady Illingworth had again dropped hints about Docklow. 'Mother agreed, but said to see how it went. Lady Illingworth was delighted.' At Docklow, the atmosphere between Susan and Michael, who were talking of getting married and buying a bigger house, had been good. 'Mother and Lady Illingworth were very close, the household was very joyous and happy.' She had returned with Marcus to York House to get more clothes for her aunt but Cathy had refused them access; it was unwise to argue with Cathy, so they had left.

She had gone to see her brother Alexander in Japan shortly afterwards, the £800 costs paid for by Aunt Puss ('Mother handed the money over. I thought Lady Illingworth wanted me to go to Japan'), and the first she heard of the will was on her return. On the crucial day, she had been told to leave, not to clutter the place up, she said, because she had wanted to show Anne Devey-Smith her holiday photographs. She often offered her aunt a glass of something.

After her aunt's arrival at Docklow, she said, their relation-ship had changed. 'I was put in my place. Mother was very close, special to Lady Illingworth. If Lady Illingworth wanted something, it was done. She seemed to be number one in our household. Mother and Lady Illingworth were a team. Mother and Lady Illingworth spent a lot of time together.'

Shortly afterwards, her mother had said she would get £100 a week to look after her aunt. She thought it was a lot for doing very little. 'Lady Illingworth wasn't present when this was said. I thought Lady Illingworth knew about this. Mother was handling her finances.' She knew nothing about bank accounts or finances. 'I trusted my mother. I didn't think she was acting dishonestly. I don't know what to think now.' Now, she said, she was 'in difficulties' over the allegations against her mother. 'I do believe my great-aunt wanted my mother to have her possessions.' It was the perfectly equivocal approach.

She had been astonished when police had told her of the amounts of money which had passed through her accounts. Some had been for work on Heath House, others for Aunt Puss; one payment had been related to her aunt's tax affairs. She had no idea about other payments her mother had made; she had never used an autobank card belonging to anyone else; she had seen Susan withdraw money from the Midland Bank twice; Lady Illingworth had been there once. Her mother had told her that the silverware bearing the Illingworth family crest was being sold to pay off a £14,000 tax bill. At the end of this lengthy exercise in denial, Sophia said: 'I never thought Mother was forging Lady Illingworth's signature. I still don't believe it . . . Mother never discussed things with us.'

Barnes began his cross-examination. Why, in view of this loving relationship between Sophia and her aunt, had she not accompanied her to the hospital? 'It all happened so quickly. I felt that I should go, but Mother said she would follow soon afterwards. That was fine by me.' She did not know her mother had refused to have Lady Illingworth back; she had been to see her two or three times when she was in hospital. She did not know her mother had told the hospital her aunt was an alcoholic.

Aunt Puss had sent lovely things to Heath House and her mother had loved her very much. She had been unhappy and lonely at York House. 'It was a pity because she was a sweetie.' Sophia never thought of inviting her to Docklow for the weekend. 'It just never happened.' She never knew where her aunt's papers were; she could think of nothing worse than going through some one else's handbag. Under cross-examination, Sophia conceded a lot of things: she did not think she knew the name of the nursing home where her aunt had been; she had not thought to tell her aunt's family; she thought they knew where she was. Her mother had always typed in her own bedroom on the windowsill; she locked the door and remained in there with Aunt Puss, said Sophia; and her mother had said that her aunt had wanted her to deal with everything. 'I felt at some times that Lady Illingworth was expected to pay for everything.'

Things had not changed much at Docklow after Aunt Puss's arrival; they had been better off because Michael was about. She had been better off by £100 a week, almost £25 a week more than she had received in London. Had she thanked Aunt Puss for this largesse? enquired Mr Barnes. I didn't get the opportunity to talk to her. At Docklow, it was a different relationship.' Although her mother had handed over the £800 for the Japanese trip, it had been her aunt's money, which was 'marvellous'. 'I did not write whilst I was in Japan. She couldn't read anyway.' When the will had been signed, she had been told to absent herself and had never enticed her aunt out of the room with a glass of sherry; it was tea-time anyway. She was not part of the will conspiracy and did not recall talking to a Mrs Luke from the hospital.

Marcus, pale, diffident, quietly spoken, took the witness stand early the following week. His involvement, Seagrott suggested, was minimal. He had hardly been at Docklow with his aunt because he had been with his father or in Europe, gardening or travelling. Decisions about his aunt had been made by his mother: 'It was her and my mother together.' His mother had told him she had discovered that Aunt Puss had not liked living with Lord Illingworth because he had been a womaniser and had only married her aunt because she was a social butter-fly. Marcus had been shown a letter which indicated that Lady Illingworth was unhappy because her husband was a divorcé.

Yes, he had helped take two statues from York House, a pair of china cheetahs, to Docklow, where his aunt had patted them on the head and said it was good to see them again. Yes, he had taken his mother to the auction rooms at Bath with a pile of assorted silver on the back seat of the car. 'Mother said it was to settle Lady Illingworth's bills – there was talk of a large tax bill.' Yes, his mother had told him that Lady Illingworth wanted to give him the Peugeot 205, though he did not know how much it had cost. Yes, he had thanked Lady Illingworth, but he could not remember the exact conversation.

The cross-examination of Marcus by Barnes was substantially more revealing. His mother had said social workers were sorting out 'a nice home' for his aunt, but there had been no discussion between Marcus, his mother and sister about the home. Asked about an episode when George Petty, the Giltspur Bullens foreman, had asked whether he could see the lady for whom he had worked nearly twenty years previously, Marcus said he had promised to fix a meeting but Mother had said they should let Aunt Puss settle at Langford House, and anyway the man was a total stranger. He denied implying to Petty that Lady Illingworth had then been living at Docklow. Although he had seen Lady Illingworth at Langford House during this period, he had not discussed the furniture with her or the fact that it had come out of store, he told Barnes. 'I didn't think she would have appreciated what I was saying.'

Barnes questioned him closely about his visit to York House with Patten and Michael. The idea had been to collect fresh clothes and ascertain what was in Lady Illingworth's room. Her papers were in an accordion file, which he took to Docklow. He was only 'a porter'. 'I assumed that the following day Lady Illingworth and Mother would go through them. I don't recall telling Lady Illingworth that her possessions had been brought up. Mother or Sophia may have told her.' He had not discussed his aunt's changing personality with anyone. He had never informed Irene. 'It wasn't my job to do so.'

Marcus did not know if a cashcard was being used on the account of Aunt Puss. He might have gone to a bank with his mother, but did not know whose it was. 'I had no idea of the mechanics of it all.' He went on: 'I knew that Lady Illingworth wanted Mother to enjoy her income. I did not know in what way.' And: 'If I needed any money, Mother would withdraw it and give me cash. The money was Lady Illingworth's, which she gave my mother. I knew nothing of the scale of withdrawals.' He had known nothing about the new will, but felt his aunt would have understood when it was explained to her. 'She never said to me how much she loved my mother, but you could see it.' He was 'surprised and amazed' at the amount of money withdrawn from the accounts and at the amount realised by the auction sales. The Spanish flat was bought with Lady Illingworth's money. She had never been told about it, he said, although he was sure she would have approved if she had known. It had never occurred to him to send a card to her when he was there, and he had no idea whether his mother and Sophia had written to Aunt Puss. And that was the case for the defence.

Later that day, Barnes rose to make the closing speech for the prosecution. He listed the key points for the jury. In Michael's case, these were the language of some of the forged documents, his finding of a particular solicitor and the priest. For Sophia, the points they should remember were the telephone call from Mrs Luke, the conversation with Barbara Smith, the handbag incident at York House and the will signing. She had lied to the police about York House, changed her story to suit the questions and had not even known the name of the nursing home where her aunt had lived. Sophia was the 'ideal lieutenant', a 'highly intelligent, highly determined' young woman who lacked any feeling for Lady Illingworth. For Marcus, said Barnes, the critical points related to the conversation with Petty and his use of cashcards in his aunt's name after she had gone into a home. All three were 'extremely devious, calculating and jealous'.

It was then the turn of the defence barristers to conclude for their clients. On behalf of Michael, Mr du Cann polished his phrase book and began with some remarkable concessions, clearly designed to win the goodwill of the jury. 'You may think', he said, 'that the man is a congenital liar. You may think that he is a monumental snob and that he comes out of this case with his reputation in shreds. The combination of these two defects of character can be lethal.' The Baron, who had lied to police about his degree and his inheritance from his father, had been in the habit of lying since childhood; he used lies and name-dropping to boost his social standing. His impeccable background concealed what the jury might consider to be 'a hopelessly inadequate character'.

But it was not evidence of any dishonesty in the affairs of Lady Illingworth. He had been unable to match Susan's 'cunning and deviousness'. 'He is, alas, a man without courage. He had not even the good sense to walk out on her or turn his back on her and she is a quite remarkably manipulative woman.' She had used him; marriage would bring her the money, title and social position she wanted, said Mr du Cann. He spoke of Susan's desire to continue her relationship with Michael and suggested that the real reason she had paid him £20,000 was as a 'financial and emotional bribe' to spend a night with her in a hotel in Paddington.

For Sophia, Wakerley conceded that she had received money knowing that it came from her aunt. The jury had to decide whether Sophia believed this had been what Lady Illingworth wanted. If Sophia had been callous and devious, why had she had conversations with Barbara Smith and her godfather, Francis Rose, about what had been going on at Docklow. She had found some of the things about her mother hard to believe. He asked: 'Why didn't Sophia line her pockets at York House? If Sophia was on the take, it was inconceivable she got so little.' He added: 'She cannot help being the daughter of her mother.'

Seagrott repeated that Marcus had not been accused of any forgeries or of any lack of care of his aunt when she had been at Docklow. He concluded with a telling passage from Oscar Wilde: 'Children love their parents at first; then they begin to judge them; they are, however, rarely forgiven.' He added: 'Sophia and Marcus were at the stage of judging their mother.'

Midway through the morning of Thursday, 12 April, Maundy Thursday, on the fourth day of the eighth week of the trial, Judge Richard Curtis began summing up the evidence for the jury. Throughout the trial he had remained largely silent, beyond conducting the formalities of the court – although in the absence of the jury, during the arguments between lawyers over what was admissible, he had been a more forceful figure.

Now, it was time for him to make his mark on the case, turning his aquiline features towards the jury.

Because of the lack of expert clinical evidence about Lady Illingworth's mental health, the judge had to draw a distinction between what the various professional and family witnesses for the prosecution were saying and the version put forward by the defence. There was a clear conflict for the jury to resolve. The issue, he said, was not whether Lady Illingworth was senile, but when she became senile.

On the will, the judge listed the questions for the jury to consider. Who had prepared the will? Certainly Susan and possibly, the prosecution alleged, Michael. Had Michael been a 'guilty messenger'? Had he or Sophia known that this had been part of a dishonest enterprise to steal Lady Illingworth's property? Why had such a drastic departure from the 1975 will been effected so soon after she arrived at Docklow? What was the point in forging the will when all three defendants said she had wanted to make a new will in their favour? Why had it been witnessed in her absence? Had it been impossible to plan the will without the defendants knowing? Had it been important to have the second will in case Lady Illingworth died before her property had been turned into cash, or so that when she did die the Docklow branch would be in a position to say to the true beneficiaries, 'She's left it all to us'?

The jury had to decide whether Sophia had lured Lady Illingworth out of the room when the will had been produced and, if she had, whether she had been acting dishonestly. Sophia had said her payments were for being a companion to Aunt Puss and for improvement work on Heath House. But the prosecution argued that they were too high for such a purpose; the dates and sums did not coincide and continued after Aunt Puss had left Docklow. The judge said there was no dispute over what Marcus had done over the property sales, but it was a question of what was going on in his mind: 'Was he intentionally stealing Lady Illingworth's property, or was he doing as his mother asked? Was he a guilty-minded porter?' Marcus had said, in effect: 'I acted on what Mother told me and believed what she said.' The judge declared: 'If this is right, then he cannot have acted dishonestly.' Marcus had also said: 'Mother made the decision what to sell. I thought the property

was Mother's and that Lady Illingworth wanted her to have it.'
The judge said that if the jury believed this to be so, he was not
dishonest.

Shortly after lunch on 18 April, the third day of his summing
up, Judge Richard Curtis reached his conclusion: 'If the defendants thought that Lady Illingworth gave her property to Susan
Wilberforce for her to do as she wished, then they would be not
guilty. If Sophia and Marcus honestly believed that the sales of
her assets were Lady Illingworth's wishes, then they would not
have been acting dishonestly. If they accepted a gift honestly,
then they would be not guilty.' The jury left and the court, the
lawyers, the defendants and the press settled down for a long
wait. Some of those who had spent many days in the public
gallery went across to wish Sophia and Marcus good luck.

While they were waiting outside, their mother made her first
appearance at the trial. Although she had pleaded guilty, the
case had to be formally opened against her. Before the judge,
and with her own counsel, Stephen Coward QC, in court,
Timothy Barnes presented the evidence against Susan, who
sat in splendid isolation in the dock. Barnes rattled through an
outline of the case, detailing the various bits of paper evidence
that supported the four charges of theft and two of forgery.
When it was over, Susan was taken back to the cells to join
in the long wait. At 5 p.m., the judge told the jury they would
spend the night in a hotel.

Twenty-four hours later, after a long, agonising, fruitless day,
with no one able to leave the building, the court reassembled.
Had the jury reached a verdict on anyone, asked the judge?
They had. At 5.25 p.m., the jury foreman pronounced a verdict
of guilty on Michael. The Baron flinched and looked down,
but otherwise covered his emotions. His daughter Tatiana, his
supporter throughout the trial, left the courtroom in tears. The
judge asked the foreman whether the jury had agreed verdicts
on Sophia and Marcus. They had not. He sent them off for
a second night. There followed another long, agonising day
without a verdict. It was Friday and the jury would have to
deliberate over the weekend. The strain for all concerned was
heavy. It was also completely unavoidable.

Saturday morning arrived. After the first ten minutes, the
judge, knowing that he might have a hung jury but unwilling

to order a retrial, said that he would accept a majority verdict. At 2.45 p.m., the jury passed a message announcing that they had reached a verdict. The court was reassembled. Sophia and Marcus were taken to a little room at the side of the dock, where they would enter once the judge and jury were ready. They came face to face with their mother, ready to be brought into the court for sentence. Sophia went up to her. The blue-black eyes were blank. Sophia looked at her and said: 'If I am convicted because of all this you have done, I will never forgive you.' Susan pretended not to hear.

They went into court and the jury took their places. The foreman rose to read the verdict. By an 11-to-1 majority both were guilty of conspiracy to steal; two jurors had clearly changed their minds. Marcus swayed; Sophia bit her lip. In the public seats, Sebastian put his head into his hands and wept.

The judge ordered that Michael and Susan be brought into the dock. Michael, who had been released on bail, stepped into the dock from the well of the court to stand beside Sophia and Marcus. As he did so, Susan too was brought in. For the first time, the full court would see the woman who had been behind it all. A silence draped itself around the courtroom as everybody – jury, barristers, ushers, press, public, Michael, Marcus and Sophia – turned as one to look at her as she walked through the pine door, accompanied by prison officers. This rather ungainly woman, with the heavily creased face, the dark eyes and black hair, wearing her usual blue cardigan and high-necked blouse, entered the dock to stand by her ex-husband and children. She seemed indifferent to it all, though a slight quiver, which could have been either a smile or a trace of nervousness, played around the corners of her mouth.

Everyone sat down to hear the pleas of mitigation from the defence barristers. Then Judge Richard Curtis came to sentencing. All four defendants were ordered to stand. The judge turned first to Marcus, who began to sway. The length of his period of imprisonment, said the judge, would reflect his lesser role in the affair. He would receive eighteen months in prison. As he said this, Marcus collapsed on to the floor of the dock. If the eyes of his mother flickered downwards from whatever far point they were examining, no one saw it happen. She stood there with her arms folded and did not move.

As Marcus was helped up by two prison officers, the judge turned to his sister. 'You and your mother were undoubtedly very close at the relevant time. You were Lady Illingworth's minder. You did not treat her cruelly but you were happy to steal her money. You played a vital part in seeing there was no trouble over the attestation of the forged will and your reward was a flat in Spain and holidays.' She would receive thirty months in prison. Sophia shook her head, saying quietly, but audibly: 'that's not true'.

The judge then pronounced on Michael. This man, he said, with clear contempt, was not clever enough to have master-minded the conspiracy: 'Stripped of your airs and flowery language, you are without doubt a conman. Your part was to put a respectable veneer on the dealings of your conspirators.' He would be sentenced to four years in prison.

The judge turned to Susan, the coldness of his glance every bit a match for hers. Susan stood there, her arms still defiantly folded, as Judge Richard Curtis spoke, choosing and delivering his words carefully. 'Your treatment of Lady Illingworth was absolutely barbarous. Having taken all her money you cast her off. Although she went to a good old people's home, you allowed her to go there in the guise of a pauper.' The fraud had been 'meticulously planned', and Susan had been 'truly wicked' in hiding her aunt's death from relatives and friends. 'One of the most grave, aggravating factors is how you involved your two children in what you were doing.' They had fallen under her 'malign and appalling influence'. She would be imprisoned for seven years.

The defendants were taken away, in the firm grip of prison officers.

In the cells, there were emotional farewells. Sophia was hugged by Richard Wakerley, with whom she had developed a close bond. Marcus had pulled himself together. Their lawyers told them that neither would be likely to spend more than six months in prison. Michael, who could expect somewhat longer, said: 'What can you expect from a working-class jury?'

Susan said nothing. She and Sophia were driven away together to Risley remand centre in Cheshire. The journey passed in silence. 'She just sat there. There was no acknowledgement anything had happened. Mother was her normal calm self.'

'I'd Rather Go to Prison . . .'

It is just possible that Susan de Stempel, her children and the Baron really stole £12 million. That was the estimated value of the gold bars seen by Aubrey Appleton, once, briefly, in the cellars of Grosvenor Square.

A month after beginning their prison sentences, Susan, Michael, Sophia and Marcus each received a bulky writ from solicitors Theodore Goddard, acting on behalf of the estate of the late Lady Illingworth, asking for the return of all the stolen property and claiming damages for 'wrongful interference'. Among page after page listing all the stolen property, carefully itemised and described, most of which had been sold at auction, there is, almost casually, the reference: '30 gold bars, each 18 inches in length; total value: £12,000,000'. Police had considered the matter resolved and no mention had been made of the bars during the nine weeks of the trial. But someone, somewhere, clearly believes they may have existed.

'We never did find out precisely how much they took,' said Mike Cowley when it was all over. No total figure was given at the trial. The main problem was knowing what was there in the first place. The Kensington bank vault had been insured for £150,000 in 1982, but no full inventory existed of this vault, or of the possessions of Lady Illingworth at York House or of the vast amounts in storage with Giltspur Bullens. Putting aside the question of the gold bars, the real value, some believe, could have been close to £1 million.

As for the bars, no one else interviewed by the police, including the National Westminster Bank, Illingworth and Wilberforce relatives and Grosvenor Square staff with access to the vault, had seen or heard of them. There are no paper references. Police doubt they ever existed and believe that Appleton was genuinely mistaken. It seems inconceivable that Lady Illingworth, then in full command of her faculties, would not have told the bank that something so important was among the other valuables sent to them. It seems unlikely that she would simply have carted them to York House. Certainly Susan and Michael never subsequently acted as though such an amount had been acquired, even allowing for the necessity of disguising the discovery. Sophia and Marcus think it laughable.

But the police do recognise that they may not have recovered everything taken. 'We think we have found most of it,' Cowley was able to say, adding a note of caution: 'It is of course entirely possible that some separate paper trail, using false names and not linked to the one we know about, was used to dispose of other property or valuables, of whose existence we were completely unaware.' As an example, family members told the police that Lady Illingworth had once had an extensive stamp collection which she had inherited from her husband, who, as Postmaster-General for so many years, would have been well placed to build up such a collection. The detectives found a few stamps, but no albums. They have no proof that one still existed at the time Lady Illingworth went to Docklow, or, even if it had, that it was worth anything at all. The police simply do not know; the possibility remains tantalising.

The question of valuation of all the property is also subject to major qualifications. A value of £500,000 was placed on the cash, valuables and shares which were either recovered, sold or otherwise accounted for. But some of the property sold at auction or via Hettich's went at prices way below its real value, possibly for speed, possibly so as not to attract attention. For example, Hettich's paid £13,392 for the Illingworth silver plate, later sold through Sotheby's in 1985 for more than £28,000. (Some was eventually purchased by Jamie Illingworth, Lady Illingworth's great-nephew.)

One of the biggest unanswered questions, which the police kept asking themselves, was: what did they spend it all on? Again, no figure was ever given in court. The detectives quickly learnt about the pleasant but unostentatious Spanish flat, the cars, the holidays, the jewellery Susan bought herself as consolation for Michael's fickleness. But this did not total much more than £75,000. As a style of spending, it was all distinctly ordinary, barely bourgeois. Not at all like the way Lord and Lady Illingworth had spent their money. For instance, none of the holidays, when examined closely, amounts to very much: although Sophia's air fares to Tokyo and New York were paid for by Aunt Puss, they were still fairly cheap tickets; Sophia was certainly working when she was in New York, and she did not leave the city. And there were better times of the year to spend three months in Spain. On top of this must be added about £50,000 paid anonymously to Michael – partially for services rendered, partially as an inducement to return. Add on perhaps £50,000 for living expenses at Docklow, the trips to the Channel Islands and the work at Heath House, and that still leaves possibly as much as £80,000 to £100,000 unaccounted for, out of what the police knew Susan had obtained and ignoring what was later retrieved or never discovered.

If there were extravagances, they were not unearthed by the police: there was certainly no suggestion of wild living, parties or really exotic holidays; Susan, who always liked smart clothes, did buy some new outfits, but neither she nor the children apparently indulged themselves. 'The food at Docklow changed from being bought in a local shop to being bought at Marks and Spencers in Hereford. We don't eat that much anyway, we are all a bit sparrow-like,' said Marcus. 'And none of us are big drinkers. There was no constant wine or anything like that.' Police do not disagree.

When they were working on Heath House, Sophia remembers her mother driving there slowly to save petrol. 'And if there was so much money, why didn't we get central heating put in at Docklow?' She also remembers working on Christmas Day 1986. 'That makes me feel very bitter, knowing all that money was supposed to have gone through my accounts.' The constant withdrawals from the cashpoints – a few hundred at a time – may simply have frittered it all away; perhaps there were some earlier debts, or more went to Michael than was ever discovered. The cash is impossible to trace. Perhaps money is still concealed, somewhere.

Other questions the police did claim to solve: did Sophia and Marcus really know what their mother was up to? 'They knew what they were doing, they knew what was going on. They were not very streetwise, admittedly, but we cannot believe they were so blinkered that they did not know what was going on.' The motivation of Susan was deemed to be a simple matter: 'The rejection by Markington and the overwhelming need for money to restore the lifestyle she had once aspired to at Heath

House.' Had the fraud been planned in advance? 'Unlikely. They seem to have seized the opportunity.' Why was the will forged if they were going to take it all anyway? 'It was an insurance policy in case Lady Illingworth died before they could get their hands on it all or something else stood in their way.' Did they keep her there against her will? 'Impossible to prove one way or the other, although some people think it was the case.' Who was the motivating force, Susan or Michael? And, if they did know what was going on, to what extent were Sophia and Marcus to blame? 'The judge got it right in the sentencing.' At the end of the day, the police were satisfied with the outcome. Justice had been done.

It has certainly been done to Sophia and Marcus. They have shared the same trials and tribulations over the past three years: their father was brutally murdered, a crime for which both they and their mother were accused; their great-aunt was stripped of her fortune and dumped in a nursing home, a crime which their mother devised and for which she is now in prison – as is their stepfather, now acrimoniously divorced from their mother; they have been released from prison after six months of their sentences for their parts in the conspiracy; their defence, such as it was, involved putting all the blame on their once beloved mother. Their family is split among itself and from their less immediate relatives. Their friends and various cousins, mostly Dormers, have stood by them throughout, they say. But their life will never be the same again; the name of Wilberforce will always cause a second's pause.

They are closer than ever. They were deeply upset when the prison authorities refused them permission to make a prison-to-prison visit to see each other. Both have lost some of the innocence which had so marked them out from their peers, which had made them so open – to quote Judge Richard Curtis – to the 'malign and appalling influence' of their mother. Neither, still, is quite like other young people of their age.

Sophia Wilberforce sits in a west London hotel. She is twenty-eight, but it is as though her development had been arrested, say when she was an eighteen-year-old, between school and university. Around her mill the varied types of modern women:

air stewardesses overnighting from Heathrow, businesswomen in shoulder pads, waitresses and a smart woman in a short skirt, accompanying an expensively dressed older man.

She is none of these. She is slim, with clear features and bright eyes. Her hair is clean, but tangled, stray locks constantly falling across her face. Her chin is the only straightforward thing about her – firm and prominent, unlike those of her brothers. She wears nondescript clothes: a floral skirt and high-necked blouse (her mother always wears high necks), a pink sweatshirt tied with a belt, woolly tights, a short black jacket. Like her mother, Sophia fidgets when nervous: her hands are always scratching each other in a curious clawing motion or rummaging underneath her chin. Sometimes her blue eyes gaze right at you; at other times they wander erratically and seem to be looking at something in the far distance. Her speech, which betrays the intonations of her background, follows a similar course: now she is speaking firmly and clearly, then suddenly everything is vague and hesitant.

Sophia smiles a lot: the action displays etched lines around her face similar to those of her mother. She seems to be undergoing some kind of inner turmoil and, while affecting nonchalance, appears restless. She often has the manner of a petulant if somewhat naive young schoolgirl, stressing certain words during the conversation, as in 'Michael was *such* a beast.' When talking about the unlikely prospect of her father 'rogering' a woman friend, she covers a smirk with her hand. If you ask her a direct question which she does not like, she will often respond only obliquely or give the curious little 'hmmm' of non-committal acknowledgement.

The experience has changed her, she says, shattering her faith in the police, the courts, the very system which has served her family so well over the generations. She was under intermittent psychiatric treatment from the time of her arrest until the start of her trial. Sophia has no idea what the future holds. Perhaps she might get some kind of secretarial work, though such jobs are not easy to find for someone with a theft conviction, even a well-educated child of the upper classes. Never mind the future – she is still having trouble coming to terms with the immediate past. Presently, she is concerned about the box she has been carrying with her all afternoon. She says: 'Would you like a rather crushed chocolate eclair?'

In her plastic overnight bag, there is the bulky writ from Theodore Goddard. Whatever assets she has are effectively frozen by this writ; she thinks she owns the flat Susan bought in her name in Spain, but cannot say for sure. Even if she wanted to go there, she has no money for a flight. She confesses she has not read the list of the property claims in the writ. She never reads these things; she did not read many of the statements used in evidence against her during her trial, including some from close members of her family and friends. 'They are all too horrible and awful and I really cannot bear to read them.' She took the same attitude towards the trial, as she sat in the dock for weeks listening to how she had helped her mother defraud Lady Illingworth. 'I just tended, you know, to switch off. I wasn't really following what was going on.' It was though, she says, 'incredible and unbelievable' that she and Marcus were both found guilty when, in fact, they were completely innocent.

When Sophia talks about her mother, her conversation swings the full pendulum between love and hate. She loves her more than anybody, she says. But when asked about the bank accounts: 'I have to believe what I see.' She repeats, again and again, her shock at the amounts of money that went through accounts she did not know she had and her astonishment at what happened to the money. She also believes, adamantly, that Aunt Puss did intend to give it all to Susan, but accepts that her mother took it in illegal ways, although adding: 'I never saw any forgeries.' Outright condemnation is somehow always around the next conversational corner: 'You don't suddenly stop loving and believing someone, whatever other people may say.' She dwells, instead, upon the effect on her: how traumatic it all was, how beastly the police were, how awful it was that she was made to spend all those days up the scaffolding painting windows when all that money was in the bank. Nevertheless, it is clear who bears the blame for all this. 'If my mother had gone into the witness box and told the truth, I would not have been found guilty.'

Since her release from prison, Sophia has not been to see her mother or replied to her letters; she does not know whether she will go to Susan when she is released some time late in 1991.

'Her problems are of her own making – I'm not spending any more time trying to help her sort them out. She spent all her time trying to involve us in her problems, involve us in Heath House in order to keep us around at home.' She stands by what she said to her mother in the last hours of her own trial. She will never forgive her.

Marcus is a wan, listless figure, aged twenty-nine, but, like his sister, could almost pass for ten years younger. His clothing is also often nondescript and well worn: tweedy jacket, jeans, sweater and shirt. He has had the same writs served upon him; like Sophia, he has apparently no assets, no job and, as an ex-con, a difficult future.

Both are staying with Sebastian at his flat in west London, although Marcus rushes back to Heath House at every opportunity. He seems slightly lost in the city, does not seem to socialise much and would perhaps be happiest pottering around the gardens at the Heath with his bees, of which he is fond. 'I always like to give honey as a gift.' Again, when he smiles, which he does slightly lopsidedly, there are those creased lines around the face, which make him seem suddenly much older. He is physically relaxed, sits with his hands and knees together, although his eyes do sometimes wander off into the distance. They are quite hazy. His hair is straw coloured and untidy.

Although Marcus was at Docklow a good deal less than Sophia, he seems to have been equally under his mother's spell. He went as porter to York House and Wickton Court, he shipped the antiques to the salerooms. What was wrong in that? It what his mother told him Aunt Puss wanted. He says he saw nothing untoward going on, though he never quite got around to talking to Aunt Puss about any of it. He was certainly 'innocent' in his replies to police questioning: they said he was quite open and ready in providing answers and information. Like Sophia, he believes his conviction unjust.

Marcus appears stronger now than before the trial and before the six months he has just spent in an open prison. He seems more positive in his actions. 'I'm amazed that I didn't break under the strain [like Sophia, he implies]. I think it taught me that I am much stronger than I thought I was.' But he is less communicative than Sophia, more inclined to let silence hang

or shrug his shoulders and stare blankly. When he does talk, it
is in the characteristic monotone, but simple and direct.

Where Sophia sometimes stumbles over the words to con-
demn her mother, they come easier to him. 'We were used,'
he says simply, which is all that he really needs to say. Like
all of them, he believes it an outrage that they or their mother
should have been charged with the murder of Simon Dale. 'I'm
still stunned that any of it happened. It all seemed so unjust. It
was a farce.' But when there is an opportunity, he is defensive
of Susan: 'Our mother only gave us the things we wanted: a
holiday for Sophia, a car for me and flying lessons for Simon.'
At another meeting, he takes a different tack: 'I don't know
the full truth. Only my mother and Aunt Puss know that. I
cannot know what Aunt Puss really wanted.' He echoes the
words used by his barrister in his defence: 'I will not judge
my mother about things I do not know.' In prison, Marcus was
refused permission to make an inter-prison visit to his mother;
now, she firmly refuses to send him a visiting order.

He feels it unlikely that the family – that is, he, Sophia, their
mother and Simon – will ever be together again, as they used
to be at Docklow. He says: 'Not because of what has happened,
you understand, but because we have learnt how to manage on
our own. We have all gone our separate ways.'

Simon lives with his girlfriend somewhere in the Midlands; he
is trying to start up a health-products business and occasionally
makes low-level parachute jumps for thrills. He has kept himself apart from all the traumas, although he is in touch with
his siblings. He was not charged with any offence. Sebastian,
now a qualified solicitor, whose silence on his personal feelings
about his mother speaks volumes, has helped, supported and
funded his brother and sister since their arrest and believes
them wrongly convicted of the defrauding of Aunt Puss.

And it is now a simple matter of opinion whether anyone else
should believe Sophia and Marcus in their vehement protestations of innocence; whether they did know their mother was
forging these documents; whether they knew the will was
forged and that Aunt Puss was so confused as to be unaware of
what they were doing. Of their physical presence at York House

and Wickton Court, or their relative absence from Hereford Hospital or Langford House, it is (as the judge said) not a question of whether they did some of these things, but what they thought when they were doing them. Only Sophia knows whether she really did stop talking to Aunt Puss when she went to Docklow or whether she really did not understand about her own bank accounts. And Marcus must know if he asked Aunt Puss about bringing all her possessions from York House or if he expressed his thanks for her later largesse. Forresters Hall is, after all, a small cottage. The facts have been set out extensively in court and a jury was not convinced of their innocence. But they are convinced themselves. Their story has been told often to the police, their lawyers and the courts; so much so that they may have become convinced almost irrespective of the truth. Or as one lawyer in the case said: 'Only three people know for sure what happened: Lady Illingworth, Susan and the cat. Aunt Puss is dead and cats can't give evidence. That leaves Susan.'

Motivation was not something the police needed to establish for the purposes of prosecution. It is not possible to say whether a single decision was made just before or soon after Lady Illingworth's arrival at Docklow to strip her of all the money and property she owned or whether Susan and Michael took one cautious step at a time until the full extent of what was possible became clear.

Perhaps it went something like this. They all knew of Lady Illingworth's wealth. It would also have become obvious when Sophia was staying at York House that Aunt Puss was going slightly dotty. Sophia was nagging her mother, apparently genuinely, to look after poor old Aunt Puss. Susan was reluctant, but may just have been persuaded by the thought, difficult to resist, that if she did look after her some of the largesse she knew was destined for brother John and family might fall her way, in belated gratitude. Certainly Aunt Puss would need to pay for her keep and she had always been used to living comfortably. They would need money to look after her. If she was just a shade too infirm to realise that her keep at Docklow was going to cost something, then why not help her to make those decisions, or make them for her? Within a few days, possibly hours, of Aunt Puss arriving at Docklow, the rubicon was crossed: the leap from guiding the hand on the cheque to doing it yourself was made. It was all so easy.

But Susan might have thought she deserved a little extra something after so many years of denial, meagre living and family handouts. Here was the opportunity to restore some of the pride and the kind of lifestyle she had aspired to at Heath House, only to be cruelly undermined by old Birdbrain. And here was the source of money that should really have been hers anyway: John had enough, he had Markington, he even had their mother's money; why should he and his children get any more? Aunt Puss had been her surrogate mother; she could take it from her.

It is entirely possible that Michael provided both catalyst and method. With his pretensions to financial wizardy, his mythical profession as an economist, his habit of dreaming up money-making schemes, he would have sensed the potential in Lady Illingworth's sudden arrival. He could have activated all these latent emotions in Susan, churned up the buried anger of the years and then shown Susan precisely how the potential could be realised: cashcard here, a bank account there, spread around various countries. He knew all the right people, he was fond of saying; Susan learnt quickly.

Some might think such a strong personality as Susan's would hardly be likely to be swayed by a man like Michael, whose hand she had rejected nearly thirty years previously because of his unreliability. Not so. He knew her weak spots. With Michael she would do strange things, act totally out of character, put up with his moods and stupid talk. Susan was, in the words of one son, 'undeniably weakened' by him, and he caught her unprepared, when she was low, her money gone, her family split. Not only would Michael help her get the money, but money would also keep him and give her a title, after all these years, to go with her new-found pride. It was an attractive prospect.

Susan knew that money was the way of keeping Michael: he had always wanted money, there was never enough, and she owed him for the Docklow years. If they had money, Michael would stay with her. And here he was, showing Susan the easy path to money – and Illingworth money at that – for them both: Aunt Puss.

But the relationship turned full circle. Once, he had pursued her; now she was frightened of being abandoned. She was weakened even more: becoming the lovelorn young woman, tolerating his oddities and infidelities, marrying him to stop him leaving and taking away the promised title. And when he did leave her, perhaps realising the enormity of what they had embarked upon, she tried to bind him to her with more money. So she carried on with the auction sales and the money transfers, packed Aunt Puss off to hospital and hauled the rest of her property out of storage. Susan knew how to do it by now. Michael never returned, but it was too late to stop.

'My father ruined my mother. Michael finished her off,' says Sophia. 'She was just not that interested in money. She would not have known how to handle all those accounts. If Michael had not been there, none of this would have happened. Mummy just accepted things from Michael that she would not have taken from anybody else.'

Unlike Susan, Michael, in Leyhill prison, has enjoyed the company and unambiguous support of his ex-spouses and children. They visit him regularly and have high hopes for his appeal. Michael is convinced a grave miscarriage of justice has occurred; he has changed his solicitor and the appeal will be made by a new barrister. This is because it will be mainly based on the comments made by Richard Du Cann in his closing speech, which Michael believes were highly detrimental towards him. Few lawyers can recall an appeal succeeding on this particular ground, although Michael is also arguing that the judge misdirected the jury. His first wife, Christina, now remarried, says Michael never got out of bed during their marriage; says it has all been blown out of proportion, laughs hysterically and abruptly puts down the telephone. Francesca Tesi entertains journalists with tapes she made of Michael's emotional telephone conversations with Susan, for whom she has little sympathy, considering her at least partly to blame for the breakdown of her own (Francesca's) marriage. She then declines to talk about it all, having taken advice from 'my Hampstead solicitor'. She has also begun signing herself 'Franca Tesi de Stempel (Baroness).' She has clearly, picked up this de Stempel trait.

In Markington and London, the Wilberforce family draws its

shutters, keeps its counsel and conducts its own communications with Theodore Goddard. There is unquestionably a collective sense of guilt over the fate of Aunt Puss. With hindsight, they must surely realise that leaving Aunt Puss at York House was, at the very least, open to misinterpretation both by the elderly woman and by others. There is also no doubt that they knew she had gone to Docklow: Cathy Whelan and Irene Wilberforce told them; Aunt Puss (or Susan) did write a postcard to Yvette, Lady Wilberforce, whose letters to Aunt Puss were not returned; Everilda Wilberforce, Lady Illingworth's cousin, had also visited Docklow.

Certainly, little effort seems to have been made to resolve the matter, despite, according to one family member, a growing sense of unfocused unease during late 1984 and 1985. Most of Lady Illingworth's relatives were spread around the country, and were ageing: Lord and Lady Wilberforce were in their late seventies in London; Everilda, eighty-one, was in Cirencester; Robert Wilberforce, in his nineties, was in a home; Michael and Lynette Wilberforce, the cousins in Datchet whom Albert Olsar had taken her to see, were in their seventies; Aunt Marion was also in her eighties, caring for and then grieving for Uncle Wee, who died in December 1984. Of the next generation down, Laura was at Markington and John in Cyprus, their children leading their own lives. They all knew that relations with Susan were strained and that she avoided any communication with them.

On the one occasion when she did see any of them together, at Uncle Wee's funeral, Susan, together with Sophia and Marcus, appeared at the church just as the service was beginning and left immediately after the burial, without more than a few words to anyone. John was abroad. The fact that Aunt Puss had not attended the funeral of her beloved brother Robert does not appear to have caused widespread concern among the family then or afterwards. At the funeral, despite both the nature of the occasion and Susan's brief appearance, no one apparently made any forceful attempt to engage her in conversation and so find out about Aunt Puss, ten months after she had gone to Docklow.

Laura would later tell police that she had had some idea that Aunt Puss was in a home and that she made unsuccessful enquiries in the area to try and locate her. Apart from Susan' call to John in Cyprus, asking him to intervene over Michael, she may not have actually spoken to any of her wider family during the period of almost three years between Aunt Puss's arrival at Docklow and her death. It is clear that none of the family had made strenuous efforts during this period to try and establish Aunt Puss's whereabouts by, say, speaking to Susan on the telephone or going to Docklow to confront her in person. A determined effort would surely have been successful. It might have uncovered what was occuring and, at the very least, would have allowed Aunt Puss the burial she desired. Even after Aunt Puss's death, during the period before police began their inquiries as a result of the murder of Simon Dale, although there were said to be murmurings of concern over the will, no serious attempt appears to have been made by her relatives to see Susan or find out why Aunt Puss died in penury. 'No. I am sorry, No,' is Lord Wilberforce's one-line letter of reply when asked to discuss the matter. 'I think we would never have found out about the fraud if the murder of Simon Dale had not taken place,' is the opinion of one senior police officer.

At the West Mercia police headquarters at Worcester, the file on the Dale murder remains open. Again, the facts were laid before the jury and the jury were not convinced.

For Simon's many new friends, the murder trial was a disgrace. In the effort to convict Susan, his bad points – the moods, the obsessiveness, the stubbornness, the barely substantiated violence – were emphasised by the prosecution at the expense of the better qualities they knew so well. And as for the nonsense about women's shoes and make-up, well . . . No one was called, although many were ready, to testify to his wit, his humanity, his gentlemanly manners, his forbearance under siege. Excluded from the funeral, the Bowaters and their circle decided to hold a memorial service for Simon in the tiny gas-lit church among the fields at Hopton Castle.

They gathered there, one bright and blustery day in May. Veronica wore her best hat and the service was led by the Revd Peter Nourse, another old friend of Simon's. Geoffrey Bowater and Christopher Hurst read the lessons, Giselle Wall and Jo Corfield were among the congregation. Also present were Sebastian and Alexander. Simon junior did not attend by choice; Marcus and Sophia were told they did not have one. No one mentioned their mother.

Sebastian gave the address, his natural slight stammer aggravated by emotion. 'Even after so long,' he said, 'there is still so much pain and grief in our hearts.' Fighting back the tears, he paid tribute to his father's intelligence, his wide range of interests and his skills as an architect and watercolourist, and recounted how his life and work had been blighted by myopia, which he had fought by research, writing and humour, rather than surrendering. It had, said Sebastian, ruined his family life. But his father's death had not been an entirely meaningless and negative affair. 'It is curious how good can come out of evil. All his children have learnt wholesomely the meaning of friendship with the support that we have all had and all continue to have from so many people.' Outside, Veronica said that, now they had grieved, they could let Simon go, in peace.

Sebastian and Alexander, both tall, sad, slimmer versions of their father, their hair receding across domed foreheads, also stood there, awkwardly and nervously in the sunlight, talking to the television cameras. It is Sebastian who most resembles his father and who is perhaps most affected by the entire episode. Custodian of his father's memory and of his ashes, his own eyesight afflicted by the same myopia, he had heard of his father's murder on the morning he began his final law examinations. Next to him is Alexander, who speaks, if anything, in even softer tones than his brother and who, distanced from affairs by his residence in Japan, pays the rent on Docklow so that his mother has somewhere to go when she is released.

They question the quality of the police investigation and stress again how terribly wrong and mistaken it had been for Marcus and Sophia and their mother to be charged with murdering their father. As they speak, their eyes are blinking, their thin voices faltering, their lips trembling and their faces contorted with the pain and grief of their family.

A few miles down the road is Heath House, shuttered, blind. Its telephone is cut off and the rabbits, squirrels and rooks have returned. The grass needs cutting, and leaves cover the paths, swirling around the wheels of a Mercedes van and a Peugeot estate. It has been burgled and now there is an alarm connected to the local police station. The house needs work, badly, on the outside again; but its owner cannot get there just at the moment. Since his release, Marcus returns at weekends to wander its rooms and passageways, and tidy the leaves, like some intermittent, restless spirit. Mostly it is unoccupied. It sits there, mute, waiting, signifying the good and the bad, the sunlight and the shadow of life. It will most likely survive them all, as it has survived the centuries.

Nearby, Oats the cat, unable to talk in ways understandable to a jury, is cared for by a friend of Sophia and Marcus.

Susan eventually got what she had always wanted: a large mansion house in Yorkshire, but one that was even more of a prison than Heath House. She waves, hesitantly, from the upstairs window of Askham Grange women's prison, which sits in the middle of a pretty village outside York. She shares a room with other prisoners, mostly young women on drugs or fraud offences.

This is the woman who dreams up all these childish nick-names and coy phrases and then defeats the interrogation of specialist barristers and hardened detectives. This is the shy woman whose emotions were inhibited by both breeding and family circumstances but whose dominant personality could intimidate her husband and his friends, press her children into crime and frighten away her relatives. This is the aloof, cold woman who ignores all around her from a position of assumed superiority, when inwardly there is the kind of turmoil over Michael revealed by the frantic, imploring, sometimes anony-mous letters and an imaginary fatal illness. This is the woman who could plan with such relentless efficiency the disposal of her aunt's assets but who lapses into the language of an upper-class teenage girl in letters to her daughter: 'Aunt Puss became ultra-panty' and 'Michael is such a bore'. This is also the supposedly devoted mother who says she pleaded guilty to ease the courtroom ordeal of 'my children' as though it had not been her 'malign and appalling influence' that had put them there in the first place.

Susan's instructions to visitors are not to park inside the prison gates, because 'they' always note the numbers, and not to write anything down because you will be thrown out immediately; she adds that she is allowed to send only one single-sheet letter at a time. This might be appropriate elsewhere; at the lowest-security-classification women's prison in the country, which does not even boast a secure fence, it is a sign of paranoia. There is more: 'I'm not applying for parole. I'll go when my term is up. If you go out on parole they can keep an eye on you.'

In the visitors' room, Susan, now fifty-six, stands in greeting. This middle-aged woman is taller and bulkier than her pictures, still wearing the characteristic blue, this time a sort of sailor's smock over a high-necked blouse and knotted scarf; she has thick ankles and heavy shoes. There is a trace of make-up, but the skin is pale; it emphasises the deep-brown, grey-flecked hair and the bright, blue-black eyes. In a hesitant, nervous fashion, her thin lips quivering slightly, she smiles, not without a certain warmth. Perhaps she is, as her children maintain, just a shy person. Her pallor could be tiredness but more likely it is the washed-out effect prison induces. She sits straight-backed, almost primly, but her hands can be restless, playing around her neck, clawing each other in front of her face or grasping her Styrofoam coffee cup. On her finger is a gold ring, presumably Michael's. With a smile, she offers thanks for the requested mug to replace her chipped enamel one. A table in the middle of the room is chosen, away from guards and from the few other visitors. It is difficult to hear her anyway, the voice is so quiet, and it is so flat that any emotional cadences are lost.

Susan has two curious mannerisms: one is an almost silent laugh, so that when she tilts her head back and opens her mouth slightly and smiles, only a faintly audible sound emerges. The second is when she does not want to answer a question: she will just perceptibly turn her chin away, letting her eyes wander and making it clear that her mind simply does not see any reason to deal with this.

For the present her chosen name is Cecilia, for some reason to do with the potential for enemies in prison. 'But I've made lots of friends, really.' She refers easily and in the accents of her background to 'screws' and 'being nicked'. She has had lots of visitors, but, since the fraud trial, only the youngest of her children has been. Alexander and Marcus she also talks about,

Sophia she finds hard to mention. For Sebastian she has only one comment: 'He is a real Simon Dale in the making.'

Susan/Cecilia talks comfortably about her early life, Markington, London, her debutante phase ('I met Noël Coward and those sort of people') and then Simon. She cannot remember which church they were married in; but it was 'a quiet wedding'. At Heath House, they had thirty builders for years. Will she return there? She shrugs her shoulders – probably not. She knows it will have to be sold anyway to deal with the writs. Marriage was 'a mistake'. She would have left Simon before, but believed in keeping the family together. Did she murder him? Susan is adamant and unblinking in maintaining her innocence; she refused to plead guilty to the lesser charge of manslaughter although the police said she would get a light sentence. She says: 'I'd rather go to prison than admit to something I did not do.'

At a later visit Susan/Cecilia bridles when there is a suggestion that she might have exhibited weakness. She laughs, fully: 'You forget, I am a Yorkshirewoman.' And Aunt Puss? 'She seized upon me. She always wanted me to come out. She loved all that sort of thing, embassies and parties.' And later? 'She was very happy everywhere. She would have eaten bread and cold baked beans if you had asked her and she would have been quite happy.'

It is time to go. She rises, as if to usher her guest to the door and then sits, with another tremulous, but now confidential, little smile of apology, realising she cannot. The face realigns itself and she stares bleakly in front of her, her eyes drilling into the wall.

Before Susan decides that, on legal advice, she cannot answer any more questions, she writes, in capital letters: 'Please stress how utterly monstrous it is that Sophia and Xenophon were imprisoned. They should not have even been arrested. And as to them being charged with murder . . .' In another letter, she says how sick and tired she is of being called snobbish. 'I know who I am and I am quite happy to leave it at that. . . . the one thing money cannot buy is breeding, don't you agree?'

A Selected List of Non-Fiction Available from Mandarin

☐	7493 0109 0	**The Warrior Queens**	Antonia Fraser £4.99
☐	7493 0108 2	**Mary Queen of Scots**	Antonia Fraser £5.99
☐	7493 0010 8	**Cromwell**	Antonia Fraser £7.50
☐	7493 0106 6	**The Weaker Vessel**	Antonia Fraser £5.99
☐	7493 0014 0	**The Demon Drink**	Jancis Robinson £4.99
☐	7493 0016 7	**Vietnam – The 10,000 Day War**	Michael Maclear £3.99
☐	7493 0061 2	**Voyager**	Yeager/Rutan £3.99
☐	7493 0113 9	**Peggy Ashcroft**	Michael Billington £3.99
☐	7493 0177 5	**The Troubles**	Mick O'Connor £4.99
☐	7493 0004 3	**South Africa**	Graham Leach £3.99
☐	7493 0254 2	**Families and How to Survive Them**	Creese/Skynner £5.99
☐	7493 0060 4	**The Fashion Conspiracy**	Nicolas Coleridge £3.99
☐	7493 0179 1	**The Tao of Pooh**	Benjamin Hoff £2.99
☐	7493 0000 0	**Moonwalk**	Michael Jackson £2.99